n Vernon 25th. Nov 84.

ave had the pleasure
tters from you since
in France, and cat
quis de la Fayette
t an acknowledge:
altho' his doing it is
he same time am sur
mpany —
have a little more
ever should be) I
h the occurrences
that have come under

The Founding Fathers

ARMIES OF THE U.S. OF AMERICA & PRESIDENT OF THE CONVENTION OF 1787 ☆ HIS EXCEL: G: WASHINGTON ESQ: LL.D. LATE COMMANDER IN CHIEF OF THE

Painted & Engraved by C.W.Peale. 1787.

The Founding Fathers

GEORGE WASHINGTON

A Biography in His Own Words

VOLUME 1

Edited by
RALPH K. ANDRIST

With an Introduction by
DONALD JACKSON
Editor, *The Papers of George Washington*

JOAN PATERSON KERR
Picture Editor

NEWSWEEK
New York

We dedicate this series of books to the memory of
Frederick S. Beebe
friend, mentor, and "Founding Father" of Newsweek Books

George Washington, *A Biography in His Own Words,*
has been produced by the Newsweek Book Division:

Joseph L. Gardner, Editor

Janet Czarnetzki, Art Director

S. Arthur Dembner, Publisher

This book is based on *The Papers of George Washington,*
edited by Donald Jackson and published by the University Press of Virginia.
The texts of Washington documents in this edition have been
supplied by Mr. Jackson, and permission to reproduce excerpts
from these documents has been obtained from their owners.

ISBN: Clothbound Edition 0-88225-035-3; ISBN: Deluxe Edition 0-88225-036-1
Library of Congress Catalog Card Number 72-76000
Copyright © 1972 by Newsweek, Inc.
All rights reserved. Printed and bound in the United States of America
ENDPAPERS: WASHINGTON TO DAVID HUMPHREYS, NOV. 25, 1784;
HENRY E. HUNTINGTON LIBRARY AND ART GALLERY

Contents

Introduction

by Donald Jackson
Editor of The Papers of George Washington

Among the nation's finest historical treasures is the collection of letters, diaries, military records, and financial documents left to us by George Washington. The wonder is that so many have survived, considering how the ravages of time and the carelessness of human hands have dealt with them.

The Library of Congress now holds a large share of these papers, and they are treated with professional care. Hundreds of others are lodged in libraries and archives, and in private collections; these, too, are given the respectful custodianship they deserve. But it was not always so.

Washington himself was the first to realize that his lifetime of public service had generated a body of papers well worth preserving. He hired secretaries and copyists, took care to see that his correspondence was boxed in sturdy trunks and shipped to safety during the Revolution, and even planned to build a small library at Mount Vernon where the records of a young nation and its first President could be stored and organized. Although the library never was built, the attention that Washington paid to his papers was without doubt the greatest factor in their survival. He could not have predicted that his heirs and fellow countrymen would be less dedicated to keeping the collection intact and available to posterity.

When Washington died in 1799, he bequeathed most of his papers to his nephew Bushrod Washington, a justice of the Supreme Court, who also was to have the Mount Vernon mansion and some of the lands around it after the death of Martha Washington. There is no reason to believe that Bushrod was not fully devoted to the preservation of the papers—although he had a habit of giving away samples to autograph seekers. Perhaps he merely failed to appreciate how zealous a stewardship is required to prevent such a collection from eroding away at the hands of well-meaning persons.

Martha Washington had a widow's prerogative to destroy the letters she had exchanged with her husband, and destroy them she did. At least, her granddaughter said that Martha burned them, and no more than two letters from Washington to his wife are known to have survived.

Bushrod planned to write a biography of his uncle—was planning it, in fact, within two weeks after Washington's death—but somehow he never got to the writing stage. Instead, he agreed that the work should be written by John Marshall, who was then Secretary of State and later would become Chief Justice. By 1807 Marshall had completed the five volumes entitled *The Life of George Washington*, the first extensive biography of our first President. During his work on these volumes, he borrowed large quantities of the original papers and kept them in Richmond, some for more than twenty years. Improper storage caused heavy damage from rodents, dampness, and other enemies of paper and ink.

If Bushrod was too generous in giving away samples of Washington's letters to autograph collectors and souvenir hunters, he was far outdistanced in this endeavor by the next biographer of Washington. Jared Sparks, editor of the *North American Review*, had decided by 1826 that he wished to publish a large edition of Washington's writings. Bushrod hesitated to make the material available because he and Marshall had been working on a similar undertaking, but in 1827 he agreed to Sparks's proposal. Thus the precious archive fell into the temporary possession of a man who could not only rewrite Washington's words without a qualm but could also mutilate and give away pages, partial pages, and even single lines of text to anyone who asked.

Sparks's editorial method must be viewed against the background of his times, when strict procedures for the arrangement and publication of historical documents had not been well developed. Writing to Bushrod at the beginning of his editorial work in 1827, he said: "I believe it may be set down as a rule, that in every case it will be safe to print, even with the names, whatever reflects credit upon all persons concerned, but whenever the heat of party, or local causes, give an unfavorable tone to the writer's feelings and sentiments, and lead him into harsh reflections upon others, there will be room for deliberation, and perhaps a motive for passing by letters in other respects highly interesting." That is not the way in which valid history is written.

The willingness of Jared Sparks to distribute free samples is shown in this letter to Richard Henry Dana, Jr., in 1861, long years after his need to have access to the manuscripts was ended: "I regret that I cannot furnish you with an autograph letter of Washington. I have had many such, but the collectors have long ago exhausted my stock. The best I can do is to enclose a very small specimen of his handwriting." The specimen, of course, represented a letter mutilated and destroyed.

This literary carnage was made easier by the fact that Sparks was allowed to take great quantities of letters to his home in Boston. What the world gained from it all was a twelve-volume edition called *The Writings of George Washington* (Boston, 1834–37). Because Sparks was so selective, so prone to revise, and so eager not to publish anything that he thought might show Washington in an improper light, the edition is far less useful than it might have been.

Bushrod Washington died in 1829 and the papers passed into the hands of his nephew, George Corbin Washington. Because officers of the United States Government had long recognized the value of the manuscripts, the Secretary of State asked the new owner in 1833 if he would consider placing them on deposit with the Government. After some negotiation, which included getting Sparks to begin returning the papers in his possession, an actual sale, not a deposit, was arranged in 1834. George C. Washington spent two more years, and made a trip to Sparks's home in Boston, before he had convinced himself that he had rounded up all the public papers of the first President. A parcel of private papers was sold to the Government later.

Now the safety of the papers was assured. They might suffer a bit from the damp summers and the dry winter heat of government buildings in the District of Columbia, but they were at least protected from the snip-snip of Jared Sparks's scissors.

It is obvious that Washington's heirs could not have turned over all the manuscripts, including incoming and outgoing correspondence. Washington failed to retain copies of many letters that he wrote; those he received were subject to loss. Even after a substantial portion had been acquired by the Government, hundreds more remained unknown or unavailable.

Through the years these papers have slowly accumulated in collections large and small. Well-known institutions such as the New York Public Library, the Historical Society of Pennsylvania, the Massachusetts Historical Society, and the Huntington Library have acquired great collections. Autograph collectors still maintain a lively interest in Washington letters, and most of these are eventually donated or sold to public institutions, where they become available for study. Although it will be many years before copies of every extant Washington document are assembled in one place, it is now possible to estimate that 95 per cent of such papers are known.

Publication of Washingtoniana continued sporadically after the Jared Sparks edition. A formidable but selective edition was edited by Worthington C. Ford and published between 1889 and 1893. Today most students of Washington rely upon *The Writings of George Washington*, edited by John C. Fitzpatrick and published in thirty-nine volumes (1931–44) by the George Washington Bicentennial Commission. Fitzpatrick's labors were enormous, and performed under difficult circumstances, including a limited staff and considerable pressure to hold down costs during the Depression years. It was inevitable that he should miss many important documents. What is more significant, however, is the fact that he was able to publish only letters and other documents written by Washington. None of the incoming correspondence was reproduced. As someone has said, reading the volumes is a bit like listening to only one side of a conversation.

By 1966 the feeling was growing among historians, librarians, and archivists that a new edition of Washington papers was very much needed. Scholars no longer would settle for one side of a correspondence. The United States was looking forward to a series of Bicentennial observances in the 1970's, and no figure was more important than Washington in the forging of a new, young nation. It seemed regrettable that no intensive work was being done on Washington's papers, especially since the papers of other Founding Fathers—Franklin, Adams, Jefferson, Hamilton, and Madison—were the subject of vigorous publishing programs. Washington's home state of Virginia soon offered the most suitable combination of sponsors for such a new, comprehensive edition of Washington's papers. The Mount Vernon Ladies' Association of the Union, which has owned and preserved Washington's home along the Potomac for more than a century, volunteered financial support and expert guidance. The University of Virginia in Charlottesville offered office space, staff, additional financing, and the facilities of the famed Alderman Library. Federal agencies are participating. A statewide institution, the University Press of

Virginia, will begin publication of the edition in 1975, and the complete work will require more than sixty volumes.

Ever since John Marshall's day, books dealing with Washington have appeared regularly. These have ranged from the quaint fantasies of Mason Weems, who gave us the hatchet and the cherry tree, to serious studies by men such as Washington Irving, Woodrow Wilson, Douglas Southall Freeman, and James Thomas Flexner. The best of these have one thing in common: reliance on that priceless creation of Washington and the men of his times, the papers so miraculously preserved in the face of heavy odds.

In this biography prepared by the Newsweek Book Division, Ralph Andrist has chosen to let Washington speak mainly for himself. His letters are always wise, sometimes eloquent, and never dull to a generation that has taken renewed interest in one of the greatest historical figures of all time.

EDITORIAL NOTE

Most of the Washington writings reprinted in this biography have been excerpted from the longer original documents being published in their entirety by the University Press of Virginia. Omissions at the beginning or ending of a document are indicated by ellipses only if the extract begins or ends in the middle of a sentence; omissions within a quoted passage are also indicated by ellipses. The original spellings have been retained; editorial insertions are set within square brackets.

Chronology of Washington and His Times

George Washington born at Popes Creek, Virginia, February 22 (February 11, Old Style)	1732	Charter granted to Colony of Georgia
	1739	War of Jenkins' Ear, 1739–42
	1740	King George's War, 1740–48
Father dies	1743	
Travels west with surveying party	1748	
Helps lay out town of Alexandria	1749	
Sails to Barbados with brother Lawrence	1751	
Courts Elizabeth Fauntleroy; Lawrence Washington dies	1752	Iroquois cede land south of Ohio River to Virginia; French move to defend Ohio territory
Adjutant in provincial militia; leads mission to French in Ohio country	1753	Fort Duquesne erected by French; Albany Congress
Battle of Fort Necessity; resigns commission; leases Mount Vernon	1754	French and Indian War, 1754–63
Fort Duquesne expedition; commander of Virginia forces; Dagworthy dispute	1755	Braddock assumes British command in America
Visits Boston to appeal to Shirley	1756	Hostilities spread to Europe, Seven Years' War, 1756–63
Illness forces retirement from field	1757	
Proposes to Martha Custis; action in Ohio; resigns commission	1758	French abandon Fort Duquesne
Marries Martha Custis, January 6; enters House of Burgesses	1759	
	1760	Reign of George III of England, 1760–1820
Visits Dismal Swamp	1763	Proclamation of 1763
	1764	Sugar Act and Colonial Currency Act
	1765	Stamp Act
	1767	Townshend duties adopted
Wins Ohio land grant; signs Association	1769	Burgesses pass Virginia Resolutions and Association
Tours Ohio with James Craik	1770	Lord North's ministry, 1770–82; Boston Massacre
	1772	Revival of committees of correspondence
John Custis enters King's College; Martha Parke Custis dies	1773	Tea Act; Boston Tea Party
First Continental Congress	1774	Intolerable Acts; reign of Louis XVI of France, 1774–92
Second Continental Congress; named Commander in Chief of Army; siege of Boston	1775	Battles of Lexington and Concord; capture of Ticonderoga; Bunker Hill; Olive Branch petition; Howe succeeds Gage as British commander; Montgomery and Arnold attack Quebec
Seizes Dorchester Heights; British evacuate Boston; Battles of Long Island and Harlem Heights; retreat through New Jersey; attacks Trenton	1776	Charles Lee holds Charleston; Declaration of Independence
Battles of Princeton, Brandywine, and Germantown; winter at Valley Forge	1777	Howe moves on Philadelphia; Battle of Saratoga; Congress adopts Articles of Confederation

Disclosure of Conway Cabal; Battle of Monmouth	1778	Clinton named British commander; France enters war; Congress rejects North's peace plan; Savannah falls to British
Battle of Stony Point	1779	Spain joins war; *Bonhomme Richard* defeats *Serapis*; Franco-American forces fail to recapture Savannah
Connecticut troops mutiny; Lafayette returns from France; Rochambeau conference; Arnold's treason	1780	British occupy Charleston; Battle of Camden
Battle of Yorktown; John Custis dies	1781	Mutiny of Pennsylvania and New Jersey troops; Congress creates executive departments; Articles of Confederation ratified; America names peace mission
Carleton-Digby peace proposals; French troops sail to West Indies	1782	North ministry ends; Carleton replaces Howe; British evacuate Savannah; preliminary peace treaty signed
Newburgh Addresses; visits northern New York; New York City evacuated; farewell to officers; returns to Mount Vernon	1783	Cessation of hostilities; Pennsylvania militia march on Congress
Heads Potomac Company	1785	
	1786	Annapolis Convention; Shays' Rebellion
President of Philadelphia Convention	1787	Northwest Ordinance; *Federalist* papers published, 1787–88
	1788	Ratification of Constitution
First inaugural as President; tours New England and New York	1789	Organization of First Congress; opening of French Revolution
Assumption debate ends in compromise; capital moved to Philadelphia; Beckwith mission	1790	Hamilton's first Report on Public Credit; Harmar expedition; Hamilton's report on the Bank
Cabinet divides on constitutionality of Bank; travels through southern states	1791	Congress passes excise tax on whiskey; Report on Manufactures; Legislative Assembly governs France, 1791–92
Tries to end Jefferson-Hamilton feud; Madison drafts a farewell address; Washington re-elected	1792	Resistance to excise; presidential electors chosen; abolition of French monarchy and institution of National Convention, 1792–95; War of First Coalition against France, 1792–97; Lafayette is imprisoned
Second inaugural; Neutrality Proclamation; Genêt and the *Little Sarah* incident; Jefferson resigns	1793	Execution of Louis XVI; France declares war on Britain; Republican majority in Second Congress, 1793–95
Proclaims embargo; Jay mission to England; Monroe sent to Paris; Whisky Rebellion	1794	Neutrality Act; Battle of Fallen Timbers
Hamilton leaves Cabinet; Jay's Treaty controversy; Fauchet-Randolph incident; Lafayette's son reaches America	1795	Treaty of San Lorenzo; Directory rules France, 1795–99
Pinckney replaces Monroe; Washington issues Farewell Address	1796	Supreme Court first rules an act of Congress unconstitutional; presidential election; Directory refuses to receive Pinckney
Retires to Mount Vernon	1797	Inauguration of Adams and Jefferson; special mission to France; XYZ Affair
Accepts command of Army; dispute over Hamilton's rank; confers with generals in Philadelphia	1798	Quasi war with France, 1798–1800
Concern over McHenry's competence; troubled by dispatch of commissioners to France; George Washington dies at Mount Vernon, December 14	1799	France ruled by Consulate headed by Napoleon Bonaparte, 1799–1804

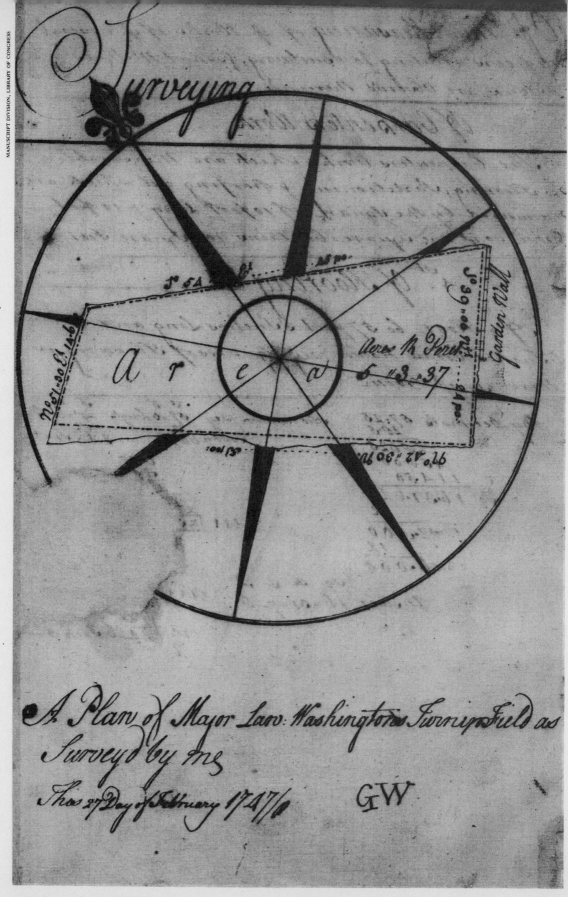

At sixteen George Washington made this survey drawing of his brother Lawrence's turnip field.

Chapter 1

Coming of Age in Virginia

George Washington gazes serenely upon us from portraits and stares empty-eyed from marble busts, as he has done upon many generations of Americans. Jaw firm in obvious resoluteness of purpose, the Washington of the portraits and statues does not smile. His life, one feels, is too dedicated to inspiring ragged troops so that they will fight one more day, too preoccupied with leading the nation through the shoals of early independence, to allow time for smiling. This Washington who has been bequeathed to us, however, is not only impossibly noble, he is not even a man of flesh and blood. All the warmth, the human foibles, the earthiness, have been excised, for in acclaiming a great man, America created a paragon that never existed. Facts that might detract from the image of a demigod were suppressed; particulars that would enhance the picture were magnified and even invented.

The George Washington of fable was coming into being even before the man himself was dead, and after his death the legend grew to absurd proportions. Even today the myth of the hatchet and the cherry tree refuses to die, although there is not the slightest doubt that it was stitched together out of whole cloth by Mason Weems, a book peddler and sometime preacher, in the 1806 edition of his life of Washington. Parson Weems is also responsible for other persistent items of folklore: the youthful Washington throwing a stone across the Rappahannock River (not a dollar across the Potomac); General Washington observed by a Quaker farmer as he knelt to pray in the snow at Valley Forge.

It is not easy to take the Father of his Country down from his pedestal and seek out what kind of human being he was. Even while he was alive, he wore a cloak of dignity that discouraged familiarity, and the blurring effects of time have made the search for the man more difficult. But once the obscuring layers are peeled away, an individual does stand revealed, a man of weaknesses as well as strengths, of enthusiasms, warmths, antagonisms. If such things as a love for dancing and the theater, and a weakness for cardplaying and fox hunting, were marks of frivolity, then George Washington was frivolous to that extent. He was frail enough to cherish a love for the wife of a close friend, but strong enough to keep his passion within circumspect bounds. He was not the military genius he is sometimes credited with having been, for some of his battles, especially the early ones, were not always models of strategic subtlety. In other words, he was a more interesting and more complex person than the one created by the mythmakers. If in time Washington occasionally did come to resemble the dedicated man of the portraits, it was largely because he accepted duty as his hard taskmaster and forced himself to surmount his frailties. As for his military abilities, he became immeasurably wiser with experience, while his foes were learning little; he discovered how to use his ragged Continentals on the half-wild American terrain, while the British and Hessians persisted in trying to fight as though they were on Europe's open fields and meadows. And as the nation's first President, he established major precedents that have endured for two centuries.

Biographers have found it difficult to obtain a revealing perspective on Washington. His contemporaries saw him in different lights; his towering presence and multiple accomplishments filled some with uncritical adoration, but to others they were cause for jealous denigration. Even those who strove to be impartial were hard put to get at the essence of the man, because Washington's reserve made him keep his thoughts and feelings largely to himself. When a friend asked him to set down his memoirs for future generations, he declined, saying he had no talent for that kind of writing. Fortunately he left a large body of other writings that provide material for a portrait of himself in his own words. It is not a portrait seen full face—for he is not addressing himself to us—but a composite made up of a hundred glimpses seen from many angles: Washington writing to a friend, instructing his farm manager, pleading with Congress, addressing his troops, occasionally putting private thoughts in his diary. His family genealogy and the record of his early years, however, must be given in conventional historical narrative.

Anyone who searches among Washington's forebears for the seeds of his greatness will be disappointed. By the time of his birth in 1732, the Washington family was well established on Virginia's Northern Neck, the long peninsula lying between the Rappahannock and Potomac rivers. But though they were good and respectable people, they were not outstanding; they were men of property, but their holdings were very modest compared to those of many Virginia landowners. The Washingtons were the kind of men who provided county justices, vestrymen for the parish churches, and, frequently, members for the House of Burgesses, the lower house of Virginia's General Assembly, but made little mark on the history of the Colony. The first Washington to settle on American soil—George's great-grandfather John—came to Virginia in 1657 as mate on a ship. John married well, prospered, and willed the bulk of his fifty-seven-hundred-acre estate to his eldest son, Lawrence. A good manager, a man who could extract money from what he had, Lawrence Washington increased his inheritance by only a few hundred acres and died at the young age of thirty-eight, leaving a widow and three children, John, Augustine, and Mildred. Augustine Washington would be the father of George.

Since he was a second son, Augustine Washington's bequest in his father's will was small. But soon after he came of age in 1715, he married Jane Butler, who added a modest inheritance to his, so that the young couple began their life together with some 1,740 acres. It was still small by Virginia standards, but Augustine began to add to it. His first purchase was a farm on the south bank of the Potomac between Bridges Creek and Popes Creek, which had once belonged to his grandfather John. There, on Popes Creek, Augustine built a home several years later. It must have been quite a small house, for it was described as having only four rooms, and the contractor agreed to build it for five thousand pounds of tobacco, a modest sum. Not much else is known about it, but this house would be the birthplace of George Washington. Augustine Washington also prospered, building a gristmill on Popes Creek near his home and becoming a justice of the peace, a church warden, and a sheriff. He acquired more land, including a twenty-five-hundred-acre tract farther up the Potomac where Little Hunting Creek emptied into the river. This he bought from his sister Mildred and her husband; it had been her inheritance and also had once belonged to John Washington. In time it would be known as Mount Vernon. Augustine became active in the development of iron ore and in iron smelting. He and his wife had three children, Lawrence, Augustine, and Jane. He was only thirty-five, and the future looked bright. Then in May, 1730, he returned from an extended trip to England on iron-furnace business to learn that his wife had died the previous November.

Augustine Washington's situation helps to explain why widowed men and women of the period usually remarried so quickly. Marriage was for practical as well as romantic reasons. It was a two-person job to manage a home and fields, watch over the slaves, take care of the children. Augustine's eye soon rested on Mary Ball, rather succinctly described as healthy, of moderate height, with a rounded figure and a pleasant voice. Mary was the sole offspring of the union of Joseph Ball, a widower nearing sixty, and Mary Johnson, a widow who could not even write her own name. Nor was the daughter to acquire much facility with the pen; the samples of Mary's orthography that survive are truly wonderful examples of how far phonic English can be stretched without snapping. Mary Ball's father had died when she was only three, leaving her four hundred acres of land, three slaves, cattle, and "all [the] feathers that are in the kitchen loft to be put into a bed for her." Her mother married again, was widowed, and herself departed this world when Mary was twelve, leaving her an orphan but bequeathing her more land and other property. Thus Mary brought a considerable amount of property to her union with Augustine Washington.

The couple was married in March of 1731. He was thirty-six, Mary was twenty-three. The following February 11 (Old Style, changed to February 22, when England adopted the Gregorian calendar in 1752), in the house on Popes Creek, was born a son whom they named George. The historian can only guess about the events of George Washington's childhood. At Popes Creek he would have become familiar with farm animals probably as soon as he was aware of the world around him, and he came to accept the enslavement of black human beings as part of the normal order of things. He undoubtedly was taken at some time to his father's nearby gristmill with its rumbling machinery, and there were certainly visits to neighbors with his parents. There was the birth of a new sister, Betty, when he was not quite a year and a half old, and before another year and a half there was Samuel, who had scarcely become part of the family when George—not yet three—had to try to comprehend that his half-sister Jane had died. His half-brothers Lawrence and Augustine, Jr., both much older than he, could have been no more than dim and unreal creatures, for they

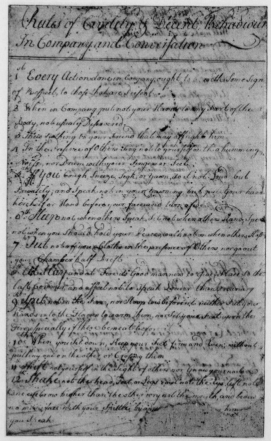

were in England at school. In 1735 Augustine Washington moved his family to the land he had bought along Little Hunting Creek on the Potomac. In the new home two more brothers were born: John Augustine, who would be known as Jack, and Charles.

In 1738 George's half-brother Lawrence returned from England. He was twenty—fourteen years older than George—urbane, educated, traveled; and the younger brother quickly idolized him. Despite the difference in age, they were to become close friends. Late that same year Augustine Washington bought a tract of land on the Rappahannock about two miles from the village of Fredericksburg, the first town George had ever seen. The place was called Ferry Farm because it was near a crossing of the river, and the family moved there on December 1, 1738. The following year Britain and Spain went to war, and Lawrence Washington became an officer in the volunteer "American Regiment" that took part in a disastrous assault on the Spanish stronghold of Cartagena on the northwest coast of what is now Colombia. Lawrence's war tales made him even more of a hero to his younger brother, and George's enthusiasm for things military apparently dated from this time.

From the age of about seven until he was eleven George received what schooling he got probably in part from a tutor and very likely for a time at a school in nearby Fredericksburg. He learned arithmetic, how to read, and how to spell after a fashion. His strong point was figures: he went on to study trigonometry, and then surveying. The very earliest specimens of Washington's handwriting that survive are his school copybooks. In them, in a firm, bold hand, he solved arithmetic problems; copied down forms for a typical will, a tobacco receipt, a land lease, and other legal papers; and wrote out tables for finding the date Easter will fall on in any given year and similar useful and useless information. Unhappily, most of these entries tell us little about the boy himself. The following exercises are among those written when George Washington was thirteen.

[August 13, 1745]

SURVEYING

Is the Art of Measuring Land and it consists of 3 Parts 1st. The going round and Measuring a Piece of Wood Land. 2d Plotting the Same and 3d To find the Content thereof and first how to Measure a Piece of Land....

Two pages from Washington's school copybooks show his early interest in surveying and the first twelve of 110 maxims he copied out under the heading of "Rules of Civility and Decent Behavior in Company and Conversation." Ink from reverse pages makes them difficult to read.

SOLID MEASURE

Is that of Timber, Stone Digging, and Liquods, and the Rule for Working is

To Multiply the Length & Breadth together; & that Product by the Depth or thickness & the Last Product will be the Content in Cubick Inches which if Timber or Stone divide by 1728 (the Cubick Inches in a Foot

Solid) & the Quotient gives the Content in Solid Feet....

Mount Vernon and its Associations BY BENSON J. LOSSING, 1883

Destroyed in 1779, Washington's birthplace, "a four-roomed house, with a chimney at each end," was described and depicted by Lossing in his book on Mount Vernon.

A DESCRIPTION OF THE LEAP YEAR, DOMINICAL LETTER, GOLDEN NUMBER, CYCLE OF THE SUN ROMON INDICTION EPACT &C. WITH MEMORIAL VERSES ON THE ECCLESIASTICAL AND CIVIL KALENDER

The Golden Number or Prime is a Circular Revolution of 19 years in which term of years it hath been anciently Supposed that the Sun & Moon do make all the Variety of Aspects one to another....

GEOGRAPHICAL DEFINITIONS

Defin. 1st. The Globe of the Earth is a Spherical Body Composed of Earth & Water &c. Divided into Contenants Islands & Seas.

2d. A Contenent is a great Quantity of Land not Divided nor Seperated by the Sea wherein are many Kingdoms & Principalities, as Europe, Asia & Africa is one Contenent & America is Another....

7 The Ocean is a general Collection of the Waters wch. environeth the Earth on every side....

The Provinces of North America are

New France	New Jersey	Carolina North & South
New England	Mary Land	Terra Florida
New York	Virginia	Mexico or New Spain
Pensylvania		

The Chief Islands are

Iselands	Hispaniola	Jamaica
Greenland	Cuba	Barbadoes & the rest of
Colofornia	Porto Rico	the Caribbee Iselands

Augustine Washington died on April 12, 1743, at the age of forty-eight. He left more than ten thousand acres, divided into at least seven tracts. Although all of his children were well remembered in his will, Lawrence, as the eldest son, got by far the largest share, including the plantation on Little Hunting Creek. George, the third son, received the Ferry Farm and, like the others, some slaves and personal property. His inheritance—neither especially large nor productive—made little difference, for his mother did not yield it to him when he became twenty-one; he had to wait another eighteen years after that before she would consent to move elsewhere. Mary Ball Washington did not remarry, was a poor manager, made frequent demands on her children, and later evinced not the slightest pride in her illustrious son's accomplishments.

Lawrence Washington renamed his Little Hunting Creek home Mount Vernon, in honor of Admiral Edward Vernon, who had led the Cartagena expedition against the Spanish. Not long after his father's death he married Anne Fairfax, the daughter of Colonel William Fairfax, whose impressive home, Belvoir, neighbored on Mount Vernon. And so, as young George came to visit at Mount Vernon, the doors of Belvoir were also opened to him. Belvoir was an important influence on the boy, who was rapidly growing into a young man, large of hands and feet, unusually strong, taller than those about him, and undoubtedly awkward and unsure of himself. At Belvoir and Mount Vernon he acquired the social graces so necessary to a member of Virginia's Northern Neck society.

In 1747 a notable event occurred at Belvoir: the arrival from England of Thomas, Lord Fairfax, cousin of Colonel Fairfax, a fox-hunting, woman-hating nobleman. He was proprietor of the Northern Neck, which meant that because of a royal grant to a forebear he was virtually feudal lord of all the expanse of land lying between the Potomac and the Rappahannock, to their most remote sources in the mountains, a huge domain of more than five million acres. When a surveying party was sent into his lordship's western land, George Washington, then sixteen, was permitted to go. Although he was qualified to run simple surveys, he did not go as a working member of the party but rather as a companion to George William, the son of Colonel Fairfax and a nephew of Lord Fairfax, who was with the party to represent his lordship's interests. George's diary account of the adventure is the earliest existing spontaneous writing from his hand.

A Journal of my Journey over the Mountains began Fryday the 11th. of March 1747/8

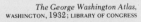
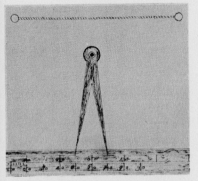

The George Washington Atlas,
WASHINGTON, 1932; LIBRARY OF CONGRESS

A chain, dividers, and scale drawn by Washington when he was fourteen

Fryday March 11th. 1747/8. Began my Journey in Company with George Fairfax Esqr.; we travelld this day 40 Miles to Mr. George Neavels in Prince William County.

Saturday March 12th. This Morning Mr. James Genn the surveyor came to us. We traveld over the Blue Ridge to Capt. Ashbys on Shannondoah River. Nothing remarkable happen'd.

Sunday March 13th. Rode to Lordships Quarter about 4 Miles higher up the River. We went through most beautiful Groves of Sugar Trees & spent the best part of the Day in admiring the Trees & richness of the Land.

Monday 14th. We sent our Baggage to Capt. Hites (near Frederick Town). Went ourselves down the River about 16 Miles to Capt. Isaac Pennington (the Land exceeding Rich & Fertile all the way produces abundance of Grain Hemp Tobacco &ca.) in order to Lay of some Lands on Cates Marsh & Long Marsh.

Tuesday 15th.   We set out early with Intent to Run round the s[ai]d. Land but being taken in a Rain & it Increasing very fast obliged us to return it clearing about one oClock. Our time being too Precious to Loose we a second time ventured out & Worked hard till Night & Then returnd to Penningtons. We got our Suppers & was Lighted into a Room & I not being so good a Woodsman as the rest of my Company I striped my self very orderly & went into the Bed as they call'd it when to my Surprize I found it to be nothing but a Little Straw Matted together without Sheets or any thing else but only one Thread Bear blanket with double its Weight of Vermin such as Lice Fleas &c. I was glad to get up (as soon as the Light was carried from us) & put on my Cloths & Lay as my Companions. Had we not have been very tired I am sure we should not have slep'd much that night. I made a Promise not to sleep so from that time forward chusing rather to sleep in the open Air before a fire as will appear hereafter.

Wednesday 16th.   We set out early & finish'd about one oClock & then Travell'd up to Frederick Town where our Baggage came to us. We cleaned ourselves (to get Rid of the Game we had catched the Night before) & took a Review of the Town & thence return'd to our Lodgings where we had a good Dinner prepar'd for us Wine & Rum Punch in Plenty & a good Feather Bed with clean Sheets which was a very agreeable regale.

Thursday 17th.   Rain'd till Ten oClock & then clearing we reached as far as Major Campbells one of there Burgesses about 25 Miles from Town. Nothing Remarkable this day nor Night but that we had a Tolerable good Bed [to] lay on.

Fryday 18th.   We Travell'd up about 35 Miles to Thomas Barwicks in Potomack where we found the River so excessively high by Reason of the Great Rains that had fallen up about the Allegany Mountains as they told us which was then bringing down the melt'd Snow & that it would not be fordable for severall Days it was then above Six foot Higher than usual & was Rising we agreed to stay till Monday. We this day calld to see the Fam'd Warm

Belvoir, home of the Fairfaxes, was destroyed in 1783 but looked much like this artist's rendering when Washington knew and loved it.

Springs. We camped out in the field this Night. Nothing Remarkable happen'd till sonday the 20th.

Sonday 20th.   Finding the River not much abated we in the Evening Swam our horses over & carried them to Charles Polks in Maryland for Pasturage till the next Morning.

Monday 21st.   We went over in a Canoe & Travell'd up Maryland side all the Day in a Continued Rain to Collo. Cresaps right against the Mouth of the South Bra[nch] about 40 Miles from Polks I believe the worst Road that ever was trod by Man or Beast.

Tuesday 22d.   Continued Rain and the Freshes kept us at Cresaps.

Wednesday 23d.   Rain'd till about two oClock & Clear'd when we were agreeably surprisd at the sight of thirty odd Indians coming from War with only one Scalp. We had some Liquor with us of which we gave them Part it elevating there Spirits put them in the Humour of Dauncing of whom we had a War Daunce. There Manner of Dauncing is as follows Viz. They clear a Large Circle & make a great Fire in the Middle then seats themselves around it the Speaker makes a grand Speech telling them in what Manner they are to Daunce. After he has finish'd the best Dauncer Jumps up as one awaked out of a Sleep & Runs & Jumps about the Ring in a most comicle Manner. He is followd by the Rest then begins there Musicians to Play. The Music is a Pot half [full] of Water with a Deerskin Streched over it as tight as it can & a Goard with some Shott in it to Rattle & a Piece of an horses Tail tied to it to make it look fine. The one keeps Rattling and the other Drumming all the While the other is Dauncing.

Fryday 25th. 1748.   Nothing Remarkable on thursday but only being with the Indians all day so shall slip it. This day left Cresaps & went up to the Mouth of Patersons Creek & there swum our Horses over got over ourselves in a Canoe & traveld up the following Part of the Day to Abram Johnstones 15 Miles from the Mouth where we crossed.

Saterday 26. Travelld up the Creek to Solemon Hedges Esqr. one of his Majestys Justices of the Peace

Thomas, Lord Fairfax

for the County of Frederick where we camped. When we came to Supper there was neither a Cloth upon the Table nor a Knife to eat with but as good luck would have it we had Knives of own. . . .

Fryday April the 1st. 1748. This Morning Shot twice at Wild Turkies but killd none. Run of three Lots & returnd to Camp.

Saterday April 2d. Last Night was a blowing Rainy night. Our Straw catch'd a Fire that we were laying upon & was luckily Preserv'd by one of our Mens awaking when it was in a [blaze]. We run of four Lots this day which Reached below Stumps.

Sunday 3d. Last Night was a much more blostering night than the former. We had our Tent Carried Quite of with the Wind and was obliged to Lie the Latter part of the Night without covering. There came several Persons to see us this day. One of our Men Shot a Wild Turkie.

[George was completely unsympathetic when German settlers from Pennsylvania followed the surveying party. He apparently did not understand that these people, squatters on the land, knew the surveyors were the forerunners of trouble.]

Monday 4th. This morning Mr. Fairfax left us with Intent to go down to the Mouth of the Branch. We did two Lots & was attended by a great Company of People Men Women & Children that attended us through the Woods as we went shewing there Antick tricks. I really think they seem to be as Ignorant a Set of People as the Indians. They would never speak English but when spoken to they speak all Dutch. This day our Tent was blown down by the Violentness of the Wind. . . .

Wednesday 6th. Last Night was so Intolerably smoaky that we were obliged all hands to leave the Tent to the Mercy of the Wind and Fire. This day was attended by our afore[mentione]d. Company untill about 12 oClock when we finish'd we travelld down the Branch to Henry Vanmetriss on our Journey was catchd in a very heavy Rain. We got under a Straw House untill the Worst of it was over & then continued our Journey.

Relics of Washington's early surveying and military expeditions include his telescope (above), and his drawing instruments, pack saddle, and camp chest (right).

RIGHT: *Century Magazine*, MAY 1890
OTHERS: *Mount Vernon*, LOSSING

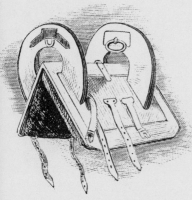

Thursday 7th. Rain'd Successively all Last night. This Morning one of our men Killed a Wild Turky that weight 20 Pounds. We went & Surveyd 15 Hundred Acres of Land & Returnd to Vanmetriss about 1 oClock. About two I heard that Mr. Fairfax was come up & at 1 Peter Casseys about 2 Miles of in the same Old Field. I then took my Horse & went up to see him. We eat our Dinners & Walked down to Vanmetriss. We stayed about two Hours & Walked back again and slept in Casseys House which was the first Night I had slept in a House since I came to the Branch.

Fryday 8th. We breakfasted at Casseys & Rode down to Vanmetriss to get all our Company together which when we had accomplished we Rode down below the Trough in order to Lay of Lots there. We laid of one this day. The Trough is [a] couple of Ledges of Mountain Impassable running side & side together for above 7 or 8 Miles & the River down between them. You must Ride Round the back of the Mountain for to get below them. We Camped this Night in the Woods near a Wild Meadow where was a Large Stack of Hay. After we had Pitched our Tent & made a very Large Fire we pull'd out our Knapsack in order to Recruit ourselves every [one] was his own Cook. Our Spits was forked sticks. Our Plates was a Large Chip. As for Dishes we had none.

[Fairfax and Washington either tired of the adventure, or the former considered his duty done, for they left the surveyors to carry on by themselves and headed for home, becoming lost once on the way.]

Saterday 9th. Set the Surveyors to work whilst Mr. Fairfax & myself stayed at the Tent. Our Provision being all exhausted & the Person that was to bring us a Recruit disappointing us we were obliged to go without untill we could get some from the Neighbours which was not till about 4 or 5 oClock in the Evening. We then took our Leaves of the Rest of our Company. Road Down to John Colins in order to set off next Day homewards.

Sunday 10th. We took our farewell of the Branch & travelld over Hills and Mountains to 1 Coddys on Great Cacapehon about 40 Miles.

Monday 11th. We Travelld from Coddys down to

Frederick Town where we Reached about 12 oClock. We dined in Town and then went to Capt. Hites & Lodged.

Tuesday 12th.   We set of from Capt. Hites in order to go over Wms. Gap about 20 Miles and after Riding about 20 Miles we had 20 to go for we had lost ourselves & got up as High as Ashbys Bent. We did get over Wms. Gap that Night and as low as Wm. Wests in Fairfax County 18 Miles from the Top of the Ridge. This day see a Rattled Snake the first we had seen in all our Journey.

Wednesday the 13th. of April 1748. Mr. Fairfax got safe home and I myself safe to my Brothers which concludes my Journal.

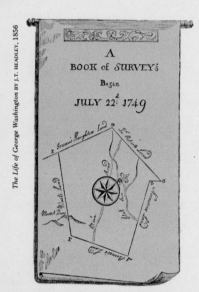

The Life of George Washington by J.T. Headley, 1856

Title page of a book of surveys started by Washington when he was seventeen and, at right, as a later artist imagined him at that age

Toward the end of that year, 1748, George William Fairfax married a charming young lady named Sarah Cary and brought her home to live at Belvoir. Sally, as she was known, was almost two years older than George; but from then, almost to the time of his death, George

Washington would hold the image of Sally Fairfax somewhere in his heart.

Other concerns in George's life were more worrisome or somber. His beloved brother Lawrence was suffering from a cough that worsened steadily and was ominously suggesting consumption. Mary Ball Washington was showing no disposition to make a home on her own land but was giving every sign of settling permanently on George's patrimony, the Ferry Farm. And by 1749 seventeen-year-old George was already occupied with earning a living, working as a surveyor and doing well. Through midsummer of that year he was helping to lay out the new town of Alexandria on the Potomac, and then he became the county surveyor of Culpeper County. In November he was on the frontier again, doing some work for Lord Fairfax, who had moved into the Shenandoah Valley. He wrote about it to a friend.

[November, 1749]

Dear Richard

The Receipt of your kind favor of the 2d. of this Instant afforded Me unspeakable pleasure as I am convinced I am still in the Memory of so Worthy a friend a friendship I shall ever be proud of Increasing. You gave me the more pleasure as I receiv'd it amongst a parcel of Barbarians and an uncooth set of People. The like favour often repeated would give me Pleasure altho I seem to be in a Place where no real Satis: be had. Since you receid my Letter on October Last I have not sleep'd above three Nights or four in a bed but after Walking a good deal all the Day lay down before the fire upon a Little Hay Straw Fodder or bairskin which ever is to be had with Man Wife and Children like a Parcel of Dogs or Catts & happy's he that gets the Birth nearest the fire. There's nothing would make it pass of tolerably but a good Reward. A Dubbleloon is my constant gain every Day that the Weather will permit my going out and some time Six Pistoles. The coldness of the Weather will not allow my making a long stay as the Lodging is rather too cold for the time of Year. I have never had my Cloths of but lay and sleep in them like a Negro except the few Nights I have lay'n in Frederick Town.

orge Washington Atlas, WASHINGTON 1932; LIBRARY OF CONGRESS

Washington's plan of the new town of Alexandria, Virginia, made in 1749 while he was helping to lay it out

During this same period George became acutely conscious of girls, and, like most young men on their first discovery of the fascinating subject, he tended to get a little purple and flowery in writing about it, as this somewhat rambling and obscure letter to a friend named Robin indicates. It was written from the frontier in late 1749 or the spring of 1750; the "Low Land Beauty" has never been identified.

As its the greatest mark of friendship and esteem absent Friends can shew each other in Writing, and often communicating their thoughts to his fellow companions makes me endeavour to signalize myself in acquainting you from time to time and at all times my situation and employments of Life, and could Wish you would take half the Pain of contriving me a Letter by any oppertunity as you may be well assured of its meeting with a very welcome reception. My Place of Residence is at present at his Lordships where I might was my heart disengag'd pass my time very pleasantly as there's a very agreeable Young Lady Lives in the same house (Colo. George Fairfax's Wife's sister) but as thats only adding Fuel to fire it makes me the more uneasy for by often and unavoidably being in Company with her revives my former Passion for your Low Land Beauty whereas was I to live more retired from young Women I might in some measure eliviate my sorrows by burying that chast and troublesome Passion in the grave of oblivion or etarnall forgetfulness for as I am very well assured that's the only antidote or remedy that I ever shall be releivd by or only recess that can administer any cure or help to me as I am well convinced was I ever to attempt any thing I should only get a denial which would be only adding grief to uneasiness.

Photograph of a lost portrait of Sally Cary, wife of Washington's friend and neighbor, George William Fairfax, and his first real love

During this vulnerable time, Washington was guilty of writing nebulous and moonstruck love poems. One such, which celebrated the charms of a passing fancy named Frances Alexander, was written as an acrostic, but before he quite finished it, George wearied either of the poem or of Frances.

From your bright sparkling Eyes, I was undone;
Rays, you have more transparent than the Sun,
A midst its glory in the rising Day,
None can you equal in your bright array;
Constant in your calm and unspotted mind;
Equal to all, but will to none Prove kind,
So knowing, seldom one so Young, you'l Find.
Ah! woe's me, that I should love and conceil
Long have I wish'd, but never dare reveal
Even though severely Loves Pains I feel;
Xerxes that great, was't free from Cupids Dart,
And all the greatest Heroes, felt His mark.

The young surveyor's work was so profitable that in October, 1750, he was able to purchase two pieces of land on Bullskin Creek, a tributary of the Shenandoah, and before the year was over he bought another tract, totaling almost fifteen hundred acres. As soon as winter ended in 1751, George was at work again, on surveys that sometimes took him to the frontier but often enough occupied him near enough at home so that he could visit brothers, sister, mother, and friends. Meanwhile, Lawrence's worsening health was casting a shadow. He had gone to London in the summer of 1749 to consult doctors but without result. Twice George accompanied him to the warm springs at Berkeley up the Potomac, the same springs George had seen on his 1748 trip. The spring waters, though reputed to have curative powers, helped Lawrence little, and it was decided that he should go to Barbados in the West Indies, whose winter climate was believed to be beneficial for lung ailments. Once again his half-brother dropped his own activities to go along. The pair left Virginia near the end of September, 1751; the following excerpts are from the diary George kept during the only trip he was ever to make outside of what would become the continental United States.

Eighteenth-century map with the island of Barbados at lower right

7 October 1751. But Little Wind at S Wt. & So. with calm smooth Sea and fair Weather. Saw many fish swimming abt. us of which a Dalphin we catchd. at Noon but cou'd not intice with a baited hook two Baricoota's which played under our Stern for some Hours. The Dalpin being small we had it dressed for Supper. . . .

19 October 1751. Hard Squals of Wind and Rain with a f[?]mented Sea jostling in heaps occasion[ed] by the Wavering wind which in 24 hours Veer'd the Compass not remaining 2 hours in any point. The Seamen seem'd disheartned confessing they never had seen such weather before. It was universally surmis'd there had been a violent hurricane not far distant. A prodigy in the West appear'd towards the suns setting abt. 6 [P.M.] remarkable for its extraordinary redness. . . .

[2 November 1751.] We were grea[tly al]arm'd with the cry of Land at 4 A:M: we quitted our Beds with Surpprise and found the land plainly appearing at [a]bout 3 leagues distance wh[en] by our reckonings we shou'd have been near 150 Leaugues to the Windward we to Leeward [abt.] the distance above mention[ed] and had we been but 3 or 4 leaugues more we shoud have been [o]ut of sight of the Island run down the Latit[ude a]nd probably not have discove[red the] Error in time to have gaind [l]and for 3 Weeks or More.

The land so narrowly sighted was Barbados. Two days after they arrived, a physician examined Lawrence and announced that his tuberculosis could be cured, and for a time the brothers were happy. They were constantly asked out, though George accepted the invitations of one of their frequent hosts with qualms because there was smallpox in the household (Lawrence was immune). The inevitable happened; George came down with the disease. It left his face somewhat pockmarked, but one day in the future it would let him move unafraid in army camps where soldiers were dying from the dreaded disease. It soon became apparent, however, that Barbados was doing Lawrence's racking cough no good, and he decided as a last resort to try the climate of Bermuda. There was nothing George could do for him, and on December 21, 1751, the two parted and the younger brother left for home, where he arrived early in February.

George busied himself again with his surveying work. In March, 1752, he added another 552 acres to his holdings on Bullskin Creek. And for the first time he considered himself not only enough in love, but old enough—he was twenty—and with sufficiently promising prospects, to think about addressing himself seriously to a young lady, Elizabeth ("Betsy") Fauntleroy, daughter of a man of high position in the Colony; she previously had spurned him. Now young Washington wrote, through her father, asking for a second chance.

May 20th. 1752

Sir

I shoud have been down long before this but my business in Frederick detain'd me somewhat longer than I expected and imediately upon my return from thence I was taken with a Violent Pleurisie which has reduced me very low but purpose as soon as I recover my strength to wait on Miss Betsy, in hopes of a Revocation of the former, cruel sentence, and see if I can meet with [any alter]ation in my favor. I have inclos'd a letter to her which I shoud be much obligd to you for the delivery of it. I have nothing to add but my best Respects to your good Lady and Family and that I am Sir, Yr. most Obedient Hble. Servt.

G WASHINGTON

Betsy Fauntleroy

Whatever the enclosed letter said, it apparently left Betsy unmoved. So far as we know, George gave up the pursuit then and there; Betsy went on to marry another. In mid-June of 1752, Lawrence arrived home. During his months on Barbados and Bermuda he had grown worse. He bravely set about trying to put his affairs in order, and on July 26, 1752, at Mount Vernon, he came to the end of his young life.

Chapter *2*

Wilderness Warrior

L awrence Washington had been Adjutant General of Virginia, the
commanding officer of the Colony's militia, and even before his
brother's death George had begun a campaign to obtain the office for
himself. It made no difference to him that he had never worn a uniform,
never drilled a corporal's guard of soldiers, never seen a fortification except
one he had visited in Barbados. With the bumptious optimism of youth he
argued his case with Robert Dinwiddie, Lieutenant Governor of Virginia,
and with others who might have influence, and in the end was in a degree
successful. When it was decided to divide Virginia into four military districts, he was appointed one of the district adjutants—and thus, before his
twenty-first birthday, became Major George Washington in 1753.

One of his principal duties as district adjutant was to travel about his
Southern District, teaching county militia officers how to drill their men;
but before he had time to do anything about his new chores—or even to
learn much about tactics himself—a more pressing matter arose. At that
time France and Great Britain were in a period of truce in their series of
wars for dominance not only of Europe but of North America and other
parts of the world. In 1753 France controlled Canada and the country west
of the Mississippi; Britain, the thirteen Colonies. Both nations claimed
the upper Ohio Valley.

In the spring of 1753 the French built a chain of forts between the shores
of Lake Erie and the Allegheny River. The forts were on land now part of
Pennsylvania but then claimed by Virginia, and word came from London to
Governor Dinwiddie of Virginia to warn the French off. Dinwiddie had his
own special reasons for being concerned: he was a member of the Ohio
Company, a group of land speculators who planned to build a fort as a
center for trade and settlement at the Forks of the Ohio, where the Allegheny
and Monongahela rivers join to form the Ohio, the site of today's Pittsburgh.
Having learned that Dinwiddie intended to send a message ordering the

French commander out of British territory, Washington rode to Williamsburg, the capital of Virginia, to volunteer to carry the letter. Dinwiddie accepted his offer at once, and Washington set out at the end of October. At Fredericksburg he picked up Jacob van Braam as his French interpreter, and at Wills Creek (now Cumberland), Maryland, he was joined by frontiersman Christopher Gist and also hired four men as "servitors."

During the rigors of his fall and winter journey, Washington kept a rough diary. On his return to Williamsburg, the Governor asked him to turn his notes into a connected account for the House of Burgesses. He had a single day for the task; his rush job in turn was given to the public printer, and the printed version is the one that survives (the printer's editing is undoubtedly responsible for removing most of Washington's frequent errors in spelling).

Wednesday, October 31st, 1753,
I was commissioned and appointed by the Honourable *Robert Dinwiddie,* Esq; Governor, &c., of *Virginia,* to visit and deliver a Letter to the Commandant of the *French* Forces on the *Ohio,* and set out on the intended Journey the same Day; the next, I arrived at *Fredericksburg,* and engaged Mr. *Jacob Vanbraam,* to be my *French* Interpreter; and proceeded with him to *Alexandria,* where we provided Necessaries; from thence we went to *Winchester,* and got Baggage, Horses, &c. and from thence we pursued the new Road to *Wills*-Creek, where we arrived the 14th of *November.*

Here I engaged Mr. *Gist* to pilot us out, and also hired four others as Servitors, *Barnaby Currin,* and *John MacQuire,* Indian Traders, *Henry Steward,* and *William Jenkins,* and in Company with those Persons, left the Inhabitants the Day following.

The excessive Rains and vast Quantity of Snow that had fallen, prevented our reaching Mr. *Frazier's* an Indian Trader, at the Mouth of *Turtle*-Creek, on *Monongahela* [River], till *Thursday* the 22d. We were informed here, that Expresses were sent a few Days ago to the Traders down the River, to acquaint them with the *French* General's [Sieur de Marin, sent to build a fort at the Forks of the Ohio] death, and the Return of the major Part of the *French* Army into Winter Quarters.

The Waters were quite impassible, without swimming our Horses; which obliged us to get the Loan of a Canoe from *Frazier,* and to send *Barnaby Currin,* and *Henry Steward,* down *Monongahela,* with our Baggage, to meet us at the Forks of *Ohio,* about 10 Miles, to cross *Aligany.*

Washington's headquarters at Wills Creek, from Lossing's Mount Vernon

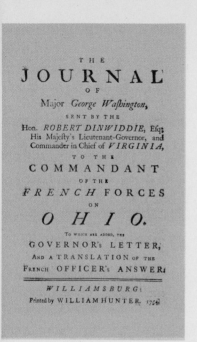

Title page of the printed Journal
*that Washington wrote for the House
of Burgesses at Dinwiddie's request*

As I got down before the Canoe, I spent some Time in viewing the Rivers, and the Land in the Fork, which I think extremely well situated for a Fort, as it has the absolute Command of both Rivers. The Land at the Point is 20 or 25 Feet above the common Surface of the Water, and a considerable Bottom of flat, well-timbered Land all around it, very convenient for Building: The Rivers are each a Quarter of a Mile, or more, across, and run here very near at right Angles: *Aligany* bearing N.E. and *Monongahela* S.E. the former of these two is a very rapid and swift running Water, the other deep and still, without any perceptible Fall.

About two Miles from this, on the South East Side of the River, at the Place where the *Ohio* Company intended to erect a Fort, lives *Shingiss,* King of the *Delawares;* We call'd upon him, to invite him to Council at the *Loggs*-Town.

[Washington proceeded to Logstown, seventeen miles below the Forks. It was a village of Delaware, Mingo, and Shawnee Indians, but its most important chief was Tanachariston, whom the English always called the Half King, an Oneida acting as a proconsul of the Iroquois Six Nations confederacy that maintained authority over the other tribes.]

25th [November, 1753]. Came to Town four of ten *Frenchmen* that deserted from a Company at the *Cuscuscas* [an Indian village], which lies at the Mouth of this River. I got the following Account from them. They were sent from *New Orleans* with 100 Men, and 8 Canoe Loads of Provisions to this Place; where they expected to have met the same Number of Men, from the Forts this Side Lake *Erie*, to convoy them and the Stores up, who were not arrived when they ran off.

I enquired into the Situation of the *French,* on the *Missisippi,* their Number, and what Forts they had built: They inform'd me, That there were four small Forts between *New-Orleans* and the *Black-Islands* [Van Braam evidently mistook the strange word "Illinois" to be *Isles Noires,* "Black Islands"], garrison'd with about 30 or 40 Men, and a few small Pieces, in each. That at *New-Orleans,* which is near the Mouth of the *Missisippi,* there are 35 Companies, of 40 Men each, with a pretty

Our Country BY BENSON J. LOSSING, 1877

Nineteenth-century depiction of "Major Washington on his mission to the French commander"

strong Fort mounting 8 Carriage Guns; and at the *Black-Islands* there are several Companies, and a Fort with 6 Guns. The *Black-Islands* are about 130 Leagues above the Mouth of the *Ohio*, which is about 350 above *New-Orleans*: They also acquainted me, that there was a small pallisado'd Fort on the *Ohio*, at the Mouth of the *Obaish* [Wabash] about 60 Leagues from the *Missisippi*: The *Obaish* heads near the West End of Lake *Erie*, and affords the Communication between the *French* on *Missisippi* and those on the Lakes. These Deserters came up from the lower *Shanoah* [Shawanoe, now Shawnee] Town with one *Brown,* an *Indian* Trader, and were going to *Philadelphia.*

About 3 o'Clock this Evening the Half-King came to Town; I went up and invited him and *Davison,* privately, to my Tent, and desir'd him to relate some of the Particulars of his Journey to the *French* Commandant, and Reception there; and to give me an Account of the Ways and Distance. He told me, that the nearest and levellest Way was now impassable, by Reason of many large miry Savannas; that we must be obliged to go by *Venango* [an Indian village on the Allegheny], and should not get to the near Fort under 5 or 6 Night's Sleep, good Travelling. When he went to the Fort, he said he was received in a very stern Manner by the late Commander; Who ask'd him very abruptly, what he had come about, and to declare his Business, which he said he did. . . .

[Washington was elated at the chief's recounting of his speech, for the Half King told of expressing his anger at the French; on the other hand, Washington was taken aback when the Half King told of expressing his vehement opposition to having either the French or the English settle in the Ohio country. Washington said nothing of this, however, when he spoke to the Indians in council the next day. Despite his impatience to be on his way, he yielded to the Half King's request that he wait until a guard be arranged for them and took the delay with better heart when told the Indians meant to warn the French to leave.]

30th [November, 1753]. Last Night the great Men assembled to their Council-House, to consult further about this Journey, and who were to go; the Result of which was, that only three of their Chiefs, with one of their best Hunters, should be our Convoy: The Reason which they gave for not sending more, after what had been proposed at Council the 26th, was, that a greater Number might give the *French* Suspicions of some bad Design, and cause them to be treated rudely: But I rather think they could not get their Hunters in.

We set out about 9 o'Clock with the Half-King, *Jeska-kake, White Thunder*, and the Hunter, and travelled on the Road to *Venango*, where we arrived the 4th of *December*, without any Thing remarkable happening but a continued Series of bad Weather.

[December 4]. This is an old *Indian* Town, situated at the Mouth of *French* Creek on *Ohio*, and lies near N. about 60 Miles from the *Loggs*-Town, but more than 70 the Way we were obliged to go.

We found the *French* Colours hoisted at a House which they drove Mr. *John Frazier*, an *English* Subject, from; I immediately repaired to it, to know where the Commander resided. There were three Officers, one of whom, Capt. *Joncaire*, inform'd me, that he had the Command of the *Ohio*, but that there was a General Officer at the near Fort, which he advised me to for an Answer. He invited us to sup with them, and treated us with the greatest Complaisance.

The Wine, as they dosed themselves pretty plentifully with it, soon banished the Restraint which at first appear'd in their Conversation, and gave a License to their Tongues to reveal their Sentiments more freely.

They told me, That it was their absolute Design to take Possession of the *Ohio*, and by G—— they would do it; for that they were sensible the *English* could raise two Men for their one; yet they knew, their Motions were too slow and dilatory to prevent any Under-taking of theirs. They pretend to have an undoubted Right to the River, from a Discovery made by one *La Sol* [La Salle] 60 Years ago; and the Rise of this Expedi-tion is, to prevent our settling on the River or Waters of it, as they have heard of some Families moving out in Order thereto. From the best Intelligence I could get, there have been 1500 Men on this Side *Ontario* Lake, but upon the Death of the General all were recalled to

Engraving of Tanachariston, the Half King, from The Pictorial Life of George Washington *by Frost, 1853*

about 6 or 700, who were left to garrison four Forts, 150 or there abouts in each, the first of which is on *French* Creek, near a small Lake, about 60 Miles from *Venango,* near N.N.W. the next lies on Lake *Erie,* where the greatest Part of their Stores are kept, about 15 Miles from the other; from that it is 120 Miles to the carrying Place, at the Falls of Lake *Erie* [Niagara Falls] where there is a small Fort which they lodge their Goods at, in bringing them from *Montreal,* the Place that all their Stores come from: The next Fort lies about 20 Miles from this, on *Ontario* Lake; between this Fort and *Montreal* there are three others, the first of which is near opposite to the *English* Fort *Oswego.* From the Fort on Lake *Erie* to *Montreal* is about 600 Miles, which they say requires no more, if good Weather, than four Weeks Voyage, if they go in Barks or large Vessels, that they can cross the Lake; but if they come in Canoes it will require 5 or 6 Weeks, for they are oblig'd to keep under the Shore.

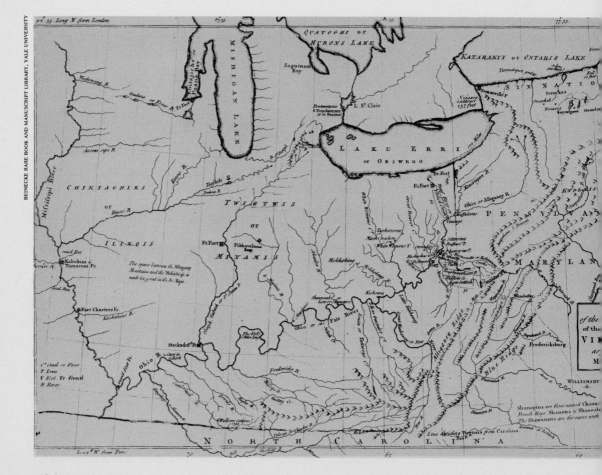

5th. Rain'd excessively all Day, which prevented our Travelling. Capt. *Joncaire* sent for the Half-King, as he had but just heard that he came with me: He affected to be much concern'd that I did not make free to bring them in before; I excused it in the best Manner I was capable, and told him I did not think their Company agreeable, as I had heard him say a good deal in Dispraise of *Indians* in general; but another Motive prevented me from bringing them into his Company; I knew he was Interpreter, and a Person of very great Influence among the *Indians,* and had lately used all possible Means to draw them over to their Interest; therefore I was desirous of giving no Opportunity that could be avoided.

When they came in, there was great Pleasure express'd at seeing them; he wonder'd how they could be so near without coming to visit him, made several trifling Presents, and applied Liquor so fast, that they were soon render'd incapable of the Business they came about, notwithstanding the Caution that was given.

6th. The Half-King came to my Tent, quite sober, and insisted very much that I should stay and hear what he had to say to the *French*; I fain would have prevented his speaking any Thing, 'til he came to the Commandant, but could not prevail: He told me, that at this Place a Council Fire was kindled, where all their Business with these People was to be transacted, and that the Management of the *Indian* Affairs was left solely to Monsieur *Joncaire.* As I was desirous of knowing the Issue of this, I agreed to stay, but sent our Horses a little Way up *French* Creek, to raft over and encamp; which I knew would make it near Night.

The version of Washington's Journal *that was printed in London included this "new map of the country as far as the Mississippi."*

About 10 o'Clock they met in Council; the King spoke much the same as he had before done to the General, and offer'd the *French* Speech-Belt [a wampum belt] which had before been demanded, with the Marks of four Towns on it, which Monsieur *Joncaire* refused to receive; but desired him to carry it to the Fort to the Commander.

7th. Monsieur *La Force,* Commissary of the *French* Stores, and three other Soldiers came over to accompany us up. We found it extremely difficult getting the *Indians* off To-day, as every Stratagem had been used to prevent

(

TRANSLATION of Legardeur de St. Piere, a [...] Officer, *in Answer to the Gove[...]*

SIR,

AS I have the Honour of commanding here in Chief, Mr. *Wafhington* delivered me the Letter which you wrote to the Commandant of the *French* Troops.

I fhould have been glad that you had given him Orders, or that he had been inclined to proceed to *Canada*, to fee our General; to whom it better belongs than to me to fet-forth the Evidence and Reality of the Rights of the King, my Mafter, upon the Lands fituated along the River *Obio*, and to conteft the Pretenfions of the King of *Great-Britain* thereto.

I fhall tranfmit your Letter to the Marquis *Duguifne*. His Anfwer will be a Law to me; and if he fhall order me to communicate it to you, Sir, you may be affured I fhall not fail to difpatch it to you forthwith.

As to the Summons you fend me to retire, I do not think myfelf obliged to obey it. Whatever may be your Inftructions, I am here by Virtue of the Orders of my General; and I intreat you, Sir, not to doubt one Moment, but that I am determin'd to conform myfelf to them with all the Exactnefs and

Translation of the letter from "Mr. Legardeur de St. Piere," in answer to Dinwiddie's, as it appeared in Washington's printed Journal, *now in damaged condition*

their going up with me. I had last Night left *John Davison* (the *Indian* Interpreter that I brought from the *Loggs-Town* with me) strictly charg'd not to be out of their Company, as I could not get them over to my Tent (they having some Business with *Custaloga,* to know the Reason why he did not deliver up the *French* Belt which he had in Keeping) but was obliged to send Mr. *Gist* over To-day to fetch them, which he did with great Persuasion.

At 11 o'Clock we set out for the Fort [Fort Le Boeuf], and were prevented from arriving there 'til the 11th. by excessive Rains, Snows, and bad Travelling, through many Mires and Swamps, which we were obliged to pass, to avoid crossing the Creek, which was impossible, either by fording or rafting, the Water was so high and rapid.

We passed over much good Land since we left *Venango,* and through several extensive and very rich Meadows; one of which I believe was near four Miles in Length, and considerably wide in some Places.

12th. I prepar'd early to wait upon the Commander, and was received and conducted to him by the second Officer in Command: I acquainted him with my Business, and offer'd my Commission and Letter, both of which he desired me to keep 'til the Arrival of Monsieur *Riparti,* Captain, at the next Fort, who was sent for and expected every Hour.

This Commander is a Knight of the military Order of St. *Lewis,* and named *Legardeur de St. Piere.* He is an elderly Gentleman, and has much the Air of a Soldier; he was sent over to take the Command, immediately upon the Death of the late General, and arrived here about seven Days before me.

At 2 o'Clock the Gentleman that was sent for arrived, when I offer'd the Letter, &c. again; which they receiv'd, and adjourn'd into a private Apartment for the Captain to translate, who understood a little *English;* after he had done it, the Commander desired I would walk in, and bring my Interpreter to peruse and correct it, which I did.

13th. The chief Officers retired, to hold a Council of War, which gave me an Opportunity of taking the Dimensions of the Fort, and making what Observations

I could.

It is situated on the South, or West Fork of *French* Creek, near the Water, and is almost surrounded by the Creek, and a small Branch of it which forms a Kind of an Island; four Houses compose the Sides; the Bastions are made of Piles driven into the Ground, and about 12 Feet above, and sharp at Top, with Port-Holes cut for Cannon and Loop-Holes for the small Arms to fire through; there are eight 6 lb. Pieces mounted, two in each Bastion, and one Piece of four Pound before the Gate; in the Bastions are a Guard-House, Chapel, Doctor's Lodging, and the Commander's private Store, round which are laid Plat-Forms for the Cannon and Men to stand on: There are several Barracks without the Fort, for the Soldiers Dwelling, covered, some with Bark, and some with Boards, and made chiefly of Loggs: There are also several other Houses, such as Stables, Smiths Shop, &c.

I could get no certain Account of the Number of Men here; but according to the best Judgment I could form, there are an Hundred exclusive of Officers, of which there are many. I also gave Orders to the People that were with me, to take an exact Account of the Canoes that were haled up to convey their Forces down in the Spring, which they did, and told 50 of Birch Bark, and 170 of Pine; besides many others that were block'd out, in Readiness to make.

Washington's critical meeting with St. Pierre, an illustration from Book of the Colonies *by Frost, 1846*

14*th.* As the Snow encreased very fast, and our Horses daily became weaker, I sent them off unloaded, under the Care of *Barnaby Currin* and two others, to make all convenient Dispatch to *Venango*, and there wait our Arrival if there was a Prospect of the Rivers freezing, if not, then to continue down to *Shanapin's* Town, at the Forks of *Ohio*, and there to wait 'til we came to cross *Aligany*, intending myself to go down by Water, as I had the Offer of a Canoe or Two....

This Evening I received an Answer to his Honour the Governor's Letter from the Commandant.

[The French commandant's letter said that he had no intention of obeying Dinwiddie's demand that the French leave the country. The officer did give Washington two canoes and provisions, but for a day the French at-

Washington descending the Ohio, from The Life of George Washington *by J. T. Headley published in 1856*

tempted unsuccessfully to cajole the Half King into remaining behind. After a cold and fatiguing seven-day trip, with four canoes of French closely following, they reached Venango on December 22.]

23d [December, 1753]. When I got Things ready to set off, I sent for the Half-King, to know whether he intended to go with us, or by Water, he told me that *White-Thunder* had hurt himself much, and was sick and unable to walk, therefore he was obliged to carry him down in a Canoe: As I found he intended to stay here a Day or two, and knew that Monsieur *Joncaire* would employ every Scheme to set him against the *English* as he had before done; I told him I hoped he would guard against his Flattery, and let no fine Speeches influence him in their Favour: He desired I might not be concerned, for he knew the *French* too well, for any Thing to engage him in their Behalf, and though he could not go down with us, he would endeavour to meet at the Forks with *Joseph Campbell,* to deliver a Speech for me to carry to his Honour the Governor. He told me he would order the young Hunter to attend us, and get Provision, *&c.* if wanted.

Our Horses were now so weak and feeble, and the Baggage heavy, as we were obliged to provide all the Necessaries that the Journey would require; that we doubted much their performing it: therefore myself and others (except the Drivers which were obliged to ride) gave up our Horses for Packs, to assist along with the Baggage; I put myself in an Indian walking Dress, and continued with them three Days, till I found there was no Probability of their getting in, in any reasonable Time; the Horses grew less able to travel every Day; the Cold increased very fast, and the Roads were becoming much worse by a deep Snow, continually freezing; and as I was uneasy to get back, to make Report of my Proceedings to his Honour the Governor, I determined to prosecute my Journey the nearest Way through the Woods, on Foot.

Accordingly I left Mr. *Vanbraam* in Charge of our Baggage, with Money and Directions, to Provide Necessaries from Place to Place for themselves and Horses, and to make the most convenient Dispatch in.

I took my necessary Papers, pulled off my Cloaths;

tied myself up in a Match Coat [a frontiersman's skin coat]; and with my Pack at my Back with my Papers and Provisions in it, and a Gun, set out with Mr. *Gist*, fitted in the same Manner, on *Wednesday* the 26th. The Day following, just after we had passed a Place called the *Murdering*-Town, where we intended to quit the Path, and steer across the Country for *Shannapins* Town, we fell in with a Party of *French* Indians, who had lain in Wait for us; one of them fired at Mr. *Gist* or me, not 15 Steps, but fortunately missed. We took this Fellow into Custody, and kept him till about 9 o'Clock at Night, and then let him go, and walked all the remaining Part of the Night without making any Stop, that we might get the Start, so far, as to be out of the Reach of their Pursuit the next Day, as we were well assured they would follow our Tract as soon as it was light: The next Day we continued travelling till quite dark, and got to the River [Allegheny] about two Miles above *Shannapins;* we expected to have found the River frozen, but it was not, only about 50 Yards from each Shore; the Ice I suppose had broken up above, for it was driving in vast Quantities.

There was no way for getting over but on a Raft, which we set about, with but one poor Hatchet, and got finished just after Sun-setting, after a whole Days Work; we got it launched, and on Board of it, and set off; but before we were Half Way over, we were jammed in the Ice in such a Manner that we expected every Moment our Raft to sink, and ourselves to perish; I put out my setting Pole to try to stop the Raft, that the Ice might pass by; when the Rapidity of the Stream threw it with so much Violence against the Pole, that it jirked me out into ten Feet Water, but I fortunately saved myself by catching hold of one of the Raft Logs; notwithstanding all our Efforts we could not get the Raft to either Shore, but were obliged, as we were near an Island, to quit our Raft and make to it.

Headley's version of Washington and Gist crossing the Allegheny River

The Cold was so extremely severe, that Mr. *Gist*, had all his Fingers, and some of his Toes frozen, and the Water was shut up so hard, that we found no Difficulty in getting off the Island, on the Ice, in the Morning, and went to Mr. *Frazier's*. We met here with 20 Warriors who were going to the *Southward* to War, but coming to a Place upon the Head of the great *Cunnaway* [Great

Kanawha River], where they found seven People killed
and scalped, all but one Woman with very light Hair,
they turned about and ran back, for fear the Inhabitants
should rise and take them as the Authors of the Murder:
They report that the People were lying about the House,
and some of them much torn and eaten by Hogs: By the
Marks that were left, they say they were *French* Indians
of the *Ottoway* Nation, &c., that did it.

As we intended to take Horses here, and it required
some Time to find them, I went up about three Miles
to the Mouth of *Yaughyaughgane* [Youghiogheny River]
to visit Queen *Alliquippa* [of the Delaware Nation],
who had expressed great Concern that we passed her
in going to the Fort. I made her a Present of a Matchcoat
and a Bottle of Rum, which latter was thought much the
best Present of the Two.

Tuesday the 1st. Day of *January* [1754], we left Mr.
Frazier's House, and arrived at Mr. *Gist's* at *Monongahela* the 2d, where I bought Horse, Saddle, &c. the 6th
we met 17 Horses loaded with Materials and Stores for
a Fort at the Forks of *Ohio,* and the Day after some
Families going out to settle: This Day we arrived at
Wills-Creek, after as fatiguing a Journey as it is possible to conceive, rendered so by excessive bad Weather:
From the first Day of *December* to the 15th, there was
but one Day but it rained or snowed incessantly; and
throughout the whole Journey we met with nothing but
one continued Series of cold wet Weather, which occasioned very uncomfortable Lodgings, especially after
we had left our Tent, which was some Screen from the
Inclemency of it.

On the 11th I got to *Belvoir* where I stopped one Day
to take necessary Rest, and then set out, and arrived in
Williamsburg the 16th, and waited upon his Honour the
Governor with the Letter I had brought from the *French*
Commandant, and to give an Account of the Proceedings
of my Journey, which I beg Leave to do by offering the
foregoing, as it contains the most remarkable Occurences
that happened to me.

I hope it will be sufficient to satisfy your Honour
with my Proceedings; for that was my Aim in under-
taking the Journey, and chief Study throughout the
Prosecution of it.

Washington's accomplishment had been a noteworthy one. Although a tenderfoot, he had borne well the rigors of travel in the bitter wilderness. Sent to deliver a letter, he had found himself involved in a diplomatic battle for the allegiance of an Indian chief and had done well for an amateur against professionals. Only once had his steps lagged, the one-day stop at Belvoir "to take necessary Rest"; and it may well be that it was the captivating Sally Fairfax more than fatigue that made him break his journey there.

The news he brought was extremely upsetting to Governor Dinwiddie and others in Williamsburg, but Washington was chagrined to find that many read his report with skepticism, as largely fiction designed to gain backing for the Ohio Company. The House of Burgesses showed little interest in the Ohio country, but eventually an expedition of three hundred men was authorized. These men, it was promised, would have the help of a thousand Cherokee and Catawba warriors from the Carolinas, and the Government in London informed the Governor that three companies of regulars would also be sent from other Colonies. The expedition was to hurry to the Forks, to aid William Trent, an Indian trader, who with forty men had already begun building a fort at the juncture of the Allegheny and Monongahela rivers.

Colonel Joshua Fry was in command; George Washington, commissioned a lieutenant colonel, was second in rank. Recruiting went slowly, and it was decided that Washington should go ahead with the vanguard, leaving Colonel Fry to follow later. On April 2, 1754, Washington led 120 men out of Alexandria. He found about forty more waiting at Winchester, but had an almost impossible time obtaining transport from the farmers, who hid all but their most broken-down wagons and decrepit horses. Two weeks later, at Wills Creek, he reported extremely disheartening news to Governor Dinwiddie.

Will's Creek [Maryland] April 25, 1754
Captain Trent's ensign, Mr. Ward, has this day arrived from the Fork of the Monongahela, and brings the disagreeable account, that the fort, on the 17th instant, was surrendered at the summons of Monsieur Contrecœur to a body of French, consisting of upwards of one thousand men, who came from Venango with eighteen pieces of cannon, sixty batteaux, and three hundred canoes. They gave him liberty to bring off all his men and working-tools, which he accordingly did the same day.

Immediately upon this information I called a council of war, to advise on proper measures to be taken in this exigency. A copy of their resolves, with the proceedings, I herewith enclose by the bearer, whom I have continued express to your Honor for more minute

Cartouche from a map drawn in 1751 by Joshua Fry, who three years later led the expedition to the Forks, and Peter Jefferson, father of Thomas

intelligence.

Mr. Ward has the summons with him, and a speech from the Half-King, which I also enclose, with the wampum. He is accompanied by one of the Indians mentioned therein, who were sent to see where we were, what was our strength, and to know the time to expect us out. The other young man I have prevailed upon to return to the Half-King with the following speech [pledging British friendship to the Half King and his people].

I hope my proceedings in these affairs will be satisfactory to your Honor, as I have, to the utmost of my knowledge, consulted the interest of the expedition and good of my country; whose rights, while they are asserted in so just a cause, I will defend to the last remains of life.

Hitherto the difficulties I have met with in marching have been greater, than I expect to encounter on the Ohio, when possibly I may be surrounded by the enemy, and these difficulties have been occasioned by those, who, had they acted as becomes every good subject, would have exerted their utmost abilities to forward our just designs. Out of seventy-four wagons impressed at Winchester, we got but ten after waiting a week, and some of those so badly provided with teams, that the soldiers were obliged to assist them up the hills, although it was known they had better teams at home. I doubt not that in some points I may have strained the law; but I hope, as my sole motive was to expedite the march, I shall be supported in it, should my authority be questioned, which at present I do not apprehend, unless some busybody intermeddles.

Your Honor will see by the resolves in council, that I am destined to the Monongahela with all the diligent despatch in my power. We will endeavour to make the road sufficiently good for the heaviest artillery to pass, and when we arrive at Red-stone Creek [site of an Ohio Company storehouse], fortify ourselves as strongly as the short time will allow. I doubt not that we can maintain a possession there, till we are reinforced, unless the rising of the waters shall admit the enemy's cannon to be conveyed up in canoes, and then I flatter myself we shall not be so destitute of intelligence, as not to get timely notice of it, and make a good retreat.

Governor Robert Dinwiddie

I hope you will see the absolute necessity for our having, as soon as our forces are collected, a number of cannon, some of heavy metal, with mortars and grenadoes to attack the French, and put us on an equal footing with them.

Perhaps it may also be thought advisable to invite the Cherokees, Catawbas, and Chickasaws to march to our assistance, as we are informed that six hundred Chippewas and Ottawas are marching down Scioto Creek to join the French, who are coming up the Ohio. In that case I would beg leave to recommend their being ordered to this place first, that a peace may be concluded between them and the Six Nations; for I am informed by several persons, that, as no good harmony subsists between them, their coming first to the Ohio may create great disorders, and turn out much to our disadvantage.

On May 9 Washington was reporting his new woes to Dinwiddie: promised pack horses had not been waiting when the column arrived at Wills Creek, roadmaking was slow, Indian allies had not appeared, Captain William Trent's men returning from the Forks had been troublemakers.

Little Meadows [Pennsylvania]
9th. of May 1754

Honble. Sir

I acquainted your Honour by Mr. Ward with the determinations, which we prosecuted in 24 Days after his Departure, as soon as Waggons arrived to convey our Provisions. The want of proper Conveyances has much retarded this Expedition, and at this time, unfortunately delay'd the Detachment I have the Honour to command. Even when we came to Wills Ck. my disappointments were not less than before, for there I expected to have found a sufficient number of pack Horses provided by Captn. Trent conformable to his Promise, Majr. Carlyles Letter's and my own (that I might prosecute my first intention with light expeditious Marches) but instd. of tht., there was none in readiness, nor any in expectation, that I could perceive, which reducd me to the necessity of waitg. till Waggon's cd. be procur'd from the Branch (40 Miles distant). However in the mean time I detach'd a party of 60 Men to make and amend the Road, which party since the 25th. of Apl., and the main body since the 1st. Instt. have been laboriously employ'd, and have got no further than these Meadows abt. 20 Miles from the new Store; where we have been two Days making a Bridge across and are not done yet. The great difficulty and labour that it requires to amend and alter the Roads, prevents our Marchg. above 2, 3, or 4 Miles a Day, and I fear (tho. no diligence shall be neglected) we shall be detained some considerable time before it can be made good for the Carriages of the Artillery with Colo. Fry.

We Daily receive Intelligence from Ohio by one or other of the Trader's that are continually retreating to the Inhabitants with their Effects; they all concur, that the French are reinforced with 800 Men; and this Day by one Kalender I receiv'd an acct. which he sets forth as certain, that there is 600 Men building at the Falls of Ohio, from whence they intd. to move up to the lower Shawno Town at the Mouth of Sciodo Ck. to Erect their Fortresses. He likewise says that these forces at the Forks are Erectg. their works with their whole Force, and as he was coming met at Mr. Gists new settlemt. Monsieur La-Force with 4 Soldrs. who under the specious pretence of hunting Deserters were reconnoitreg. and discovering the Country. He also brings the agreeable news that the Half King has receiv'd, & is much pleas'd with the speech I sent them, and is now upon their March with 50 Men to meet us.

The French down the River are sending presents and invitations to all the neighbouring Indians, and practiseing every means to influence them in their Interest.

We have heard nothing from the Cawtaba's or any of the Southern Indians tho. this is the time we mostly need their assistance. I have not above 160 Effective Men with me since Captn. Trent have left us, who I discharg'd from this Detacht. & order'd them to wait your Honour's Comds. at Captn. Trents for I found them rather injurious to the other Men than Serviceable to the Expn. till they could be upon the same Establisht. with us and come under the rigr. of the Martial Law.

I am Honble. Sir with the most profound respect yr. Honour's most obt. & most Hbl. Servt.

GO: WASHINGTON

P.S. I hope yr. Hr. will excuse the papr. & wg. the want of conveniences obliges me to this.

More frustrations followed. Washington explored the Youghiogheny as a possible water route but found it obstructed by a falls. On May 27 he was writing to the Governor from a place called Great Meadows.

Gt. Meadws. [Pennsylvania]
27th. May 1754

I hereupon hurried to this place as a convenient spot. We have with Natures assistance made a good Intrenchment and by clearing the Bushes out of these Meadows prepar'd a charming field for an Encounter. I detach'd imediately upon my arrival here small light partys of horse (Wagn. Horses) to reconnoitre the Enemy and discover their strength & motion who returnd Yesterday witht. seeing any thing of them. Nevertheless we were alarmd at Night and remain under Arms from two OClock till near Sun rise. We conceive it was our own Men as 6 of them Deserted but can't be certain whether it was them or other Enemy's. Be it as it will they were fired at by the Centrys but I believe without damage.

This Morning Mr. Gist arrivd from his place where a Detachment of 50 Men was seen Yesterday at Noon Comd. by Monsr. Laforce. He afterwards saw their tracks within 5 Miles of our Camp. I imediately detachd 75 Men in pursuit of them who I hope will overtake them before they get to red Stone where their Canoes Lie. Mr. Gist being an Eye witness of our proceedings hereupon, and waiting for this witht. knowing till just now that he intended to wait upon your Honr. obliges me to refer to him for particulars. As I expect my Messenger in to Night from the Half King I shall write more fully to morrow by the Express that came from Colo. Fry.

But before I conclude I must take the Liberty of mentioning to your Honour the gt. necessity there is for having goods out here to give for Services of the Indians. They all expect it and refuse to Scout or do any thing without saying these Services are paid well by the French. I really think was 5 or 600 Pounds worth of proper goods sent it wd. tend more to our Interest than so many Thousands given in a Lump at a treaty. I have been obligd to pay Shirts for what they have already done which I cannot continue to do.

The Numbers of the French have been greatly magnified as your Honour may see by a copy of the inclosd journal who I sent out to gain intelligence. I have receivd

Letter's from the Governor's of Pensylvania & Maryland
Copys of which I also send. I am Yr. Honrs. most Obt. &
most Hble. Servt.

Go: Washington

P.S. I hope your Honr. will excuse the Haste with which
I was obligd. to use in writing this.

Two days later Washington was writing the Governor
again from Great Meadows. After he complained at great length about the
miserable pay of Colonial officers, he eventually got around to a matter
of some importance.

[Great Meadows, Pennsylvania,
May 29, 1754]

Now, Sir, as I have answer'd your Honour's Letter, I
shall beg leave to acq't you with what has happen'd
since I wrote by Mr. Gist. I then acquainted you, that I
had detach'd a party of 75 Men to meet with 50 of the
French, who, we had Intelligence, were upon their
March towards us to Reconnoitre &ca. Ab't 9 O'clock
the same night, I receiv'd an express from the Half
King, who was Incamp'd with several of his People ab't
6 Miles of, that he had seen the Tract of two French
Men x'ing the road, and believ'd the whole body were
lying not far off, as he had an acc't of that number passing Mr. Gist.

I set out with 40 Men before 10, and was from that
time till near Sun rise before we reach'd the Indian's
Camp, hav'g March'd in [a] small path, a heavy Rain,
and a Night as Dark as it is possible to conceive. We
were frequently tumbling one over another, and often
so lost, that 15 or 20 Minutes' search would not find
the path again.

When we came to the Half King, I council'd with
him, and got his assent to go hand in hand and strike
the French. Accordingly, himself, Monacatoocha, and
a few other Indians set out with us; and when we came
to the place where the Tracts were, the Half King sent
two Indians to follow their tracts, and discover their
lodgement, which they did ab't half a mile from the Road,
in a very obscure place surrounded with Rocks. I there-
upon, in conjunction with the Half King and Monacatoocha, form'd a disposition to attack y'm on all sides,
which we accordingly did, and, after an Engagement of

ab't 15 Minutes, we killed 10, wounded one, and took 21 Prisoners. Amongst those that were killed was Monsieur Jumonville, the Commander, princip'l Officers taken is Monsieur Druillong and Mons'r La force, who your Honour has often heard me speak of as a bold Enterprising Man, and a person of great sublity and cunning. With these are two Cadets.

These Officers pretend they were coming on an Embassy; but the absurdity of this pretext is too glaring, as your Honour will see by the Instructions and Summons inclos'd. These Instructions were to reconnoitre the Country, Roads, Creeks, &ca. to Potomack, which they were ab't to do. These Enterprising Men were purposely choose out to get intelligence, which they were to send Back by some brisk dispatches, with mention of the Day that they were to serve the Summons; which could be through no other view, than to get sufficient Reinforcements to fall upon us immediately after. This, with several other Reasons, induc'd all the Officers to believe firmly, that they were sent as spys, rather than any thing else, and has occasion'd my sending them as prisoners, tho' they expected (or at least had some faint hope, of being continued as ambassadors).

They, finding where we were Incamp'd, instead of coming up in a Publick manner, sought out one of the most secret Retirements, fitter for a Deserter than an Imbassador to incamp in, and s[t]ay'd there two or 3 Days, sent Spies to Reconnoitre our Camp, as we are told, tho' they deny it. Their whole Body mov'd back near 2 miles, sent off two runners to acquaint Contrecoeur with our Strength, and where we were Incamp'd. &ca. Now 36 Men w'd almost have been a Retinue for a Princely Ambassador, instead of Petit, why did they, if their designs were open, stay so long within 5 Miles of us, with't delivering his Ambassy, or acquainting me with it; His waiting c'd be with no other design, than to get Detachm't to enforce the Summons, as soon as it was given, they had no occasion to send out Spys, for the Name of Ambassador is Sacred among all Nations; but it was by the tract of these Spys, they were discover'd, and we got Intelligence of them. They w'd not have retir'd two Miles back with't delivering the Summons, and sought a sculking place (which, to do them justice, was done with g't Judgment) but for some

Death of M. Jumonville from Headley's Life of George Washington

especial reason: Besides The Summons is so insolent and savours so much of Gascoigny that if two Men only had come openly to deliver it. It was too great Indulgence to have sent them back. . . .

In this Engagement we had only one Man kill'd, and two or three wounded, among which was Lieutt. Waggener slightly, a most miraculous escape, as Our Right Wing was much expos'd to their Fire and receiv'd it all. . . .

Your Honour may depend I will not be surprized let them come what hour they will; and this is as much as I can promise, but my best endeavour's shall not be wanting to deserve more, I doubt not if you hear I am beaten, but you will at the same [time,] hear that we have done our duty in fighting as long [as] there was a possibility of hope.

Washington, with his little forest skirmish, had fired the opening gun of the Seven Years' War (1754–63), whose American phase is called the French and Indian War. At the moment, however, he was concerned only with his immediate problems, which increased on May 31 when Colonel Fry died after a horseback accident and Washington assumed command of all Virginia troops. Soon after, at the age of twenty-two, he was promoted to colonel.

At Great Meadows he built Fort Necessity, a stronghold that to his untrained eye appeared sturdy enough so that he need "not fear the attack of 500 men." Indian allies drifted in, but most were women and children who consumed great amounts of scarce provisions. In mid-June Captain James MacKay arrived from South Carolina with a company of the regular British army, but he refused to take orders from Washington, since any officer holding a commission from the King outranked any Colonial officer.

Washington resumed his slow advance toward Fort Duquesne, which the French had built at the Forks of the Ohio. The Virginians had scarcely begun fortifying an advanced position when word came that the French, greatly reinforced, were moving on them. There was a hasty retreat to Fort Necessity, which was hurriedly extended and strengthened, while the Indian allies quietly vanished. Despite what Washington had written about the place being "a charming field for an encounter," the position was poor. It was low, and trenches filled with water from a steady rain that began on the morning of July 3. Before the morning was over, the French attacked.

If Washington wrote a contemporary record of the engagement, it has been lost. Long afterward, in 1786, however, he sent a memorandum to a would-be biographer, describing the fight but warning that after so many years his memory was vague on some details.

The surrender of Fort Necessity, drafted in French, was signed by Washington and dated July 3, 1754.

[October, 1786]

About 9 Oclock on the 3d. of July the Enemy advanced with Shouts, and dismal Indian yells to our Intrenchments, but was opposed by so warm, spirited, and constant a fire, that to force the works in *that way* was abandoned by them; they then, from every little rising, tree, stump, Stone, and bush kept up a constant galding fire upon us; which was returned in the best manner we could till late in the Afternn. when their fell the most tremendous rain that can be conceived, filled our trenches with Water, Wet, not only the Ammunition in the Cartouch boxes and firelocks, but that which was in a small temporary Stockade in the middle of the Intrenchment called Fort Necessity erected for the sole purpose of its security, and that of the few stores we had; and left us nothing but a few (for all were not provided with them) Bayonets for defence. In this situation and *no* prospt. of bettering it terms of capitulation were offered to us by the enemy wch. with some alterations that were insisted upon were the more readily acceded to, as we had no Salt provisions, and but indifferently supplied with fresh; which, from the heat of the weather, would not keep; and because a full third of our numbers Officers as well as privates were, by this time, killed or wounded. The next Morning we marched out with the honors of War, but were soon plundered contrary to the Articles of capitulation of great part of our Baggage by the Savages. Our Sick and wounded were left with a detachment under the care, and command of the worthy Doctr. Craik (for he was not only Surgeon to the Regiment but a lieutt. therein) with such necessaries as we could collect and the Remains of the Regimt., and the detachment of Regulars, took up their line for the interior Country. And at Winchester met 2 Companies from No. Carolina on their March to join them. These being fresh, and properly provided, were ordered to proceed to Wills's Creek and establish a post (afterwards called Fort Cumberland) for the purpose of covering the Frontiers. Where they were joined by a Company from Maryland, which, about this time, had been raized, Captn. McKay with his detachment remd. at Winchester; and the Virginia Regiment proceedd. to Alexandria in order to recruit, and get supplied with cloathing and necessarys of which they stood much in need. In this manner the Winter was

49

employed, when advice was recd. of the force destined for this Service under the ordrs. of G. B. [General Braddock] and the arrival of Sir Jno. St. Clair the Q:Mastr. Genl with some new arrangement of Rank by which no Officer who did not *immediately* derive his Comn. from the *King* could command one *who did.* This was too degrading for G. W to submit to; accordingly, he resigned his Military employment; determining to serve the next campaign as a Volunteer.

Washington had lost thirty men killed and seventy wounded; the French admitted to two killed and seventeen wounded. Washington became something of a hero despite his defeat, although experienced military men criticized many aspects of his campaign. Moreover, the fight at Fort Necessity had wide reverberations. From the Crown in England came a promise of money and arms. Governor Horatio Sharpe of Maryland was given a King's commission and put in command of all forces that were to "be raised on this part of the continent to protect His Majesty's Dominions from the encroachments of his presumptuous enemies."

Word came that Washington's Virginia Regiment was to be broken up into independent companies, each led by a captain holding a regular commission. The plan would have reduced Washington in rank from colonel to captain; if he were unable to obtain a King's commission as captain he would have ranked below every officer, of whatever rank, who held such a commission. It was too much for his pride, and in late October of 1754 he handed his resignation to Dinwiddie.

Governor Sharpe, however, needed Washington's knowledge of the wilderness and wanted him along on the campaign he was trying to organize. He suggested that Washington might keep the title of colonel and assured him that the company he commanded would be kept on separate assignment, so that the proud Virginian would not be under the command of anyone he would have commanded as colonel. Washington refused, in a somewhat emotional letter to Sharpe's military aide.

Belvoir [Virginia], November 15th. 1754
I was favoured with your letter, from Rousby-Hall, of the 4th. Instant. It demands my best acknowledgments, for the particular marks of Esteem you have expressed therein; and for the kind assurances of his Excellency, Governour Sharp's good wishes towards me. I also thank you, and sincerely, Sir, for your friendly intention of making my situation easy, if I return to the Service; and do not doubt, could I submit to the Terms, that I should be as happy under your command, in the absence

of the General, as under any gentleman's whatever: but, I think, the disparity between the present offer of a Company, and my former Rank, too great to expect any real satisfaction or enjoyment in a Corps, where I once did, or thought I had a right to, command; even if his Excellency had power to suspend the Orders received in the Secretary of Wars' Letter; which, by the bye, I am very far from thinking he either has or will attempt to do, without fuller Instructions than I believe he has: especially, too, as there has been a representation of this matter by Governour Dinwiddie, and, I believe, the Assembly of this State; we have advices, that it was received before Demmarree obtained his Letter.

All that I presume the General can do, is, to prevent the different Corps from interfering, which will occasion the Duty to be done by Corps, instead of Detachments; a very inconvenient way, as is found by experience.

You make mention in your letter of my continuing in the Service, and retaining my Colo.'s Commission. This idea has filled me with surprise: for if you think me capable of holding a Commission that has neither rank or emolument annexed to it; you must entertain a very contemptible opinion of my weakness, and believe me to be more empty than the Commission itself.

Besides, Sir, if I had time, I could enumerate many good reasons, that forbid all thoughts of my Returning; and which, to you, or any other, would, upon the strictest scrutiny, appear to be well-founded. I must be reduced to a very low Command, and subjected to that of many who have acted as my inferior Officers. In short, every Captain, bearing the Kings' Commission; every half-pay Officer, or other, appearing with such commission, would rank before me; for these reasons, I choose to submit to the loss of Health, which I have, however, already sustained (not to mention that of Effects) and the fatigue I have undergone in our first Efforts; than subject myself to the same inconveniences, and run the risque of a second disappointment. I shall have the consolation itself, of knowing, that I have opened the way when the smallness of our numbers exposed us to the attacks of a Superior Enemy; That I have hitherto stood the heat and brunt of the Day, and escaped untouched, in time of extreme danger; and that I have the Thanks of my Country, for the Services I have rendered it.

It shall not sleep in silence, my having received information, that those peremptory Orders from Home, which, you say, could not be dispensed with, for reducing the Regiments into Independant Companies, were generated, hatched, & brought from Will's-Creek. Ingenuous treatment, & plain dealing, I at least expected. It is to be hoped the project will answer; it shall meet with my acquiescence in every thing except personal Services. I herewith enclose Governour Sharp's Letter, which I beg you will return to him, with my Acknowledgments for the favour he intended me; assure him, Sir, as you truly may, of my reluctance to quit the Service, and of the pleasure I should have received in attending his Fortunes: also, inform him, that it was to obey the call of Honour, and the advice of my Friends, I declined it, and not to gratify any desire I had to leave the military line.

My inclinations are strongly bent to arms.

The length of this, & the small room I have left, tell me how necessary it is to conclude, which I will do as you always shall find Truly & sincerely, Your most hble. Servant,

GEO. WASHINGTON

General Edward Braddock

With his military career over, at least for the time being, Washington turned to his land. Ferry Farm was to have become his on his twenty-first birthday, but he was now nearing twenty-three and his mother gave no sign of moving out. Lawrence, in his will, had left Mount Vernon to his baby daughter, with the provision that if there were no surviving children it would go to his widow until her death and then pass on to his brother George. Washington's chances of obtaining the plantation appeared thin; but Lawrence's daughter died in 1754, and his widow, who had remarried less than six months after Lawrence's death, had gone elsewhere to live with her new husband. George leased Mount Vernon from her, with eighteen resident slaves, for fifteen thousand pounds of tobacco yearly.

Thus, in December, 1754, George became the squire of Mount Vernon. But about the same time word spread through Virginia that an expedition commanded by Major General Edward Braddock was coming from Britain to drive the French from Fort Duquesne and so expel them from the upper Ohio country. Although George had resigned his commission, he still yearned for a military career, and he sent a letter when Braddock landed, congratulating him on his arrival in America—and incidentally letting him know that George Washington existed.

Washington's experience in wilderness fighting was not to be ignored, and Braddock's aide wrote to him, offering the Virginian a place on the General's staff, where he would not be subject to the humiliating distinction between regular and Colonial officers. In the latter part of March, 1755, Washington went to Alexandria, Virginia, where Braddock was organizing his expedition. He met the General, and it was agreed that Washington would join Braddock's staff at Wills Creek, Maryland. He was fascinated by his first contact with a professional army, and with the comings and goings of important Colonial leaders, and after having returned to Mount Vernon he wrote a letter to his confidant and adviser Colonel William Fairfax that reflected his pride at being part of the exciting scene.

[Mount Vernon, April 23, 1755]

I cannot think of quitting Fairfax, without embracing this last opportunity of bidding you farewell.

I this day set out for Wills Creek, where I expect to meet the Genl., and to stay — I fear too long, as our March must be regulated by the slow movements of the Train, which I am sorry to say, I think, will be tedious in advancing — very tedious indeed — as [agreeable] to the expectation I have long conceived, tho' few believ'd.

Alexandria has been honourd with 5 Governors in Consultation — a happy presage I hope, not only of the success of this Expedition, but for our little Town; for surely, such honours must have arisen from the Commodious, and pleasant situation of this place, the best constitutional qualitys for Popularity and encrease of a (now) flourishing Trade.

I have had the Honour to be introduced to the Governors; and of being well receiv'd by them all; especially Mr. Shirley, whose Character and appearance has perfectly charm'd me, as I think his every word, and every Action discovers something of the fine Gent'n., and great Politician. I heartily wish such unanimity amongst us, as appeard to Reign between him and his Assembly; when they, to expidate the Business, and forward his Journey here, sat till eleven, and twelve o'clock at Nights.

Mount Vernon, LOSSING

Washington first met General Edward Braddock (opposite) at this house in Alexandria, which served as his Virginia organizing headquarters.

Washington rode out to inspect his Bullskin plantation on the Shenandoah before joining Braddock. While there, he wrote to Sally Fairfax, asking her to correspond with him.

[Bullskin, Virginia, April 30, 1755]

Dear Madam

In order to engage your corrispondance, I think it

expedient just to deserve it; which I shall endeavour to do, by embracing the earliest, and every oppirtunity, of Writing to you.

It will be needless to expatiate on the pleasures that a communication of this kind will afford me, as it shall suffice to say—a corrispondance with my Friends is the greatest satisfaction I expect to enjoy, in the course of the Campaigne, and that none of my Friends are able to convey more real delight than you can to whom I stand indebted for so many Obligations.

If an old Proverb can claim my belief I am certainly [close to a] share of success—for surely no Man ever made a worse beginning than I have: out of 4 Horses which we brought from home, one was killd outright, and the other 3 rinderd unfit for use; so that I have been detain here three days already, and how much longer I may continue to be so, the Womb of time must discover.

Braddock's forces moved forward at a snail's pace, methodically building a road, while the General damned the Colonists who did not deliver the wagons, horses, and supplies they had promised (only a Pennsylvanian, Benjamin Franklin, provided every one of the wagons, with teams and drivers, that he had pledged). Indians and Frenchmen wise in the ways of forest fighting struck now and then as the column moved through the woods, often at no more than two miles a day; a few men were killed, but when Washington tried to warn how unsuited the British methods were for forest warfare, he was shrugged off as the British officers expressed serene faith in their tactics and firepower. Braddock did, however, accept Washington's suggestion that a portion of the column leave some of its ponderous train of artillery and supply wagons behind and push on more rapidly before French reinforcements could reach the fort.

Washington became ill with a fever and violent head pains and had to remain behind at a supply depot on June 20 while Braddock's vanguard pushed on. Later, still painfully ill, he rejoined Braddock so as not to miss the assault on the fort, catching up with the advanced force on July 8 where it was camped only a dozen miles from Fort Duquesne. The next day the march was resumed. Early in the afternoon, the column was suddenly attacked by a much smaller force of French and Indians. The British soldiers, unable to see their enemy in the forest, hearing blood-chilling war whoops everywhere, and with their comrades falling about them, panicked completely. Only the despised Virginia Colonials, over whom Washington took command, retained some semblance of discipline. Washington wrote about it to Governor Dinwiddie.

DVERTISEMENT

Lancaſter, May 6th. 1755.

ICE is hereby given to all who have contracted to ſend Waggons and Teams, or ngle Horſes from *York* County to the Army at *Will's* Creek, that *David M'Conaughy* d *Michael Schwoope* of the ſaid County, Gentlemen, will attend on my Behalf at *York* n *Friday* next, and at *Philip Forney's* on *Saturday*, to value or appraiſe all ſuch Wag-eams and Horſes, as ſhall appear at thoſe Places on the ſaid Days for that Purpoſe; and do not then appear muſt be valued at *Will's* Creek.

Waggons that are valued at *York* and *Forney's*, are to ſet out immediately after the Va-on thence for *Will's* Creek, under the Conduct and Direction of Perſons I ſhall appoint Purpoſe.

Owner or Owners of each Waggon or Set of Horſes, ſhould bring with them to the Valuation, and deliver to the Appraiſers, a Paper containing a Deſcription of their orſes in Writing, with their ſeveral Marks natural and artificial; which Paper is to be to the Contract.

Waggon ſhould be furniſhed with a Cover, that the Goods laden therein may be n Damage by the Rain, and the Health of the Drivers preſerved, who are to lodge in aggons. And each Cover ſhould be marked with the Contractor's Name in large

Waggon, and every Horſe Driver ſhould alſo be furniſhed with a Hook or Sickle, the long Graſs that grows in the Country beyond the Mountains.

the Waggons are obliged to carry a Load of Oats, or Indian Corn, Perſons who have n to diſpoſe of, are deſired to be cautious how they hinder the King's Service, by do-an extravagant Price on this Occaſion.

B. FRANKLIN.

Bekanntmachung.

Lancaſter, 6ten May, 1755.

[German blackletter text]

B. Fränklin.

Franklin's successful advertisement for horses and wagons was printed in both English and German. The map below of General Braddock's defeat was drawn by a British engineer serving in his army.

[Fort Cumberland, Maryland, July 18, 1755]
As I am favour'd with an oppertunity, I shou'd think my-self inexcusable, was I to omit givg. you some acct. of our late Engagemt. with the French on the Monongahela the 9th. Inst.

We continued our March from Fort Cumberland to Frazer's (which is within 7 Miles of Duquisne) witht. meetg. with any extraordinary event, havg. only a strag-ler or two picked Up by the French Indians. When we came to this place, we were attackd, (very unexpectedly I must own) by abt. 300 French and Indns.; Our numbers consisted of abt. 1300 well armd Men, chiefly regular's, who were immediately struck with such a deadly Panick, that nothing but confusion and disobedience of order's prevaild amongst them. The Officer's in Genl. behavd with incomparable bravery, for which they greatly suf-ferd, there being near 60 killd and woundd. A large Proportion out of the number we had! The Virginian Companies behavd like Men, and died like Soldier's; for I believe out of 3 Companys that were there that Day, scarce 30 were left alive: Captn. Peyrouny and all his Officer's down to a Corporal, were killd; Captn. Polson shard almost as hard a Fate, for only one of his Escap'd: In short the dastardly behaviour of the English Soldiers expos'd all those who were inclin'd to do their duty, to almost certain Death; and at length, in despight of every

effort to the contrery broke & run as Sheep before the Hounds, leavg. the Artillery, Ammunition, Provisions and every individual thing we had with us a prize to the Enemy; and when we endeavourd to rally them in hopes of regaining our invaluable Loss, it was with as much Success as if we had attempted to have stopd the Wild Bears of the Mountains.

The Genl. was wounded behind the Shoulder, & into the Breast, of wch. he died three days after; his two Aids de Camp were both wounded, but are in a fair way of Recovering; Colo. Burton & Sir Jno. St. Clair are also wounded, and I hope will get over it; Sir Peter Halket, with many other brave Officers were killd in the Field. I luckily escap'd with't a Wound tho' I had four Bullets thro' my Coat & two Horses shot under me. It is supposed that we left 300 or more dead in the Field; abt. that number we brought off wounded; and it is imagin'd (I believe with good justice too) that two thirds of both those number's receiv'd their shots from our own cowardly Dogs of Soldiers, who gatherd themselves into a body contrary to orders 10 or 12 deep, woud then level, Fire, & shoot down the Men before them.

I Tremble at the consequences that this defeat may have upon our back setlers, who I suppose will all leave their habitation's unless their are proper measures taken for their security. Colo. Dunbar, who commands at present, intends as soon as his Men are recruited at this place to continue his March to Philda. into *Winter* Quarter's; so that there will be no Men left here unless it is the poor remains of the Virginia Troops; who now are, & will be too small to guard our Frontiers.

British military uniforms from the time of George II, worn by the soldiers fighting in America

RADIO TIMES HULTON PICTURE LIBRARY

The panic of defeat spread so far and so strongly that the rear force commander, Colonel Thomas Dunbar, assuming leadership from the dying Braddock, destroyed his artillery, transport, and supplies and retreated precipitately to Fort Cumberland at Wills Creek. There he decided that his forces were too few, too demoralized, and without sufficient artillery and other equipage to undertake any further action, and on August 2 he marched out of the frontier fort, heading for Philadelphia to go into winter quarters and leaving the border unprotected against the French and Indians except by the battered remnants of the Virginia Regiment. That same day, Washington at Mount Vernon was writing to a friend, expressing his disgust at the disaster in the wilderness.

Mount Vernon, August 2, 1755.

I must acknowledge you had great reason to be terrified with the first accts. that was given of our unhappy defeat, and I must own, I was not a little surpris'd to find that Governor Innis [James Innis, in charge of Fort Cumberland] was the means of alarming the Country with a report of that extraordinary nature, without having any better confirmation of the truth, than an affrighted waggoner's story. Its true, we have been beaten, most shamefully beaten, by a handful of Men! who only intended to molest and disturb our March; Victory was their smallest expectation, but see the wondrous works of Providence! the uncertainty of Human things! *We*, but a few moments before, believ'd our number's almost equal to the Canadian Force; *they* only expected to annoy us: Yet, contrary to all expectation, and even to the common course of things, we were totally defeated, sustain'd the loss of every thing; which they have got, are enrichen'd and strengthened by it. This, as you observe, must be an affecting story to the Colony; and will, no doubt, license the tongues of People to censure those they think most blamably; which by the by, often falls very wrongfully. I join very heartily with you in believing that when this story comes to be related in future Annals, it will meet with ridicule or indignation; for had I not been witness to the fact on that fatal Day, I sh'd scarce give credit to it now.

Dunbar's army was hardly out of sight before reports began to come in of Indians murdering isolated pioneer families on the Maryland and northwestern Virginia frontiers. In Williamsburg the General Assembly voted money to fill and equip the decimated Virginia Regiment, and Governor Dinwiddie offered George Washington an appointment not only as colonel commanding the regiment but as "commander of all the forces that now are or may be employed in the country's [Virginia's] service." Washington received his commission on August 14. At once he set to work. After having given his captains instructions for recruiting and training men, he hastened to Fort Cumberland. He reached that post on September 17, found its garrison almost demoralized, and immediately set about instilling discipline in his new command.

Fort Cumberland, September 19th. 1755

All the Men of the two Companies formed Yesterday, are to distinguish their Firelocks by some particular mark, which the Subaltern Officers of the Companies are to enter in a Book, which they are to keep for that purpose. And if any man changes or loses his Firelock, or other Arms, he is to be confined and severely punished. The Arms of all Deserters or Dead Men, are immediately to be delivered to the Commissary, who is to pass his Receipt for them to the Commanding Officer of the Company.

Any Soldier who is guilty of any breach of the Articles of War, by Swearing, getting Drunk, or using an Obscene Language; shall be severely Punished, without the Benefit of a Court Martial.

A Court Martial to sit immediately, for Trial of all the Prisoners in the Guard.

Captain Savage—President.

Members { Lieutenant Roe, Lieutenant Stewart; Lieutenant Linn, Lieutenant Blegg.

The Officers of the two Companies formed Yesterday, are to have their Rolls called over thrice every Day; which the Officers are to attend and see Done by turns, beginning with the Captain: and if any Soldier is absent without Leave, he is to be confined immediately, and

Letter of instruction from Governor Dinwiddie to Washington, August 14, 1755, after his appointment as commander of the Virginia Regiment

tried by a Court Martial, or punished at the Discretion of the Commanding Officer.

AFTER ORDERS

As Complaint has been made to me, that John Stewart, Soldier in Captain Bronaughs Company, keeps a Disorderly and riotous Assembly, constantly about him:

I do Order, that, for the future, he shall not presume to Sell any Liquor to any Soldier or any other Person whatsoever, under pain of the severest punishment.

From that time on, Washington's letters were largely of supplies that did not arrive, of orders disobeyed, of desertions, of multitudinous frustrations. In November he wrote to Lieutenant Colonel Adam Stephen, his second in command, about a serious situation.

Alexandria [Virginia] November 28, 1755

There has been such total negligence among the Recruiting Officers in general; such disregard of the Service they were employed in, and idle proceedings, that I am determined to send out none until we all meet; when each Officer shall have his own men and have only this alternative, to complete his number, or loose his Commission.

There are several officers who have been out six weeks or two months, without getting a man; spending their time in all the gaiety of pleasurable mirth, with their Relations and Friends; not attempting, or having a possible chance of Recruiting any but those who, out of their inclination to the service, will proffer themselves.

A month later he was reproving one of his company captains, John Ashby, in a letter that, except for the complaint about the man's wife, was typical of scores he had written and would write.

Winchester [Virginia] December 28, 1755

I am very much surprized to hear of the great irregularities which were allowed of in your Camp. The Rum, although sold by Joseph Coombs, I am credibly informed, is your property. There are continual complaints to me of the misbehaviour of your Wife; who I am told sows sedition among the men, and is chief of every mutiny. If she is not immediately sent from the Camp, or I hear any more complaints of such irregular Behaviour upon my arrival there; I shall take care to drive her out myself, and suspend *you*.

It is impossible to get clothing here for your men. I think none so proper for Rangers as Match-coats; therefore would advise you to procure them. Those who have not received clothing, for the future will receive their full pay without stoppages; and those already made, will be repaid them. . . .

I have sent you one of the mutiny Bills which you are (as far as it relates to the men) to have frequently read to them. Further; acquaint them, that if any Soldier deserts, altho' he return *himself*, he shall be hanged.

An intolerable situation prevailed at Fort Cumberland. Although vital to Virginia's defense, the fort was on the Maryland side of the Potomac, and arriving there early in October was one Captain John Dagworthy with a handful of Maryland troops. Dagworthy had once held a King's commission, and though his present status was cloudy, he attempted to order Washington and the Virginia troops about. Washington and his men were infuriated, and Washington wrote to Governor Dinwiddie, threatening to resign his commission unless the situation was corrected.

[Alexandria, January 14, 1756]

When I was down the Committee among other Things resolved that the Maryland and Carolina Companies shoud not be supported with our Provisions. This Resolve (I think) met with your Approbation; upon which I wrote to Colo. Stephen desiring him to acquaint Capt. Dagworthy thereof, who paid slight Regard to it, saying it was in the Kings Garrison and all the Troops had an equal Right to draw Provision with Us by his Order (as commanding Officer) and that We, after it was put there, had no Power to remove it without his Leave. I shoud therefore be glad of your Honours peremptory Orders what to do in this Case, as I dont care to act without Instructions lest it shoud appear to proceed from Pique & Resentment as having the Command disputed. This is one among the numberless Inconveniencies of having the Fort in Maryland. Capt. Dagworthy I dare venture to affirm is encouraged to say this by Governor Sharpe [of Maryland], who We know has wrote to him to keep the Command. This Capt. Dagworthy acquainted Colo. Stephen of himself.

As I have not yet heard how General Shirley has answered your Honrs. Request I fear the Success; especially as its next to an Impossibility (as Govr. Sharpe has been there to plead Capt. Dagworthy's Cause) by writing to make the General acquainted with the Nature of the Dispute. The officers have drawn up a Memorial to be presented to the General [Governor Shirley of Massachusetts], & that it may be properly strengthened they humbly beg your Sollicitation to have Us (as We have certain Advices that it is in his Power) put upon the Establishment. This woud at once put an End to Contention which is the Root of Evil & destructive to the best of Operations, and turn all our Movements into a free easy Channel. They have urged it in the warmest Manner to Me to appear personally before the General for this End, which I woud at this disagreeable Season gladly do Things being thus circumstanced if I have your Permission which I more freely ask since I have determined to resign a Commission which You were generously pleased to offer Me (and for which I shall always retain a grateful Sense of the Favour) rather than submit to the Command of a Person who I think has not such superlative Merit to balance the Inequality of Rank, however he adheres to what he calls his Right, & in which I know he is supported by Govr. Sharpe. He says that he has no Commission from the Province of Maryland but acts by Virtue of that from the King, that this was the Condition of his engaging in the Maryland Service, & when he was sent up there the first of last October was ordered by Governor Sharpe and Sr. John St. Clair not to give up his Right. To my certain Knowledge his Rank was disputed before General Braddock; who gave it in his Favour, and he accordingly took Place of every Captain upon the Expedition—except Capt. James Mercer and Capt. Rutherford whose Commissions were older than his so that I shoud not by any Means choose to act as your Honr. hinted in your last, lest I shoud be called to an Account myself.

I have during my Stay above from the 1st. Decr. to this, disposed of all the Men & Officers (that are not recruiting & can be spared from the Fort) in the best Manner I can for the Defence of the Inhabitants, and they will need no further Orders till I coud return, and the recruiting Officers are allowed till the 1st. of March to repair to their Rendezvous—which leaves at present nothing to do at the Fort but to train & discipline the Men, & prepare and salt the Provisions. For the better

Governor William Shirley

perfecting both these I have left full & clear Directions.

Besides in other Respects I think my going to the Northward might be of Service as I shoud thereby so far as they thought proper to communicate be acquainted with their Plan of Operations especially the Pennsylvanians so as to act as much as the Nature of Things woud admit in Concert.

When the Dagworthy affair got no better, Washington obtained permission from Dinwiddie to carry the Virginians' complaint to Governor William Shirley of Massachusetts, Commander in Chief of all Colonial forces. With two of his captains as aides and two servants, he set out in the first days of February, 1756. During five days in Philadelphia he spent a great deal on the new clothing that was always a weakness with him, and in New York he courted Polly Philipse, the sister-in-law of a friend and one of the wealthiest young ladies in the Colonies.

The little troop arrived in Boston on February 25. Governor Shirley gave Washington a letter stating unequivocally that the strutting Dagworthy ranked no higher than any other Colonial officer, but he did not give Washington a regular army commission, which the Virginian had deeply set his hopes on.

Washington had scarcely returned to Williamsburg on March 30 when urgent reports came in that the French and Indians, who had been immobilized during the winter, were attacking the frontier again. Washington hastened to the scene. His troubles were so many—insufficient men, provisions and pay that did not arrive, unwarranted criticism from officials safe in Williamsburg—that very soon he was writing to Governor Dinwiddie in a somewhat frantic tone.

Winchester [Virginia] April 22, 1756
This encloses several letters, and the minutes of a Council of War, which was held upon the receipt of them. Your Honor may see to what unhappy straits the distressed Inhabitants as well as I, am reduced. I am too little acquainted, Sir, with pathetic language, to attempt a description of the peoples distresses, though I have a generous soul, sensible of wrongs, and swelling for redress. But what can I do? If bleeding, dying! would glut their insatiate revenge, I would be a willing offering to savage fury, and die by inches, to save a people! I *see* their situation, know their danger, and participate their Sufferings, without having it in my power to give them further relief, than uncertain promises. In short, I see inevitable destruction in so clear a light, that, unless

Polly Philipse, later Mrs. Roger Morris, in a portrait by Copley

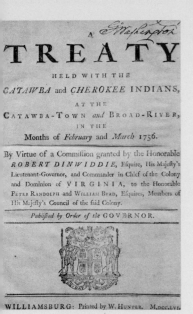

A
TREATY
HELD WITH THE
CATAWBA and CHEROKEE INDIANS,
AT THE
CATAWBA-TOWN and BROAD-RIVER,
IN THE
Months of *February* and *March* 1756.

By Virtue of a Commission granted by the Honorable
ROBERT DINWIDDIE, Esquire, His Majesty's
Lieutenant-Governor, and Commander in Chief of the Colony
and Dominion of V I R G I N I A, to the Honorable
PETER RANDOLPH and WILLIAM BYRD, Esquires, Members of
His Majesty's Council of the said Colony.

Published by Order of the G O V E R N O R.

WILLIAMSBURG: Printed by W. HUNTER. M,DCC,LVI.

*Title page of Washington's own
copy of a treaty signed with the
Indians during the winter of 1756*

vigorous measures are taken by the Assembly, and speedy assistance sent from below, the poor Inhabitants that are now in Forts, must unavoidably fall, while the remainder of the County are flying before the barbarous Foe. In fine, the melancholy situation of the people, the little prospect of assistance; The gross and scandalous abuses cast upon the Officers in general, which is reflecting upon me in particular, for suffering misconducts of such extraordinary kinds—and the distant prospects, if any, that I can see, of gaining Honor and Reputation in the Service, are motives which cause me to lament the hour that gave me a Commission, and would induce me, at any other time than this of imminent danger, to resign without one hesitating moment, a command, which I never expect to reap either Honor or Benefit from. But, on the contrary, have almost an absolute certainty of incurring displeasure below: While the murder of poor innocent Babes and helpless families, may be laid to my account here!

The supplicating tears of the women, and moving petitions from the men, melt me into such deadly sorrow, that I solemnly declare, if I know my own mind, I could offer myself a willing Sacrifice to the butchering Enemy, provided that would contribute to the people's ease.

Lord Fairfax has ordered men from the adjacent counties: But when they will come, or in what numbers, I cannot pretend to determine. If I may judge from the success we have met with here, I have but little hopes, as three days incessant endeavours have produced but twenty men....

Fortunately, the attacks soon lessened; the French and Indian parties apparently had returned in large part to Fort Duquesne. But problems continued, and one of the most pressing among many was that of widespread desertions. Washington reported on it to the Governor.

July 11, 1757.

The Deserters apprehended at Maidstone, were treated with such lenity as their subsequent behaviour convinces me was misplaced: Several of them having since deserted. This infamous practice, wherein such numbers of our own men have (by means of the villainy and ill-judged compassion of the country-people, who deem it a merit to assist Deserters) has been wonderfully successful; and is now arrived at such a height, that nothing can stop its scandalous progress, but the severest punishments, and most striking examples. Since mine of yesterday, no less than 24 more of the Draughts [drafted men] (after having received their money and clothes) deserted: notwithstanding every precaution I cou'd suggest was taken to prevent it: among others, I had all the roads way-laid in the night. Seven of those who went off last night, took that road which happened to be blocked up. Mr. Hughes (whom your Honor has been pleased to appoint adjutant) and two Soldiers, took two of them, after exchanging some Shot, and wou'd in all probability have taken them all, had he not been disabled in the right hand, & one of our Soldiers shot thro' the leg; and, it is believed, one of the Deserters was killed in the conflict.

I must again, earnestly request, your Honor will please to send me up a copy of the mutiny and desertion bill, passed the last Session of Assembly, with blank warrants to execute the Sentence of the Courts martial; without which I fear we will soon lose, not only all the draughts, but, by their going off with impunity, there is set such a bad example, as will render even the detension of the old Soldiers impracticable.

This engraving after a miniature by Charles Willson Peale was meant to show Washington at twenty-five.

Washington was a very forbearing commander but he had reached the end of his patience. Writing to Colonel John Stanwix, a regular army officer who had taken command of a new regiment on the frontier, he mentioned, among other things, a step he had taken to discourage desertions.

July 15, 1757.
No man I conceive was ever worse plagu'd than I have been with the Draughts that were sent from the several counties in this Government, to compleat its Regiment: out of 400 that were received at Fredericksburgh, and at this place, 114 have deserted, notwithstanding every precaution, except absolute confinement has been used to prevent this infamous practice. I have used the most vigorous measures to apprehend those fellows who escaped from hence (which amounted to about 30) and have succeeded so well that they are taken with the loss of one of their men, and a Soldier wounded. I have a

Gallows near 40 feet high erected (which has terrified the rest exceedingly), and I am determined, if I can be justified in the proceeding, to hang two or three on it, as an example to others.

Washington very soon put his gallows to use, as he reported in a subsequent letter to the Governor.

> Fort Loudoun [Virginia], August 3, 1757. I send your Honor a copy of the proceedings of a General Court martial. Two of those condemned, namely, Ignatious Edwards, and Wm. Smith, were hanged on thursday last, just before the companies marched for their respective posts. Your Honor will, I hope excuse my hanging, instead of shooting them: It conveyed much more terror to others; and it was for example sake, we did it. They were proper objects to suffer: Edwards had deserted twice before, and Smith was accounted one of the greatest villains upon the continent. Those who were intended to be whipped, have received their punishment accordingly; and I should be glad to know what your Honor wou'd choose to have done with the rest?

Washington submitted this plan for a line of march to General Forbes at that officer's express request.

Within three weeks, however, Washington's basically lenient nature had reasserted itself. He reported to Dinwiddie that he had freed some deserters from jail, since he found "examples of so little weight, and since those poor unhappy criminals have undergone no small pain of body and mind, in a dark room, closely ironed."

Although the chronically undermanned Virginia Regiment was never able to completely protect the frontier, it did make things more difficult for the French and Indian raiding parties. His exertions finally told on Washington; he developed a "bloody flux" (dysentery) that worsened, until by early November of 1757 he was in such distress that his physicians ordered him home at once for a long and painful convalescence. By the middle of March, 1758, he had recovered enough interest in life to call on Martha Dandridge Custis, one of the wealthiest young widows in Virginia. A week later he paid a second call, proposed marriage, and was accepted.

By the time Washington returned to duty in April, the military situation had changed. The British were making ready to put new life into their lagging war against France in America with a three-pronged offensive. One prong would be a new attempt to capture Fort Duquesne; it was to be led by Brigadier General John Forbes, and Washington would lead the Virginia Regiment (the conflict over rank had been eased by an order that any Colonial officer would be under the command of regulars only of higher rank). In late summer Washington received a letter from George William Fairfax about the progress of prenuptial remodeling at Mount Vernon. In it was enclosed a note from Sally, describing some phases of the work and also apparently teasing George about his coming marriage. Washington, as usual, burned her letter; she saved his answer, which leaves no doubt about his feelings toward her.

> Camp at Fort Cumberland [Maryland]
> 12th. Septr. 1758
>
> Dear Madam,
>
> Yesterday I was honourd with your short, but very agreable favour of the first Inst. How joyfully I catch at the happy occasion of renewing a Corrispondance which I feard was dis-relished on your part, I leave to time, that never failing Expositor of all things—and to a Monitor equally as faithful in my own Breast to Testifie. In silence I now express my joy. Silence which in some cases—I wish the present—speaks more Intelligably than the sweetest Eloquence.
>
> If you allow that any honour can be derivd from my opposition to Our present System of management you destroy the merit of it entirely in me by attributing my anxiety to the annimating prospect of possessing Mrs. Custis. When—I need not name it. Guess yourself. Shoud not my own Honour, and Country's welfare be the excitement? Tis true, I profess myself a Votary to Love. I acknowledge that a Lady is in the Case—and further I confess, that this Lady is known to you. Yes Madam, as well as she is to one, who is too sensible of her Charms to deny the Power, whose Influence he feels and must ever Submit to. I feel the force of her amiable beauties in the recollection of a thousand tender passages that I coud wish to obliterate, till I am bid to revive them. But experience alas! sadly reminds me how Impossible this is and evinces an Opinion which I have long entertaind, that there is a Destiny, which has the Sovereign controul of our Actions—not to be resisted by the strongest efforts of Human Nature.
>
> You have drawn me my dear Madam, or rather have I drawn myself, into an honest confession of a Simple Fact. Misconstrue not my meaning—'tis obvious—doubt i[t] not, nor expose it. The World has no business to know the object of my Love, declard in this manner to you when I want to conceal it. One thing above all things in this

Romanticized nineteenth-century engraving of Martha Washington

World I wish to know, and only one person of your Acquaintance can solve me that or guess my meaning. But adieu to this, till happier times, if I ever shall see them. The hours at present are melancholy dull. Neither the rugged Toils of War, nor the gentler conflict of A — B — s [Assembly Balls?] is in my choice. I dare believe you are as happy as you say. I wish I was happy also. Mirth, good Humour, ease of Mind and—what else? cannot fail to render you so, and consummate your Wishes. . . .

I cannot easily forgive the unseasonable haste of my last Express, if he deprivd me thereby of a single word you intended to add. The time of the present messenger is, as the last might have been, entirely at your disposal. I cant expect to hear from my Friends more than this once, before the Fate of the Expedition will, some how or other be determind. I therefore beg to know when you set out for Hampton, & when you expect to Return to Belvoir again—and I shoud be glad to hear also of your speedy departure, as I shall thereby hope for your return before I get down; the disappointment of seeing [the failure to see] your Family woud give me much concern. . . .

Be assured that I am Dr. Madam, with the most unfeignd regard,

Yr. Most Obedient & Most Obligd Hble Servt.

Go: Washington

Plan showing Fort Duquesne's dominance of the Forks of the Ohio

General Forbes built a new road west through Pennsylvania, while Washington protested, writing letter after letter, extolling the virtues of Braddock's road, minimizing its disadvantages, hinting that the new road was a Pennsylvania plot, and direly predicting that the expedition would never reach Fort Duquesne. Forbes was purposely moving slowly because a treaty was being arranged with the Indians; the diplomacy was successful, and the expedition reached the fort on November 25 to find that the French had burned it the night before and departed. Their Indian allies had deserted them. Washington had to leave part of his ragged Virginia Regiment in the desolate ruins to garrison the fort during the winter. He rode to Williamsburg to arrange clothing and supplies for the men who had been assigned the miserable duty. That taken care of, the young officer, not quite twenty-seven, who had once wanted a military career and had yearned to serve in the regular British army, resigned his commission as the year ended.

Chapter 3

The Squire
of Mount Vernon

Martha Custis and George Washington were married on January 6, 1759, on the Custis plantation. He was almost twenty-seven years old; she was a few months older. It was destined to be a happy marriage; she brought to it a cheerful nature, personal warmth, the ability to manage a large plantation household—all the attributes of a good companion and an excellent hostess. She was considered pretty, but she was diminutive, as small as her husband was large and strong—the contrast must have been striking.

Martha's late husband had left a large estate, 17,438 acres, with other property—cash, slaves, livestock, securities—worth some twenty thousand pounds sterling, or a little over half a million dollars, as nearly as it can be translated into today's terms. One third of this went to Martha and so became Washington's on marriage, subject to restrictions preventing him from alienating or encumbering her rights in the property. The other two thirds were the property of her two children, and Washington was made the administrator of their estate. Only in relation to her two children did Martha Washington fail to show common sense. At the time of her remarriage, her son, John Parke ("Jackie") Custis, was four; her daughter, Martha Parke ("Patsy") Custis, two. Their mother indulged them shamefully and had such a morbid anxiety about leaving them that she would not accompany George on trips unless the children went along. On February 22—the day he turned twenty-seven—Washington took his seat as a member in the House of Burgesses. He had been elected a member from Frederick County the previous July, even though he was on the Forbes expedition against Fort Duquesne at the time; his fame, the efforts of his friends, and his generous provision for potables (160 gallons of rum, punch, wine, and beer) made him an easy winner.

Leaving Williamsburg, Washington set out early in April for home with his bride, stepchildren, servants, and baggage. Not until he was almost at

Mount Vernon did it occur to him that he had made no arrangements for their arrival, and he sent a messenger galloping on ahead with urgent instructions for his manager, John Alton.

Thursday Morning [April 1, 1759]

I have sent Miles on to day, to let you know that I expect to be up to Morrow, & to get the Key from Colo. Fairfax's which I desire you will take care of. You must have the House very well clean'd, & were you to make Fires in the Rooms below it wd. Air them. You must get two of the best Bedsteads put up, one in the Hall Room, and the other in the little dining Room that use to be, & have Beds made on them against we come. You must also get out the Chairs and Tables & have them very well rubd. & Cleand. The Stair case ought also to be polishd in order to make it look well.

Enquire abt. in the Neighbourhood, & get some Egg's and Chickens, and prepare in the best manner you can for our coming. You need not however take out any more of the Furniture than the Beds Tables & Chairs in Order that they may be well rubd. & cleand.

The Custis family coat of arms, as engraved on a silver salver

In preparation for the arrival of his bride, Washington had added a story to the original story-and-a-half house at Mount Vernon, but he had found little time to furnish and decorate the enlarged mansion. Making this austere domain a home and managing a large household—there were eleven house slaves—was to be Martha's task. The land was George's responsibility. He accepted the challenge gladly; his diary entries early in the following year reveal that he was a man completely absorbed in his farming.

January 1 [1760] Tuesday. Visited my Plantations and receivd an Instance of Mr. French's great Love of Money in disappointing me of some Pork because the price had risen to 22/6 [22 shillings, 6 pence] after he had engagd to let me have it at 20/.

Calld at Mr. Posseys in my way home and desird him to engage me 100 Barl. of Corn upon the best terms he coud in Maryland.

And found Mrs. Washington upon my arrival broke out with the Meazles.

Jany. 2d. Wednesy. Mrs. Barnes who came to visit Mrs. Washington yesterday returnd home in my Chariot the Weather being too bad to Travel in an open Carriage

—which together with Mrs. Washington's Indisposition confind me to the House and gave me an oppertunity of Posting my Books and putting them in good Order.

Fearing a disappointment elsewhere in Pork I was fein to take Mr. French upon his own terms & engagd them to be delivd. at my House on Monday next.

Thursday Jany. 3d. The Weather continuing Bad & the same causes subsisting I confind myself to the House.

Morris who went to work Yesterday caught cold, and was laid up bad again—and several of the Family were taken with the Measles, but no bad Symtoms seem'd to attend any of them.

Hauled the Sein and got some fish, but was near being disappointd of my Boat by means of an Oyste[r] man who had lain at my Landing and plaged me a good deal by his disorderly behaviour.

Friday Jany. 4th. The Weather continued Drisling and Warm, and I kept the House all day. Mrs. Washington seemg. to be very ill [I] wrote to Mr. Green [a clergy-man-physician] this afternoon desiring his Company to visit her in the Morng.

Saturday Jany. 5th. Mrs. Washington appears to be something better. Mr. Green however came to see her abt. 11 Oclock and in an hour Mrs. Fairfax arrivd. Mr. Green prescribd the needful and just as we were going to Dinnr. Captn. Walter Stuart appeard with Doctr. Laurie.

The Evening being very cold, and the wind high Mr. Fairfax went home in the Chariot & soon afterwards Mulatto Jack arrivd from Fredk. with 4 Beeves.

Sunday Jany. 6th. The Chariot not returng. time enought from Colo. Fairfax's we were prevented from Church.

Mrs. Washington was a good deal better today, but the Oyster man still continued his Disorderly behaviour at my Landing I was obligd in the most preemptory manner to order him and his Compy. away which he did not Incline to obey till next morning. . . .

Tuesday Jany. 8. Directed an Indictment to be formd by Mr. Johnston against Jno. Ballendine for a fraud in some Iron he sold me.

Got a little Butter from Mr. Dalton—and wrote to Colo. West for Pork.

In the Evening 8 of Mr. French's Hogs from his Ravensworth Quarter came down one being lost on the way as the others might as well have been for their goodness.

Nothing but the disappoin[t]ments in this Article of Pork which he himself had causd and my necessities coud possibly have obligd me to take them.

Carpenter Sam was taken with the Meazles. . . .

Saturday Jany. 12th. Sett out with Mrs. Bassett on her journey to Port Royal. The morning was clear and fine but soon clouded and promisd much Rain or other falling weather wch. is generally the case after remarkable white Frosts—as it was today. We past Occoquan [Creek] witht. any great difficulty notwithstanding the Wind was something high and Lodgd at Mr. McCraes in Dumfries—sending the Horses to the Tavern.

Here I was informd that Colo. Cocke was disgusted at my House, and left it because he saw an old Negroe there resembling his own Image.

Washington wrote Martha's name on the title page of an English song book (left) during the first year of their marriage. He acquired an English gardening book (below) for his own library the following year.

NEW
PRINCIPLES
OF
GARDENING:

Or, The Laying out and Planting
PARTERRES, GROVES, WILDERNESSES,
LABYRINTHS, AVENUES, PARKS, &c.

After a more GRAND and RURAL MANNER, than
has been done before;

With Experimental Directions

For raising the several KINDS of FRUIT-TREES, FOREST-
TREES, EVER-GREENS and FLOWERING-SHRUBS
with which Gardens are adorn'd.

To which is added,

The various NAMES, DESCRIPTIONS, TEMPERATURES,
MEDICINAL VIRTUES, USES and CULTIVATIONS of
several ROOTS, PULSE, HERBS, &c. of the Kitchen and
Physick Gardens, that are absolutely necessary for the Service of
Families in general.

Illustrated with great Variety of GRAND DESIGNS, curiously
Engraven on twenty eight Folio Plates, by the best Hands.

By BATTY LANGLEY of Twickenham.

LONDON.

Printed for A. BETTESWORTH and J. BATLEY in Pater-Noster
Row, J. PEMBERTON in Fleetstreet, T. BOWLES in St. Paul's
Church-Yard, J. CLARKE, under the Royal Exchange,
and J. BOWLES at Mercer's Hall in Cheapside.
MDCCXXVIII.

Washington was not a skilled farmer at the outset. But unlike most of his fellow Virginians, he strove to preserve the land and its fertility. He ordered from London the latest books on agriculture, and he experimented with crops and farming methods, as these additional diary entries show.

Thursday April 3d [1760]. Sowd 17½ Drills of Trefoil seed in the ground adjoining the Garden, numbering from the side next the Stable (or Work shop) the residue of them viz 4 was sowd with Lucerne [alfalfa] Seed—both done with design to see how these Seeds answer in that Ground.

Sowd my Fallow Field in Oats today, and harrowd them in viz 10½ Bushels. Got done about three Oclock.

Cook Jack after laying of the Lands in this Field went to plowing in the 12 Acre Field where they were Yesterday as did the other plow abt. 5 Oclock after Pointing.

Got several Composts and laid them to dry in order to mix with the Earth brot. from the Field below to try their several Virtues.

Wind blew very fresh from South—Clouds often appeard, and sometimes threatned the near approach of Rain but a clear setting Sun seemd denoted the Contrary....

Monday Apl. 14. Fine warm day, Wind Soly. and clear till the Eveng. when it clouded;

No Fish were to be catchd today neither.

Mixd my Composts in a box with ten Apartments in the following manner viz—in No. 1 is three pecks of the Earth brought from below the Hill out of the 46 Acre Field without any mixture—in No.

2. is two pecks of the said Earth and one of Marle taken out of the said Field which Marle seemd a little Inclinable to Sand.

3. Has 2 Pecks of sd. Earth and 1 of Riverside Sand.

4. Has a Peck of Horse Dung.

5. Has Mud taken out of the Creek.

6. Has Cow Dung.

7. Marle from the Gullys on the Hillside wch. seemd. to be purer than the other.

8. Sheep Dung.

9. Black Mould taken out of the Pocoson [a swamp usually dry in summer] on the Creek side.

10. Clay got just below the Garden.

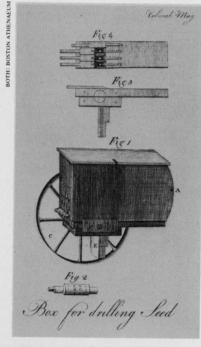

These two engravings, of a box for drilling seed and the plan for a granary (opposite), appeared in a volume of the Columbian Magazine that Washington had in his library.

All mixd with the same quantity & sort of Earth in the most effectual manner by reducing the whole to a tolerable degree of fineness & jubling them well together in a Cloth.

In each of these divisions were planted three Grains of Wheat 3 of Oats & as many of Barley all at equal distances in Rows & of equal depth (done by a Machine made for the purpose).

The Wheat Rows are next the Numberd side, the Oats in the Middle & the Barley on that side next the upper part of the Garden.

Two or three hours after sowing in this manner, and about an hour before Sun set I waterd them all equally alike with Water that had been standing in a Tub abt. two hours exposed to the Sun.

Began drawing Bricks burning Lime & Preparing for Mr. Triplet who is to be here on Wednesday to Work.

Finishd Harrowing the Clover Field, and began reharrowing of it. Got a new harrow made of smaller, and closer Tinings for Harrowing in Grain — the other being more proper for preparing the Ground for sowing.

Cook Jack's plow was stopd he being employd in setting the Lime Kiln.

Managing a plantation had its problems, but hard work usually produced results; much more frustrating was Washington's relationship with the English merchants who were his agents in selling his tobacco and in buying the endless items not available in the Colonies. Washington complained that he was underpaid for his tobacco, overcharged for the goods sent him, given inferior merchandise, and taken advantage of in various other ways. Typical of scores of laments was one to Robert Cary and Company, which handled most of Washington's overseas business.

[Mount Vernon, August 10, 1760]

By my Friend Mr. Fairfax I take the Oppertunity of acknowledging the Receipts of your several favours that have come to hand since mine of the 30th. of November last, and observe in one of them of the 14 Feby. by Crawford that you refer to another by the same Ship, but this has never yet appeard. . . .

The Insurrance on the Tobo. pr. Falman was high I think — higher than expected; And here Gentn. I cannot forbear ushering in a Complaint of the exorbitant prices of my Goods this year all of which are come to hand (except those packages put on board Hooper): For many Years I have Imported Goods from London as well as other Ports of Britain and can truely say I never had such a penny worth before. It woud be a needless Task to innumerate every Article that I have cause to except against, let it suffice to say that Woolens, Linnens, Nails &ca. are mean in quality but not in price, for in this they excel indeed, far above any I have ever had. It has always been a Custom with me when I make out my Invoices to estimate the Charge of them, this I do, for my own satisfaction, to know whether I am too fast or not, and I seldom vary much from the real prices doing it from old Notes &ca. but the amount of your Invoice exceeds my Calculations above 25 pr. Ct. & many Articles not sent that were wrote for.

I must once again beg the favour of you never to send me any Goods but in a Potomack Ship, and for this purpose let me recommend Captn. John Johnson in an annual Ship of Mr. Russels to this River. Johnson is a person I am acquainted with, know him to be very careful and he comes past my Door in his Ship: I am certain therefore of always having my Goods Landed in Good time and Order which never yet has happend when they come into another River: This year the Charming Polly went into Rappahannock & my Goods by her, recd. at different times and in bad order. The Porter entirely Drank out [by seamen during the voyage]. There came no Invoice of Mr. Dandridges Goods to me. I suppose it was forgot to be Inclosd.

Washington imported many items from London, including "Woollens" and "Linnens" such as those advertised in the trade cards above and opposite. The trade card of his own English cabinetmaker, Philip Bell, is reproduced at right.

Six weeks later Washington was penning a letter to the same agents, plaintively claiming that rapacious London shopkeepers were making Colonists their special victims.

[Mount Vernon, September 28, 1760]

By this conveyance, & under the same cover of this Letter, you will receive Invoices of such Goods as are wanting, which please to send as there directed by Capt. Johnston in the Spring—and let me beseech you Gentn. to give the necessary directions for purchasing of them upon the best Terms. It is needless for me to particularise the sorts, quality, or taste I woud choose to have them in unless it is observd; and you may believe me when I tell you that instead of getting things good and fashionable in their several kinds we often have Articles sent Us that coud only have been usd by our Forefathers in the days of yore. 'Tis a custom, I have some Reason to believe, with many Shop keepers, and Tradesmen in London when they know Goods are bespoke for Exportation to palm sometimes old, and sometimes very slight and indifferent Goods upon Us taking care at the same time to advance 10, 15 or perhaps 20 pr. Ct. upon them. My Packages pr. the Polly Captn. Hooper are not yet come to hand, & the Lord only, knows when they will without more trouble than they are worth. As to the Busts a future day will determine my choice of them if any are wrote for. Mrs. Washington sends home a Green Sack to get cleand, or fresh dyed of the same colour; made up into a handsome Sack again woud be her choice, but if the Cloth wont afford that, then to be thrown into a genteel Night Gown. The Pyramid you sent me last year got hurt, and the broken pieces I return by this oppertunity to get New ones made by them; please to order that they be securely Packd.

John Morris
LINNEN DRAPER,
at the Old Black Boy, in Norton Folgate,
(the Shop of the late
Mr. JOHN STEVENS Deceas'd)
near Bishopgate-Barrs, London.
Sells all Sorts of Hollands, Cambricks, Muslins,
Irish Linnens, Dowlas, Printed & Striped Cottons &
Linnens, wth all other sorts of Linnen Drapery Goods
Wholesale & Retail at Reasonable Rates

Mount Vernon was badly run down when Washington inherited it; he built and repaired and bought parcels of land to round out his acres and then had to buy more slaves to work the additional land. Nor did he and Martha scrimp in satisfying their desires for fine clothes, furniture, and entertaining. As a result, Robert Cary and Company informed Washington early in 1764 that instead of having a balance in his account, he was indebted to the firm. Moreover, Jackie Custis's balance—the money from his father's estate separately deposited for him in London—had also shrunk. George Washington was quite bewildered.

Williamsburg, May 1, 1764.
The Copy of your Letter of the 13th. of February—by Falman—is come to hand, but for want of the Account Inclosed in the Original I am a loss to conceive how my balance can possibly be so much as £1811.1.1 in your favour, or Master Custis's so little as £1407.14.7 in his; however as the several Accts. will shew what Articles are charged and credited—without which there can be no judging—I shall postpone an explicit answer till they arrive....

As to my own Debt I shall have no objections to allowing you Interest upon it untill it is discharged and you may charge it accordingly from this time forward, but had my Tobacco sold as I expected and the Bills been paid according to promise I was in hopes to have fallen very little in Arrears; however as it is otherwise I shall endeavour to discharge the Balle. as fast as I can, flattering myself there will be no just cause for complts. of the Tobacco this year.

Cultivating tools as depicted in an eighteenth-century encyclopedia, Maison Rustique, *which was also in George Washington's library*

Washington was forced to admit that the merchants' accounting was correct. He also at last faced up to a grim truth: no matter what he did, his Mount Vernon tobacco consistently received lower prices than that of his neighbors. Some of his 1765 diary entries reveal what he was doing about it.

[MAY]

12
13 } Sowed Hemp at Muddy hole by Swamp.

Do [Ditto] Sowed Do above the Meadow at Doeg Run
15   Sowed Do at head of the Swamp Muddy H
16   Sowed Hemp at the head of the Meadow at Doeg Run & about Southwards Houses with the Barrel

JULY

22.   Began to Sow Wheat at Rivr. Plantn.
23.   Began to Sow Do. at Muddy hole
25.   Began to Sow Do. at the Mill

AUGUST

9.   Abt. 6 Oclock put some Hemp in the Rivr. to Rot....
13.   Finish'd Sowing Wheat at the Rivr. Plantn. i.e. in the corn ground 123 Bushels it took to do it.
15.   The English Hemp i.e. the Hemp from the English Seed was picked at Muddy hole this day & was ripe.
15.   Began to seperate Hemp in the Neck....

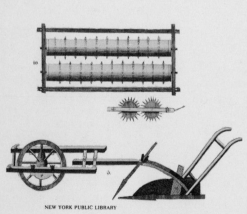

SEPTEMBER

24. Took up Flax which had been in Water since the 12th. viz 12 days.

Washington, again as can be seen from his diary, was beginning to grow hemp and flax and was greatly increasing his plantings of wheat. That year, 1765, Washington grew very little tobacco at Mount Vernon—although he continued to plant it on the Custis lands—and the next year none at all. Hemp and flax would prove unprofitable, but his production of wheat and corn greatly increased in the next three or four years; both were crops that could be sold at home, without costly shipping charges or fat commissions to London merchants. All was not work and worry at Mount Vernon, however. Washington was a social creature; he loved parties, dancing, horse races, cardplaying, the occasional drama that came to Williamsburg or Annapolis. He considered it a dull dinner when no guests were present, and once made the matter-of-fact entry in his diary, "Mrs. Possey and some young woman whose name was unknown to any body in this family dind here." In 1768 he began keeping separate entries of how his time was spent. They hardly presented a picture of a man too overworked to enjoy friends and pleasures.

JANUARY [1768]

Where, & how—my time is Spent.

1st. Fox huntg. in my own Neck with Mr. Robt. Alexander, and Mr. Colvill Catchd nothing. Captn. Posey with us.

2. Surveying some Lines of my Mt. Vernon Tract of Land.
3. At Home with Doctr. Rumney.
4. Rid to Muddy hole, D:Run, and Mill Plantn.
5. Went into the Neck.
6. Rid to Doeg Run and the Mill before Dinner. Mr. B. Fairfax and Mr. Robt. Alexander here.
7. Fox hunting with the above two Gentn. and Captn. Posey. Started but catchd nothing.
8. Hunting again in the same Comp'y. Started a Fox and run him 4 hours. Took the Hounds off at Night.
9. At Home with Mr. B: Fairfax.
10. At Home alone.
11. Running some Lines between me and Mr. Willm. Triplet.

Nineteenth-century print showing Washington and friends after a hunt

12. Attempted to go into the Neck on the Ice but it wd. not bear. In the Evening Mr. Chs. Dick, Mr. Muse & my Brother Charles came here.

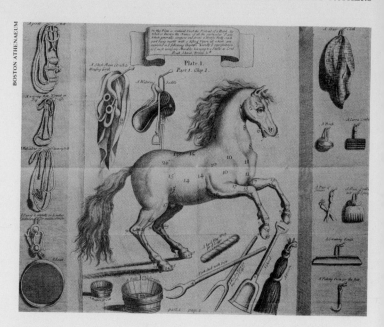

BOSTON ATHENAEUM

Washington, a superb horseman, owned a copy of The Compleat Horseman *containing this plate.*

13. At Home with them—Col. Fairfax, Lady, &ca.
14. Ditto—Do. Colo. Fx & famy went home in the Evening.
15. At Home with the above Gentlemen and Shooting together.
16. At home all day at Cards—it snowing.
17. At Home with Mr. Dick, &ca.
18. Went to Court and sold Colo. Colvil's L[an]d, returnd again at Night.
19. Went to Belvoir with Mr. Dick, my Bro. &ca.
20. Returnd from Do. by the Mill, Doeg Run and Muddy hole.
21. Surveyd the Water courses of my Mt. Vernon Tract of Land—taking advant. of the Ice.
22. Fox hunting with Capt. Posey, started but catchd. nothing.
23. Rid to Muddy hole & directed paths to be cut for Fox hunting.
24. Rid up to Toulston in order to Fox hunt it.
25. Confind by Rain with Mr. Fairfax and Mr. Alexander.
26. Went out with the Hounds but started no Fox. Some of the Hounds run of upon a Deer.
27. Went out again. Started a Fox ab. 10. Run him till 3 and lost him.
28. Returnd Home—found Mr. Tomi Elsey there.
29. Went to Belvoir with Mrs. W[ashingto]n, &ca. after Dinnr. Left Mr. Ellzey at home.

30. Dined at Belvoir and returnd in the Afternoon. Borrowed a hound from Mr. Whiting, as I did 2 from Mr. Alexr. the 28th.

31. At Home alone all day.

The humor in Washington's writings was infrequent and sometimes a bit heavy. One party he attended, however, did call forth some wry comments in his diary.

Friday Feby. 15th [1760]. A Small fine Rain from No. Et. wet the Top of my Hay that had been landed last Night. It was all carted up however to the Barn & the Wet and dry seperated.

Went to a Ball at Alexandria—where Musick and Dancing was the chief Entertainment. However in a convenient Room detachd for the purpose abounded great plenty of Bread and Butter, some Biscuets with Tea, & Coffee which the Drinkers of coud not Distinguish from Hot water sweetned. Be it rememberd that pocket hankerchiefs servd the purposes of Table Cloths & Napkins and that no Apologies were made for either.* (*I shall therefore distinguish this Ball by the Stile & title of the Bread & Butter Ball.)

Washington never was to father any children of his own. As a stepfather he was affectionate but overly indulgent, showing little firmness to counter Martha's doting attitude toward her children. As a result, his stepson, Jack Custis, a pleasant enough boy, grew up with little purpose in life beyond horses and clothes. Washington's concern that Jack should not lack for the best comes through clearly in a letter to the Reverend Jonathan Boucher, headmaster of a school for boys in Caroline County.

[Mount Vernon] May 30th. 1768

Mr. Magowan who lived several years in my Family a Tutor to Master Custis (my Son in law & Ward) having taken his departure for England leaves the young Gentleman without any Master at all at this time. I shoud be glad there fore to know if it woud be convenient for you to add him to the number of your Pupils. He is a boy of good genius, about 14 yrs. of age, untainted in his Morals, & of innocent Manners. Two yrs. and upwards he has been reading of Virgil, and was (at the time Mr. Magowan left him) entered upon the Greek Testament, tho' I presume he has grown not a little rusty in both;

Jack Custis and his sister, Patsy (opposite), in twin oval portraits painted in 1772 by C. W. Peale

having had no benefit of his Tutor since Christmas, notwithstanding he left the Country in March only.

If he come, he will have a boy [a personal slave] (well acquainted with House business, which may be made as useful as possible in your Family to keep him out of Idleness) and two Horses, to furnish him with the means of getting to Church, and elsewhere as you may permit; for he will be put entirely, and absolutely under your Tuition, and direction to manage as you think proper in all respects.

Now Sir, if you Incline to take Master Custis I shoud be glad to know what conveniencies it may be necessary for him to bring & how soon he may come, for as to his Board & Schooling (provendar for his Horses he may lay in himself) I do not think it necessary to enquire into, and will chearfully pay Ten or Twelve pounds a year extraordinary to engage your peculiar care of, and a watchful eye to him, as he is a promising boy—the last of his Family—& will possess a very large Fortune; add to this my anxiety to make him fit for more useful purposes, than a horse Racer &ca.

In May of 1773, when Jack was eighteen, Washington took him to New York, entered him in King's College (later Columbia), and rented comfortable lodgings for him and his servant. At college the youth dined with the faculty, a privilege doubtless arranged by his stepfather, for Jack boasted that no one else was similarly favored. But Jack tired of school, withdrew from college, and was married early in 1774 to Eleanor Calvert, member of a prominent Maryland family. Meanwhile Patsy Custis had been indulged as excessively as her brother, but her story was a tragic one. Washington's diary on June 14, 1768, noted that Patsy had been "seized with fitts." The fits—possibly epilepsy—continued. The family doctor did no good, nor did desperate resort to primitive remedies. An inevitable day came; Washington wrote of it to Burwell Bassett, Martha's brother-in-law.

Mount Vernon, 20th June, 1773.

It is an easier matter to conceive, than to describe the distress of this Family; especially that of the unhappy Parent of our Dear Patsy Custis, when I inform you that yesterday removed the Sweet Innocent Girl Entered into a more happy & peaceful abode than any she has met with in the afflicted Path she hitherto has trod.

She rose from Dinner about four o'clock in better health and spirits than she appeared to have been in

for some time; soon after which she was seized with one of her usual Fits, & expired in it, in less than two minutes without uttering a word, a groan, or scarce a sigh. This sudden, and unexpected blow, I scarce need add has almost reduced my poor Wife to the lowest ebb of Misery; which is encreas'd by the absence of her son, (whom I have just fixed at the College in New York from whence I returned the 8th. Inst.) and want of the balmy consolation of her Relations; which leads me more than ever to wish she could see them, and that I was Master of Arguments powerful enough to prevail upon Mrs. Dandridge [Martha's mother] to make this place her entire & absolute home. I should think as she lives a lonesome life (Betsey being married) it might suit her well, & be agreeable, both to herself & my Wife, to me most assuredly it would.

I do not purpose to add more at present, the end of my writing being only to inform you of this unhappy change.

One notable aspect of Washington's character was his insatiable desire to acquire land. By 1763 his total holdings were 9,381 acres, but he was thinking in much larger terms, and late in the summer of 1763 he entered a scheme to obtain a huge tract on the Mississippi from the Crown—a plan that eventually fell through. That same year he twice visited the Dismal Swamp, which straddles the Virginia–North Carolina border, convinced that a region of such lush vegetation must have rich soil. His summary of his trip into the Dismal Swamp was an unemotional appraisal of the area's soil and drainage possibilities.

15 *October*—1763 Memm. From Suffolk to Pocoson Swamp is reckoned about 6 Miles, and something better than 4 perhaps 5 miles from Collo. Reddick's Mill run (where the Road x's it). The land within this distance especially after passing Willis Reddicks is Level & not bad. The banks down to this (Pocoson) Swamp declines gradually, and the Swamp appears to be near 75 yds. over, but no Water in it at present. Note. Willis Reddick's Plantn. seems to be a good one, the land being level and stiff. So does Henry Riddick's above.

From Pocoson Swamp to Cyprus Swamp (which conducts more Water into the Great Dismal than any one of the many that leads into it) is about 2½ Miles. This also is dry at present, but appears to be 60 or 65 yards across in the wettest part.

The next Swamp to this is calld Mossey Swamp and distant about 3 Miles. Near this place lives Jno. Reddick on good Land, but hitherto from Pocoson Swamp, the land lies flat, wet, & poor. This Swamp is 60 yards over and dry.

Between Cyprus Swamp, and the last mentioned one we went on horse back not less than ½ a mile into the great Swamp (Dismal) without any sort of difficulty the horse not sinking over the fetlocks. The first quarter however abounding in Pine and Galebury bushes, the Soil being much intermixed with Sand but afterwards it grew blacker and richer with many young Reeds & few pines and this it may be observed here is the nature of the Swamp in general.

From Mossey Swamp to a branch and a large one it is, of Oropeak (not less than 80 yards over) is reckoned 4 Miles—two Miles short of which is a large Plantation belonging to one Brindle near to which (on the south side) passes the Carolina line.

The Main Swamp of Oropeak is about ½ a Mile from this, where stands the Widow Norflets Mi[ll] and luke Sumners Plantations. This Sw[am]p cannot be less than 200 yards across but does not nevertheless discharge as much water as Cyprus Swamp.

At the Mouth of this Swamp is a very large Meadow of 2 or 3000 Acres held by Sumner, Widow Norflet, Marmaduke Norflet, Powel and others and valuable ground it is....

...we crossed from Elias Stallens (one Mile above the upper bridge on Pequemin) across to a set of People which Inhabit a small slipe of Land between the said River Pequemen & the Dismal Swamp and from thence along a new cut path through the Main Swamp a Northerly course for 5 Miles to the Inhabitants of what they call new found land which is thick settled, very rich Land, and about 6 Miles from the aforesaid River Bridge of Paspetank. The Arm of the Dismal which we passed through to get to this New land (as it is called) is 3¼ Miles Measured—Little or no timber in it, but very full of Reeds & excessive rich. Thro this we carried horses without any great difficulty.

This Land was formerly esteemed part of the Dismal but being higher tho' full of Reeds People ventured to

A romantic engraving of George Washington at Lake Drummond in the Dismal Swamp

settle upon it and as it became more open, it became more dry & is now prodigeous fine land, but subject to wets and unhealthiness.

It is to be observed here that the tide, or still Water that comes out of the Sound up Pequemen River flows up as high as Stallens, and the River does not widen much untill it passes the lower Bridge some little distance. At Ralphs ferry upon Paspetank the River is Said to be 2 Miles over, and decreases in width gradually to the bridge called River bridge where it is about 30 yards across and affords sufficient Water for New England Vessels to come up and Load.

From what observations we were capable of making it appeared, as if the Swamp had very little fall—(I mean the Waters out of the great Sw[am]p) into the heads of these Rivers which seems to be a demonstration that the Swamp is much lower on the South & East Sides because it is well known that there is a pretty considerable fall on the West side through all the drains that make into Nansemond River & the Western Branch of Elizabeth at the North End of the Dismal....

This Arm of the Dismal is equaly good & Rich like the rest & runs (as we were informed) 15 or 20 Miles Easterly, and has an outlet (as some say) into Curratuck Inlet by No. West River, or Tulls Ck. but these accts, were given so indistinctly as not to be relied upon. However it is certain I believe that the Water does drain of at the East end somewhere, in which case a common causay through at the crossing place woud most certainly lay all that Arm dry.

Washington and several partners formed a company to drain and develop the Dismal Swamp and the next year, 1764, sent slaves to begin the work. Although returns from the enterprise were to be small, all his life Washington was to consider it one of his most valuable investments. There were other opportunities to be seized. When surveyors Charles Mason and Jeremiah Dixon surveyed and fixed the western limit of Pennsylvania, lands hitherto in dispute became patentable, that is, the Colony now had clear title and could make grants of land. Washington at once wrote to William Crawford, an old comrade from the Forbes expedition, who was then settled in western Pennsylvania—and was not above suggesting a bit of subterfuge if such would help obtain land.

[Mount Vernon, September 21, 1767]
From a sudden hint of your Brother Val[entin]e I wrote to you a few days ago in a hurry, since which having had more time for reflection, I am now set down in order to write more deliberately, & with greater precision to you on the Subject of my last Letter; desiring that if any thing in this shoud be found contradictory to that Letter you will wholely be governd by what I am now going to add.

I then desird the favour of you (as I understood Rights might now be had for the Lands which have fallen within the Pennsylvania Line) to look me out a Tract of about 1500, 2000, or more Acres somewhere in your Neighbourhood meaning only by this that it may be as contiguous to your own Settlemt. as such a body of good Land coud be found and about Jacobs Cabbins or somewhere on those Waters I am told this might be done. It will be easy for you to conceive that Ordinary, or even middling Land woud never answer my purpose or expectation so far from Navigation & under such a load of Expense those Lands are incumbred with. No: A Tract to please me must be rich (of which no Person can be a better judge than yourself) & if possible to be good & level; Coud such a piece of Land as this be found you woud do me a singular favour in falling upon some method to secure it immediately from the attempts of any other as nothing is more certain than that the lands cannot remain long ungranted when once it is known that Rights are to be had for them. What mode of proceeding is necessary in order to accomplish this design I am utterly at a loss to point out to you but as your own Lands are under the same Circumstances self Interest will naturally lead you to an enquiry. I am told the Land, or Surveyors Office is kept at Carlyle, if so I am of Opinion that Colo. Armstrong (an Acquaintance of mine) has something to do in the management of it & I am perswaded woud readily serve me. To him therefore at all events I will write by the first oppertunity on that Subject that the way may be prepard for your application if you shoud find it necessary to make one to him. Whatever trouble or expence you may be engagd in on my behalf you may depend upon being thankfully repaid. It is possible (but I do not know that it really is the case) that Pensylvania Customs will not admit so large a quantity of Land as I

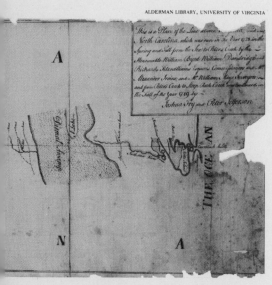

Detail from a manuscript map of 1749 by Joshua Fry and Peter Jefferson, showing the Dismal Swamp

require, to be entered together if so this may possibly be evaded by making several Entrys to the same amount if the expence of doing which is not too heavy but this I only drop as a hint leaving the whole to your discretion & good management. If the Land can only be securd from others it is all I want at present. The Surveying I would choose to postpone, at least till the Spring, when if you can give me any Satisfactory Account of this matter and of what I am next going to propose I expect to pay you a visit about the last of April.

The other matter just now hinted at and which I proposed in my last is to join you in attempting to secure some of the most valuable Lands in the Kings part which I think may be accomplished after a while notwithstanding the Proclamation [the Proclamation of 1763 forbade settlement west of the Appalachians] that restrains it at present & prohibits the Settling of them at all for I can never look upon that Proclamation in any other light (but this I say between ourselves) than as a temporary expedient to quiet the Minds of the Indians & must fall of course in a few years especially when those Indians are consenting to our Occupying the Lands. Any person therefore who neglects the present oppertunity of hunting out good Lands & in some measure Marking & distinguishing them for their own (in order to keep others from settling them) will never regain it. If therefore you will be at the trouble of seeking out the Lands I will take upon me the part of securing them so soon as there is a possibility of doing it & will moreover be at all the Cost & charges of Surveying Patenting &c. after which you shall have such a reasonable proportion of the whole as we may fix upon at our first meeting as I shall find it absolutely necessary & convenient for the better furthering of the design to let some few of my friends be concernd in the Scheme & who must also partake of the advantages....

I woud recommend it to you to keep this whole matter a profound Secret, or Trust it only with those in whom you can confide & who can assist you in bringing it to bear by their discoveries of Land and this Advice proceeds from several very good Reasons, and in the first place because I might be censurd for the Opinion I have given in respect to the King's Proclamation & then if the Scheme I am now proposing to you was known it might

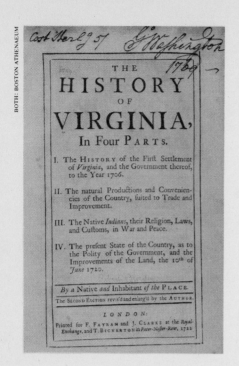

give the alarm to others & by putting them upon a Plan of the same nature (before we coud lay a proper foundation for success ourselves) set the different Interests a clashing and very probably in the end overturn the whole all which may be avoided by a Silent management & the [operation] snugly carried on by you under the pretence of hunting other Game which you may I presume effectually do at the same time you are in pursuit of Land which when fully discovered advise me of it, & if there appears but a bear possibility of succeeding any time hence I will have the Lands immediately Surveyed to keep others off & leave the rest to time & my own Assiduity to Accomplish.

If this Letter shoud reach your hands before you set out I shoud be glad to have your thoughts fully expressd on the Plan I have proposd or as soon afterwards as conveniently may be as I am desirous of knowing in time how you approve of the Scheme.

In 1754, as an incentive to recruit men for the Virginia Regiment—which eventually bled so at Fort Necessity—Governor Dinwiddie had promised 200,000 acres of frontier land as a bounty. Fifteen years later, in 1769, Washington reminded Lord Botetourt, the latest of Dinwiddie's successors, of that promise and obtained a grant of lands down the Ohio River, wherever a suitable tract might be found. The next autumn Washington set out with Dr. James Craik, who had served with him on the frontier, to select the land. By mid-October the pair was passing through an area very familiar to Washington—who was so absorbed in evaluating the land that he failed even to mention that Great Meadows had been the site of Fort Necessity and of his battle with the French sixteen years earlier. Later, however, he acquired an area including the site of his baptism in blood, just possibly from sentiment.

[October, 1770]

13. Set out about Sunrise, breakfasted at the Great Meadows 13 miles of & reachd Captn. Crawfords about 5 Oclock.

The Lands we travelld over today till we had crossed the Laurel Hill (except in small spots) was very Mountainous & indifferent—but when we came down the Hill to the Plantation of Mr. Thos. Gist the Ld. appeard charming; that which lay level being as rich & black as any thing coud possibly be. The more Hilly kind, tho of a different complexion must be good, as well from the

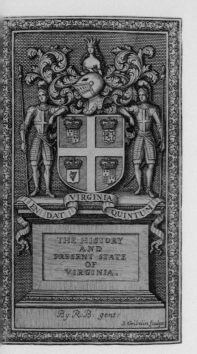

Crops it produces, as from the beautiful white Oaks that grows thereon. The white Oak in genl. indicates poor Land, yet this does not appear to be of that cold kind. The Land from Gists to Crawford's is very broken tho not Mountainous—in Spots exceeding Rich, & in general free from Stone. Crawfords is very fine Land; lying on Yaughyaughgani at a place commonly called Stewarts Crossing.

Sunday 14th. At Captn. Crawfords all day. Went to see a Coal Mine not far from his house on the Banks of the River. The Coal seemd to be of the very best kind, burning freely & abundance of it.

Monday 15th. Went to view some Land which Captn. Crawford had taken up for me near the Yaughyaughgani distant about 12 miles. This Tract which contains about 1600 Acres Includes some as fine Land as ever I saw—a great deal of Rich Meadow—and in general, is leveller than the Country about it. This Tract is well waterd, and has a valuable Mill Seat [Washington built a mill there five years later] (except that the Stream is rather too slight, and it is said not constant more than 7 or 8 months in the Year; but on acct. of the Fall, & other conveniences, no place can exceed it).

In going to this Land I passd through two other Tracts which Captn. Crawford had taken up for my Brothers Saml. and John. That belonging to the former, was not so rich as some I had seen; but very valuable on acct. of its levelness and little Stone, the Soil and Timber being good; that of the latter had some Bottom Land up on sml. Runs that was very good (tho narrow) the Hills very rich, but the Land in genl. broken. I intended to have visited the Land which Crawford had procurd for Lund Washington [a cousin] this day also, but time falling short, I was obligd to Postpone it making it in the Night before I got back to Crawfords where I found Colo. Stephen.

The Lands which I passed over to day were generally Hilly, and the growth chiefly white Oak, but very good notwithstanding; and what is extraordinary, & contrary to the property of all other Lands I ever saw before, the Hills are the richest Land, the Soil upon the sides and Summits of them, being as black as a Coal, & the Growth Walnut, Cherry, Spice Bushes, &ca. The flats are not so rich, and a good deal more mixd with stone.

[Two days later Washington arrived at Fort Pitt, having passed Turtle Creek on the way. Again he was too absorbed in land to note that this was memorable ground, for Braddock had suffered his ghastly defeat where Turtle Creek entered the Monongahela.]

Wednesday 17.   Doctr. Craik and myself with Captn. Crawford and others arrivd at Fort Pitt, distant from the Crossing 43½ Measurd Miles. In Riding this distance we pass over a great deal of exceeding fine Land (chiefly White Oak) especially from Sweigley Creek to Turtle Creek but the whole broken; resembling (as I think all the Lands in this country does) the Loudoun Lands for Hills.

We lodgd in what is calld the Town, distant abt. 300 yards from the Fort at one Mr. Semples who keeps a very good House of Publick Entertainment; these Houses which are built of Logs, & rangd into Streets are on the Monongahela, & I suppose may be abt. 20 in Number and inhabited by Indian Traders, &ca.

The Fort [Fort Pitt] is built in the point between the Rivers Alligany & Monongahela, but not so near the pitch of it as Fort Duquesne stood. It is 5 sided & regular, two of which (next the Land) are of Brick; the others stockade. A Mote incompasses it. The Garrison consists of two Companies of Royal Irish Commanded by one Captn. Edmondson. . . .

Saturday 20.   We Imbarkd in a large Canoe with sufficient stores of Provision & Necessaries, & the following Persons (besides Doctr. Craik & myself) to wit: Captn. Crawford Josh. Nicholson Robt. Bell—William Harrison—Chs. Morgan & Danl. Reardon a boy of Captn. Crawfords, & the Indians who went in a Canoe by themselves. . . .

We passd several large Island[s] which appeared to [be] very good, as the bottoms also did on each side of the River alternately; the Hills on one side being opposite to the bottoms on the other which seem generally to be abt. 3 and 4 hundred yards wide, & so vice versa. . . .

Monday 22d.   As it began to Snow about Midnight, & continued pretty steadily at it, it was about 1/2 after Seven before we left our Incampment. At the distance of about 8 Miles we came to the Mouth of Yellow Creek (to the west) opposite to, or rather below which, appears to be a long bottom of very good Land, and the Assent to the Hills apparently gradual. There is another pretty large bottom of very good Land about two or 3 Miles above this. About 11 or 12 Miles from this, & just above what is called the long Island (which tho so distinguished is not very remarkable for length, breadth or goodness) comes in on the east side the River, a small Creek or Run, the name of which I coud not learn; and a Mile or two below the Island, on the West side, comes in big stony Creek (not larger in appearance than the other) on neither of which does there seem to be any large bottoms or body's of good Land. About 7 Miles from the last Mentiond Creek 28 from our last Incampment, and about 75 from Pittsburg, we came to the Mingo Town Situate on the West Side a little above the Cross Creeks.

This place contains abt. Twenty Cabbins, & 70 Inhabitants of the Six Nations.

Had we set of early, & kept pretty constantly at it, we might have reachd lower than this place Today; as the Water in many places run pretty swift, in general more so than yesterday....

Upon our arrival at the Mingo Town we receivd the disagreeable news of two Traders being killd at a Town calld the Grape Vine Town, 38. miles below this; which causd us to hesitate whether we shoud proceed or not, and wait for further Intelligence.

Tuesday 23. Several imperfect accts. coming in, agreeing that only one Person was killd, & the Indians not supposing it to be done by their People, we resolvd to pursue our passage, till we coud get some more distinct Acct. of this Transaction. Accordingly abt. 2 Oclock we set out with the two Indians which was to accompany us, in our Canoe, and in about 4 Miles came to the Mouth of a Creek calld Seulf [Sewell] Creek, on the East side; at the Mouth of which is a bottom of very good Land, as I am told there likewise is up it.

The Cross Creeks (as they are calld) are not large, that on the West side however is biggest. At the Mingo Town we found, and left, 60 odd Warriors of the Six Nations going to the Cherokee Country to proceed to war against the Cuttaba's [Catawbas]. About 10 Miles below the Town we came to two other cross Creeks

Detail of a 1761 map of Pittsburgh showing Fort Pitt on the point of land where Fort Duquesne had stood

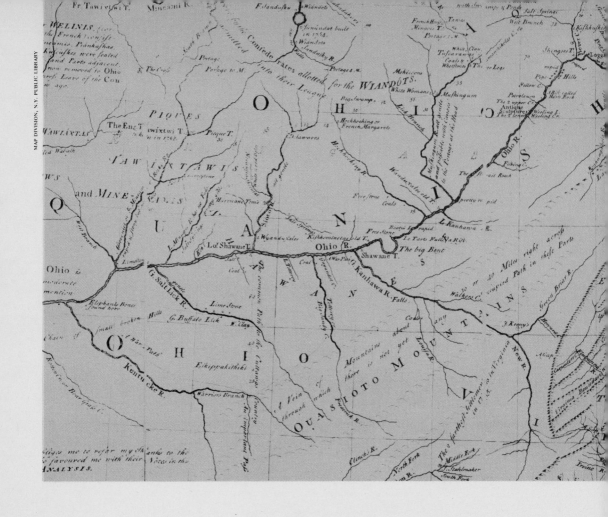

that on the West side largest, but not big; and calld by Nicholson, French Creek. About 3 Miles or a little better below this, at the lower point of some Islands which stand contiguous to each other, we were told by the Indians with us that three men from Virginia (by Virginians they mean all the People settled upon Redstone, &ca.) had markd the Land from hence all the way to Redstone—that there was a body of exceeding fine Land lying about this place and up opposite to the Mingo Town—as also down to the Mouth of Fishing Creek. At this Place we Incampd.

[They continued downriver, with George appraising the land along the way. They learned that the trader had not been slain but had drowned trying to ford the Ohio. There was a council with friendly Indians. About 160 miles by river below Pittsburgh they came to the Great Bend, at whose foot the Great Kanawha River enters. Washington began tentatively selecting tracts of rich bottomland.]

Portion of a map made in 1755 by L. Evans showing the junction of the Ohio and Kanawha rivers

Monday 29th. ... Opposite to the Creek just below wch. we Incampd, is a pretty long bottom, & I believe tolerable wide; but abt. 8 or 9 Miles below the aforemend. Creek, & just below a pavement of Rocks on the west side, comes in a Creek with fallen Timber at the Mouth, on which the Indians say there is wide bottom's, & good Land.... Six Miles below this comes in a small Creek on the west side at the end of a small naked Island, and just above another pavement of Rocks. This Creek comes thro a Bottom of fine Land, & opposite to it (on the East side of the River) appears to be a large bottom of very fine Land also. At this place begins what they call the great Bent. 5 Miles below this again on the East side comes in (abt. 200 yds. above a little stream or Gut) another Creek; which is just below an Island, on the upper point of which are some dead standing trees, & a parcel of white bodied Sycamores. In the Mouth of this Creek lyes a Sycamore blown down by the wind; from hence an East line may be run 3 or 4 Miles; thence a North Line till it strikes the River, which I apprehend would Include about 3 or 4000 Acres of exceeding valuable Land....

Tuesday 30. We set out at 50 Minutes passed Seven; the Weather being windy and cloudy (after a Night of Rain)....

About 10 Miles below our Incampment & a little lower down than the bottom described to lye in the shape of a horse Shoe comes in a small Creek on the West side, and opposite to this on the East begins a body of flat Land which the Indians tell us runs quite across the Fork to the Falls in the Kanhawa, and must at least be 3 days walk across. If so the Flat Land containd therein must be very considerable. A Mile or two below this we Landed, and after getting a little distance from the River we came (without any rising) to a pretty lively kind of Land grown up with Hicky. & Oaks of different kinds, intermixd with Walnut, &ca. here and there. We also found many shallow Ponds, the sides of which abounding in grass, invited innumerable quantities of wild fowl among which I saw a Couple of Birds in size between a Swan and a Goose; & in colour somewhat between the two; being darker than the young Swan and of a more sutty Colour. The cry of these was as

91

unusual as the Bird itself, as I never heard any noize resembling it before. About 5 Miles below this we Incampd in a bottom of Good Land which holds tolerably flat & rich some distance out.

Wednesday 31st. I sent the Canoe along down to the Junction of the two Rivers abt. 5 Miles, that is the Kanhawa with the Ohio—and set out upon a hunting Party to view the Land. We steerd nearly East for about 8 or 9 Miles then bore Southwardly, & westwardly, till we came to our Camp at the confluence of the Rivers. The Land from the Rivers appeard but indifferent, & very broken; whether these ridges might not be those that divide the Waters of the Ohio from the Kanhawa is not certain, but I believe they are. If so the Lands may yet be good. If not, that which lyes of the River bottoms is good for little.

November 1st. A little before eight Oclock we set of with our Canoe up the River to discover what kind of Lands lay upon the Kanhawa. The Land on both sides this River just at the Mouth is very fine; but on the East side when you get towards the Hills (which I judge to be about 6 or 700 yards from the River) it appears to be wet, & better adapted for Meadow than tillage. This bottom continues up the East side for about 2 Miles, & by going up the Ohio a good Tract might be got of bottom Land Including the old Shawna Town, which is about 3 Miles up the Ohio just above the Mouth of a Ck. where the aforementiond bottom ends on the East side the Kanhawa, which extends up it at least 50 Miles by the Indns. acct. and of great width (to be ascertaind, as we come down) in many places very rich; in others somewhat wet and pondy; fit for Meadow, but upon the whole exceeding valuable, as the Land after you get out of the Rich bottom is very good for Grain, tho not rich. We judgd we went up this River about 10 Miles today. On the East side appear to be some good bottoms but small—neither long nor wide, & the Hills back of them rather steep & poor.

Novr. 2d. We proceeded up the River with the Canoe about 4 Miles more, & then incampd & went a Hunting; killd 5 Buffaloes & wounded some others—three deer, &ca. This Country abounds in Buffalo & Wild game of

In 1773 Washington placed an ad in The Pennsylvania Gazette *offering 20,000 acres of his land on the Ohio and Great Kanawha for lease to people willing to clear and till it.*

all kinds; as also in all kinds of wild fowl, there being in the Bottoms a great many small grassy Ponds or Lakes which are full of Swans, Geese, & Ducks of different kinds.

Some of our People went up the River 4 or 5 Miles higher & found the same kind of bottom on the west side, & we were told by the Indians that it continued to the Falls which they judgd to be 50 or 60 Miles higher up. This Bottom next the Water (in most places) is very rich. As you approach to the Hills you come (in many) to a thin white Oak Land, & poor. The hills as far as we coud judge were from half a Mile to a Mile from the River; poor & steep in the parts we see, with Pine growing on them. Whether they are generally so, or not, we cannot tell but I fear they are.

Saturday 3d.   We set of down the River on our return homewards, and Incampd at the Mouth; at the Beginning of the Bottom above the junction of the Rivers, and at the Mouth of a branch on the East side, I markd two Maples, an Elm, & Hoopwood Tree as A Cornr. of the Soldiers Ld. (if we can get it) intending to take all the bottom from hence to the Rapids in the Great Bent into one Survey. I also markd at the Mouth of another Gut lower down on the West side (at the lower end of the long bottom) an Ash and hoopwood for the Beginning of another of the Soldiers Survey, to extend up so as to Include all the Bottom (in a body) on the west side.

The party returned home without incident. Although Washington never saw the lands on the Great Kanawha again, his acres there would be a prized possession until the year of his death. He assumed responsibility for pressing the claims of the veterans of 1754 and had the land surveyed. Grants were made according to rank; Washington, a colonel, received fifteen thousand acres (and bought the grants of two other men for another fifty-six hundred acres). There was some grumbling later about the division. One dissatisfied veteran was George Muse, a former major, who had applied for and been given his land, though he had been a coward at Fort Necessity. When Muse complained he had received short measure, Washington fired back a letter giving a rare picture of him in anger.

[Mount Vernon, January 29, 1774]
Your impertinent Letter of the 24th. ulto., was delivered to me yesterday by Mr. Smith. As I am not accustomed

to receive such from any Man, nor would have taken the same language from you personally, without letting you feel some marks of my resentment; I would advise you to be cautious in writing me a second of the same tenour; for though I understand you were drunk when you did it, yet give me leave to tell you, that drunkness is no excuse for rudeness; and that, but for your stupidity and sottishness you might have known, by attending to the public Gazettes, (particularly Rinds of the 14th. of January last) that you had your full quantity of ten thousand acres of Land allowed you; that is, 9073 acres in the great Tract of 51,302 acres, and the remainder in the small tract of 927 acres; whilst I wanted near 500 acres of my quantity, Doctr. Craik of his, and almost every other claimant little or much of theirs. But suppose you had really fallen short 73 acres of your 10,000, do you think your superlative merit entitles you to greater indulgences than others? or that I was to make it good to you, if it did? when it was at the option of the Governor and Council to have allowed you but 500 acres in the whole, if they had been inclin'd so to do. If either of these should happen to be your opinion, I am very well convinced you will stand singular in it; & all my concern is, that I ever engag'd in behalf of so ungrateful and dirty a fellow as you are. But you may still stand in need of my assistance, as I can inform you that your affairs, in respect to these Lands, do not stand upon so solid a basis as you may imagine, & this you may take by way of hint; as your coming in for *any,* much less a *full share* may still be a disputed point, by a Gentleman who is not in this Country at this time, & who is exceedingly dissatisfyed therewith. I wrote to you [him?] a few days ago concerning the other distribution, proposing an easy method of dividing our Lands; but since I find in what temper you are, I am sorry I took the trouble of mentioning the Land, or your name in a Letter, as I do not think you merit the least assistance from

G: WASHINGTON.

Washington later described the land awarded the veterans as "the cream of the country." He had first look at the surveys and selected well: the richest land in the choice locations. He got the Governor's agreement to a plan to divide among those who had had the trouble and expense of surveying the land the acreage remaining after all claims were satisfied. There were nineteen thousand acres left over; when that pie was cut up, Washington got a 3,953-acre piece. In 1773 George was asking the Governor for still another grant, this time a bounty awarded to veterans of the French and Indian War, although his eligibility was doubtful. Only the coming of the Revolution halted this and other plans to acquire western lands.

During these years Washington showed a disinterest in political affairs beyond his immediate horizons. Even when the controversy with the mother country over taxation became a burning issue, he for a time maintained his apolitical stance. Washington was a member of the House of Burgesses when Patrick Henry made his famous speech against the Stamp Act, concluding "If *this* be treason, make the most of it." He kept no diary of his attendance and the event is not mentioned in his surviving letters. However, he was not untouched by the Stamp Act furor and wrote to Francis Dandridge, his wife's uncle, giving his measured opinion of how the act might affect trade between the Colonies and the mother country.

[Mount Vernon, September 20, 1765]

If you will permit me after six years silence—the time I have been married to your Niece—to pay my respects to you in this Epistolary way I shall think myself happy in beginning a corrispondance which cannot but be attended with pleasure on my side....

At present few things are under notice of my observation that can afford you any amusement in the recital. The Stamp Act Imposed on the Colonies by the Parliament of Great Britain engrosses the conversation of the Speculative part of the Colonists, who look upon this unconstitutional method of Taxation as a direful attack upon their Liberties, and loudly exclaim against the Violation. What may be the result of this and some other (I think I may add) ill judgd Measures, I will not undertake to determine; but this I may venture to affirm, that the advantage accrueing to the Mother Country will fall greatly short of the expectations of the Ministry; for certain it is, our whole Substance does already in a manner flow to Great Britain and that whatsoever contributes to Lesson our Importation's must be hurtful to their Manufacturers. And the Eyes of our People, already beginning to open, will perceive, that many Luxuries which we lavish our substance to Great Britain for, can well be dispensd with whilst the necessaries of Life are (mostly) to be had within ourselves. This consequently will introduce frugality, and be a necessary

German engraving of the protest in Boston against the Stamp Act

Washington did not approve of the destruction of tea at the Boston Tea Party but opposed the punishment.

stimulation to Industry. If Great Britain therefore Loads her Manufactures with heavy Taxes, will it not facilitate these Measures? They will not compel us I think to give our Money for their exports whether we will or no, & certain I am none of their Traders will part from them without a valuable consideration. Where then is the Utility of these Restrictions?

As to the Stamp Act, taken in a single view, one, & the first bad consequences attending it I take to be this. Our Courts of Judicature must inevitably be shut up; for it is impossible (or next of kin to it) under our present Circumstances that the Act of Parliam't can be complyd with were we ever so willing to enforce the execution; for not to say, which alone woud be sufficient, that we have not Money to pay the Stamps, there are many other cogent Reasons to prevent it; and if a stop be put to our judicial proceedings I fancy the Merchants of G. Britain trading to the Colonies will not be among the last to wish for a Repeal of it.

The political opinions of Washington slowly hardened. When the Crown passed new taxes on imports into the Colonies (the Townshend Acts), the Colonies resisted with nonimportation schemes. Washington sent the text of one such plan to a neighbor, George Mason; the opening portion of his letter shows a growing opposition to King and Parliament.

Mount Vernon, April 5, 1769.
Herewith you will receive a letter and Sundry papers which were forwarded to me a day or two ago by Doctor Ross of Bladensburg. I transmit them with the greater pleasure, as my own desire of knowing your sentiments upon a matter of this importance exactly coincides with the Doctors inclinations.

At a time when our lordly Masters in Great Britain will be satisfied with nothing less than the deprivation of American freedom, it seems highly necessary that some thing shou'd be done to avert the stroke and maintain the liberty which we have derived from our Ancestors; but the manner of doing it to answer the purpose effectually is the point in question.

That no man shou'd scruple, or hesitate a moment to use a-ms [arms] in defence of so valuable a blessing, on which all the good and evil of life depend; is clearly my opinion; yet A-ms I wou'd beg leave to add, should be the last resource; the denier resort. Addresses to the Throne, and remonstrances to parliament, we have already, it is said, proved the inefficacy of; how far then their attention to our rights and priviledges is to be awakened or alarmed by starving their Trade & manufactures, remains to be tryed.

Washington was present early in May, 1769, when the House of Burgesses drew up resolutions affirming, among other things, that it alone had the right to tax the people of Virginia. On receiving the resolutions, Governor Botetourt at once dissolved the House of Burgesses. Most members went to a local tavern, where they drew up an agreement to buy no taxed article from Britain. Washington was among the first to sign. Washington's point of view shifted slowly from the practical one of how parliamentary acts would affect the Colonial economy to the more philosophical one of how they infringed on the constitutional rights of citizens. Although he did not approve of the destruction of tea at the Boston Tea Party at the end of 1773, he was much opposed to the "despotick measures" laid on Boston as punishment. In the summer of 1774 Bryan Fairfax, brother of Washington's neighbor George William Fairfax, considered standing for election to the House of Burgesses. Bryan advocated a conciliatory approach to the Crown, and Washington wrote to him, commenting on Bryan's position in language showing that his own views by then were well formed.

Mount Vernon, 4 July 1774

John has just delivered to me your favor of yesterday, which I shall be obliged to answer in a more concise manner, than I could wish, as I am very much engaged in raising one of the additions to my house, which I think (perhaps it is fancy) goes on better whilst I am present, than in my absence from the workmen....

As to your political sentiments, I would heartily join you in them, so far as relates to a humble and dutiful petition to the throne, provided there was the most distant hope of success. But have we not tried this already? Have we not addressed the Lords, and remonstrated to the Commons? And to what end? Did they deign to look at our petitions? Does it not appear, as clear as the sun in its meridian brightness, that there is a regular, systematic plan formed to fix the right and practice of taxation upon us? Does not the uniform conduct of Parliament for some years past confirm this? Do not all the debates, especially those just brought to us, in the House of

The Capitol at Williamsburg, where the House of Burgesses convened

Garden house at Mount Vernon

Commons on the side of government, expressly declare that America must be taxed in aid of the British funds, and that she has no longer resources within herself? Is there any thing to be expected from petitioning after this? Is not the attack upon the liberty and property of the people of Boston, before restitution of the loss to the India Company was demanded, a plain and self-evident proof of what they are aiming at? Do not the subsequent bills (not I dare say acts), for depriving the Massachusetts Bay of its charter, and for transporting offenders into colonies or to Great Britain for trial, where it is impossible from the nature of the thing that justice can be obtained, convince us that the administration is determined to stick at nothing to carry its point? Ought we not, then, to put our virtue and fortitude to the severest test?

That summer of 1774 George busied himself in adding a new wing to the Mount Vernon mansion house. He also had a sad duty to perform, auctioning off the furniture and furnishings of Belvoir, for his neighbors George William and Sally Fairfax had gone to England to live. In late August he was off to Philadelphia as one of Virginia's seven delegates to the First Continental Congress. Following his usual habit, Washington spoke little but listened and learned during the six weeks the Congress sat; he also made it a point to become acquainted socially with delegates from other Colonies. After his return to Virginia, county after county elected him to lead its militia. That the Colonies might have to fight for their rights no longer seemed impossible. And despite his quiet showing in Philadelphia the previous year, Washington was easily elected a delegate to the Second Continental Congress, which was to meet on May 10, 1775. The first news of the clashes at Lexington and Concord reached Mount Vernon on April 27. Whether Washington had any intimation of what that distant event would do to his life we cannot know. But when he drove away seven days later, bound for Philadelphia, he was not to see Mount Vernon, except in passing through, for more than eight years.

Chapter 4

Commander in Chief

Washington had not been put on a single committee in the First Continental Congress, but his experience as a military man was in demand in the Second, which convened at Philadelphia on May 10, 1775. He was made a member of groups to study the defense of New York, to draw up rules for the government of the army, to find means to supply the Colonies with ammunition. Few of the delegates expected a long conflict. Most were hopeful that the intransigent ministry of Lord North would soon be replaced by a more conciliatory one and the unpleasantness between mother country and Colonies would quickly be forgotten. But by and large, all turned with spirit to meet the challenge to their British liberties. Despite their enthusiasm, the delegates ran into a harsh and unyielding fact: they could talk and vote all they wanted, but they had little to back up their words with. The Colonies had almost no industry; they might raise an army, but they would be hard put to clothe, arm, transport, and shelter it. But Washington, pondering the first complete accounts of the fighting at Lexington and Concord, saw that the Colonials did possess one element essential for success: the spirit to stand up to British regulars. In writing to George William Fairfax in England, whose Virginia plantation he had agreed to manage, he gave his analysis of the Lexington-Concord fight.

> Philadelphia, May 31, 1775.
>
> Before this Letter can reach you, you must, undoubtedly, have received an Account of the engagement in the Massachusetts Bay between the Ministerial Troops (for we do not, nor cannot yet prevail upon ourselves to call them the King's Troops) and the Provincials of that Government; But as you may not have heard how that affair began, I inclose you the several Affidavits that were taken after the Action.
>
> General Gage acknowledges, that the detachment un-

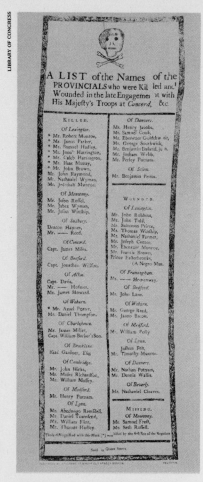

Boston broadside listing the names of "Provincials" killed at Concord

der Lieutenant Colonel Smith was sent out to destroy private property; or, in other Words, to destroy a Magazine which self preservation obliged the Inhabitants to establish. And he also confesses, in effect at least, that his Men made a very precipitate retreat from Concord, notwithstanding the reinforcement under Lord Piercy, the last of which may serve to convince Lord Sandwich (and others of the same sentiment) that the Americans will fight for their Liberties and property, however pusilanimous, in his Lordship's Eye, they may appear in other respects.

From the best Accounts I have been able to collect of that affair; indeed from every one, I believe the fact, stripped of all colouring, to be plainly this, that if the retreat had not been as precipitate as it was (and God knows it could not well have been more so) the Ministerial Troops must have surrendered, or been totally cut off: For they had not arrived in Charlestown (under cover of their Ships) half an hour, before a powerful body of Men from Marblehead and Salem were at their heels, and must, if they had happened to have been up one hour sooner, inevitably intercepted their retreat to Charleston. Unhappy it is though to reflect, that a Brother's Sword has been sheathed in a Brother's breast, and that, the once happy and peaceful plains of America are either to be drenched with Blood, or Inhabited by Slaves. Sad alternative! But can a virtuous Man hesitate in his choice?

One of the first orders of business for Congress was to aid the New England forces besieging the British in Boston. While the delegates debated they were somewhat taken aback by news that a force of Colonials led by Benedict Arnold and Ethan Allen had captured Fort Ticonderoga on Lake George. This incident could not be blamed on aggression by British troops, as Lexington and Concord had been, but at the same time the seizure of the fort cut the British route from Canada and so eased the problem of defending the Colony of New York. Some of the nimbler minds in Congress worked out a resolution justifying the seizure as necessary to avert an invasion of the Colonies being prepared (they said) in Quebec. At the same time instructions were sent to have the artillery in the fort safely stored until Britain and the Colonies should have their differences conciliated. The cannon would prove useful before many months had passed.

Congress decided early that the New England army before Boston should become part of a united Colonial army — and that raised the question of who should have the top command. Many New Englanders favored Artemas Ward, a veteran of the French and Indian War, commander in chief of Massachusetts troops, and at the moment in command of the troops laying siege to Boston. A few championed Charles Lee, a professional soldier who had served with the British and as a soldier of fortune on the Continent, and whom many considered a top military expert. There were a few local favorites. And there was Washington. Not only was he highly regarded for his military experience and his personal qualities, but his election was urged by some, and especially John Adams, because the choice of a Virginian would help to dispel a common notion that New England was attempting to dominate the rest of the Colonies. In mid-June Washington made two brief entries in his diary.

> 14 [June, 1775]. Dined at Mr. Saml. Merediths. Spent the Evening at home.
>
> 15. Dined at Burn's in the Field. Spent the Eveng. on a Committee [to draft rules and regulations for the government of the army].

The diary entries do not hint that on June 14 John Adams rose to nominate Washington for Commander in Chief (as Washington modestly slipped out a side door), or that the next day Washington, still discreetly absent, was unanimously elected. On June 16 he was formally notified and made a formal acceptance.

> [Philadelphia, June 16, 1775]
> Tho' I am truly sensible of the high Honour done me in this Appointment, yet I feel great distress from a consciousness that my abilities and Military experience may not be equal to the extensive and important Trust: However, as the Congress desires I will enter upon the momentous duty, & exert every power I Possess In their Service for the Support of the glorious Cause: I beg they will accept my most cordial thanks for this distinguished testimony of their Approbation.
>
> But lest some unlucky event should happen unfavourable to my reputation, I beg it may be remembered by every Gentn. in the room, that I this day declare with the utmost sincerity, I do not think my self equal to the Command I am honoured with.
>
> As to pay, Sir, I beg leave to Assure the Congress that as no pecuniary consideration could have tempted me to have accepted this Arduous employment at the expence of my domestk. ease & happiness I do not wish to make

John Adams

any proffit from it: I will keep an exact Account of my expences; those I doubt not they will discharge & that is all I desire.

Two days later the new General wrote his wife a troubled letter, breaking the news to her. Although he spoke of returning to Mount Vernon in the fall, the air was full of uncertainty.

Philadelphia, June 18, 1775.

My Dearest:

I am now set down to write to you on a subject, which fills me with inexpressible concern, and this concern is greatly aggravated and increased, when I reflect upon the uneasiness I know it will cause you. It has been determined in Congress, that the whole army raised for the defence of the American cause shall be put under my care, and that it is necessary for me to proceed immediately to Boston to take upon me the command of it.

You may believe me, my dear Patsy, when I assure you, in the most solemn manner that, so far from seeking this appointment, I have used every endeavor in my power to avoid it, not only from my unwillingness to part with you and the family, but from a consciousness of its being a trust too great for my capacity, and that I should enjoy more real happiness in one month with you at home, than I have the most distant prospect of finding abroad, if my stay were to be seven times seven years. But as it has been a kind of destiny, that has thrown me upon this service, I shall hope that my undertaking it is designed to answer some good purpose. You might, and I suppose did perceive, from the tenor of my letters, that I was apprehensive I could not avoid this appointment,

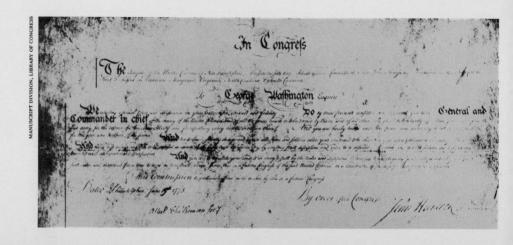

as I did not pretend to intimate when I should return. That was the case. It was utterly out of my power to refuse this appointment, without exposing my character to such censures, as would have reflected dishonor upon myself, and have given pain to my friends. This, I am sure, could not, and ought not, to be pleasing to you, and must have lessened me considerably in my own esteem. I shall rely, therefore, confidently on that Providence, which has heretofore preserved and been bountiful to me, not doubting but that I shall return safe to you in the fall. I shall feel no pain from the toil or the danger of the campaign; my unhappiness will flow from the uneasiness I know you will feel from being left alone. I therefore beg, that you will summon your whole fortitude, and pass your time as agreeably as possible. Nothing will give me so much sincere satisfaction as to hear this, and to hear it from your own pen.

If it should be your desire to remove into Alexandria (as you once mentioned upon an occasion of this sort) I am quite pleased that you should put it into practice, and Lund Washington may be directed by you to build a kitchen and other houses there proper for your reception. If on the other hand you should rather incline to spend a good part of your time among your friends below, I wish you to do so. In short my earnest and ardent desire is that you will pursue any plan that is most likely to produce content, and a tolerable degree of tranquility; as it must add greatly to my uneasy feelings to hear that you are dissatisfied or complaining at what I really could not avoid.

As life is always uncertain, and common prudence dictates to every man the necessity of settling his temporal concerns while it is in his power, and while the mind is calm and undisturbed, I have, since I came to this place (for I had not time to do it before I left home) got Colonel Pendleton to draft a will for me, by the directions I gave him, which will I now enclose. The provision made for you in case of my death will, I hope, be agreeable: I have included the money for which I sold my land (to Doctor Mercer) in the sum given you as also all my other debts. What I owe myself is very trifling, Cary's debt excepted, and this would not have been much if the bank stock had been applied without such difficulties as he made in the transference.

Washington's appointment by Congress as Commander in Chief, dated June 19, 1775

I shall add nothing more at present as I have several letters to write, but to desire that you will remember me to Milly and all friends, and to assure you that I am, with the most unfeigned regard

My dear

Patcy Yr affecte

GO WASHINGTON

A letter went to Jack Custis, urging him and his wife to move to Mount Vernon while Washington was gone. To his brother John Augustine, Washington wrote of his heavy new burden of responsibility.

Philadelphia, June 20, 1775.

I am now to bid adieu to you, & to every kind of domestick ease, for a while. I am Imbarked on a wide Ocean, boundless in its prospect, & from whence, perhaps, no safe harbour is to be found. I have been called upon by the unanimous Voice of the Colonies to take Command of the Continental Army—an honour I neither sought after, nor desired, as I am thoroughly convinced, that it requires greater Abilities, and much more experience, than I am Master of, to conduct a business so extensive in its nature, and arduous in the execution; but the partiallity of the Congress, joined to a political motive, really left me without a choice; and I am now Commissioned a Generl & Commander in Chief of all the Forces now raisd, or to be raisd, for the defence of the United Colonies. That I may discharge the Trust to the Satisfaction of my Imployers, is my first wish—that I shall aim to do it, there remains as little doubt of— how far I may succeed is another point; but this I am sure of, that in the worst event, I shall have the consolation of knowing (if I act to the best of my judgment) that the blame ought to lodge upon the appointers, not the appointed, as it was by no means a thing of my own seeking, or proceeding from any hint of my friends.

I am at liberty to inform you, that the Congress, in a Committee, (which will I dare say be agreed to when reported) have consented to a Continental Currency; have ordered two million of Dollars to be struck for payment of the Troops, &ca. and have voted 15,000 Men as a Continental Army—which number will be augmented, as the strength of the British Troops will be greater than was expected at the time of passing that vote. Genl.

John Augustine Washington

THIRTYSIX-SHILLINGS.

Decm.ʳ 7. 1775.

Paul Revere designed and engraved
this thirty-six shilling note in 1775.

Ward, Genl. Lee, Genl. Schuyler and Genl. Putnam are appointed Major Genls. under me; the Brigadier Genls. are not yet appointed. Majr. Gates Adjutant Genl. I expect to set out tomorrow for Boston & hope to be joind there in a little time by Ten Companies of Riflemen from this Province, Maryland & Virginia. For other Articles of Intelligence, I shall refer you to the Papers, as the Printers are diligent in collecting every thing that is stirring.

I shall hope that my Friends will visit, & endeavour to keep up the spirits of my Wife as much as they can, as my departure will, I know, be a cutting stroke upon her; and on this acct. alone, I have many very disagreeable sensations. I hope you & my sister (although the distance is great) will find as much leisure this Summer, as to spend a little time at Mount Vernon.

The choice of George Washington as Commanding General, seen in the light of afterthought, was a wise one, but at the time skeptics could have been excused for doubting its wisdom. He had never commanded large bodies of men, had never led troops in battle on an open field, had never handled artillery or cavalry. Yet the various other men put forward as candidates for Commander in Chief—Charles Lee, Israel Putnam, Artemas Ward, and others—were all to fall into eclipse before the end of the war through ineptitude, improper behavior, or mischance. Congress had put the fate of America in the right hands. At the moment, the fate of the Colonies lay with the citizen-soldiers before Boston, and Washington was impatient to get there. Before setting out, he penned a short note to Martha.

Phila. June 23d. 1775.

My Dearest,

As I am within a few Minutes of leaving this City, I could not think of departing from it without dropping you a line; especially as I do not know whether it may be in my power to write again till I get to the Camp at Boston. I go fully trusting in that Providence, which has been more bountiful to me than I deserve, & in full confidence of a happy Meeting with you sometime in the Fall. I have not time to add more, as I am surrounded with Company to take leave of me. I retain an unalterable affection for you, which neither time or distance can change. My best love to Jack & Nelly, & regards for the rest of the Family concludes me with the utmost truth & sincerity, Yr. entire

Go: Washington

With Charles Lee and Philip Schuyler, newly appointed major generals, Washington started for Boston. Militia guards of honor and civic groups with speeches of welcome slowed his travel. New York, a town of about twenty-two thousand souls, gave him a tumultuous ovation, and there he intercepted an express rider carrying the first news of the Battle of Bunker Hill to Congress. He left General Schuyler in command of the Colony of New York and before proceeding found time to reply reassuringly to an address from the New York legislature, which had expressed the hope that he and the other generals would exercise their military power no longer than necessary to restore peace to the land.

June 26, 1775.

At the same time that with you I deplore the unhappy necessity of such an Appointment, as that with which I am now honoured, I cannot but feel sentiments of the highest gratitude for this affecting Instance of distinction and Regard.

May your every wish be realized in the success of America, at this important and interesting Period; & be assured that the every exertion of my worthy Colleagues & myself will be equally extended to the re-establishment of Peace & Harmony between the Mother Country and the Colonies, as to the fatal, but necessary, operations of War. When we assumed the Soldier, we did not lay aside the Citizen; and we shall most sincerely rejoice with you in that happy hour when the establishment of American Liberty, upon the most firm and solid foundations, shall enable us to return to our Private Stations in the bosom of a free, peaceful and happy Country.

Washington made his headquarters in this handsome Cambridge mansion.

Pictorial Field-Book of the Revolution
BY BENSON J. LOSSING, 1852

Washington arrived at Cambridge outside Boston on July 2 and established headquarters there. The next day he assumed command of the army from Artemas Ward, reduced to second in command as one of Congress's new major generals. Washington also delivered a major general's commission to Israel Putnam, a Connecticut Yankee of little learning but who had had a life of incredible adventure and was then fresh from heroism on Bunker Hill. Then the new commander applied himself to the onerous tasks of strengthening fortifications, instilling discipline, bolstering morale, improving camp sanitation, and taking care of the multitude of other details involved in military command. Within a day he issued his first extended orders to the army. (Note: the countersign listed daily in general orders was the password that must be given to sentries to enter the lines; the parole was a special password given only to officers of the guard and inspectors of the guard.)

GENERAL ORDERS

Head Quarters, Cambridge, July 4th. 1775.
Parole Abington. Countersign Bedford.

Exact returns to be made by the proper Officers of all the Provisions Ordnance, Ordnance Stores, Powder, Lead working Tools of all kinds, Tents, Camp Kettles, and all other Stores under their respective care, belonging to the Armies at Roxbury and Cambridge. The commanding Officer of each Regiment to make a return of the number of blankets wanted to compleat every Man with one at least.

The Hon: Artemus Ward, Charles Lee, Philip Schuyler, and Israel Putnam Esquires, are appointed Major Generals of the American Army, and due obedience is to be paid them as such. The Continental Congress not having compleated the appointments of the other officers in said army nor had sufficient time to prepare and forward their Commissions; any officer is to continue to do duty in the Rank and Station he at present holds, untill further orders.

Thomas Mifflin Esqr, is appointed by the General one of his Aid-de-Camps. Joseph Reed Esqr. is in like manner appointed Secretary to the General, and they are in future to be consider'd and regarded as such.

The Continental Congress having now taken all the Troops of the several Colonies, which have been raised, or which may be hereafter raised for the support and defence of the Liberties of America; into their Pay and Service. They are now the Troops of the UNITED PROVINCES of North America; and it is hoped that all Distinctions of Colonies will be laid aside; so that one and the same Spirit may animate the whole, and the only Contest be, who shall render, on this great and trying occasion, the most essential service to the great and common cause in which we are all engaged.

It is required and expected that exact discipline be observed, and due Subordination prevail thro' the whole Army, as a Failure in these most essential points must necessarily produce extreme Hazard, Disorder and Confusion; and end in Shameful disappointment and disgrace.

The General most earnestly requires, and expects a due observance of those articles of war, established for the Government of the army, which forbid profane cursing, swearing and drunkeness; And in like manner re-

Broadside of "A Favorite New Song in the American Camp" giving a "Huzza for Ward and Washington" as Washington arrived in Cambridge

*A stylized woodcut of Washington
taking over command of his army*

quires & expects, of all Officers, and Soldiers, not engaged on actual duty, a punctual attendance on divine Service, to implore the blessings of heaven upon the means used for our safety and defence.

All Officers are required and expected to pay diligent Attention, to keep their Men neat and clean—to visit them often at their quarters, and inculcate upon them the necessity of cleanliness, as essential to their health and service. They are particularly to see, that they have Straw to lay on, if to be had, and to make it known if they are destitute of this article. They are also to take care that Necessarys be provided in the Camps and frequently filled up to prevent their being offensive and unhealthy. Proper Notice will be taken of such Officers and Men, as distinguish themselves by their attention to these necessary duties.

The commanding Officer of each Regiment is to take particular care that not more than two Men of a Company be absent on furlough at the same time, unless in very extraordinary cases.

Col. Gardner is to [be] buried to morrow at 3, O'Clock, P.M. with the military Honors due to so brave and gallant an Officer, who fought, bled and died in the Cause of his country and mankind. His own Regiment, except the company at Malden, to attend on this mournful occasion. The places of those Companies in the Lines on Prospect Hill, to be supplied by Col. Glovers regiment till the funeral is over.

No Person is to be allowed to go to Fresh-water pond a fishing or on any other occasion as there may be danger of introducing the small pox into the army.

It is strictly required and commanded that there be no firing of Cannon or small Arms from any of the Lines, or elsewhere, except in case of necessary, immediate defence, or special order given for that purpose.

All Prisoners taken, Deserters coming in, Persons coming out of Boston, who can give any Intelligence; any Captures of any kind from the Enemy, are to be immediately reported and brought up to Head Quarters in Cambridge.

Capt. Griffin is appointed Aide-de-Camp to General Lee and to be regarded as such.

The Guard for the security of the Stores at Watertown, is to be increased to thirty men immediately.

A Serjeant and six men to be set as a Guard to the Hospital, and are to apply to Doctor Rand.

Complaint having been made against John White Quarter Master of Col. Nixon's Regmt. for misdemeanors in drawing out Provisions for more Men than the Regiment consisted of; a Court Martial consisting of one Captain and four Subalterns is ordered to be held on said White, who are to enquire, determine and report.

AFTER ORDERS. 10 OCLOCK

The General desires that some Carpenters be immediately set to work at Brattle's Stables, to fix up Stalls for eight Horses, and more if the Room will admit, with suitable racks, mangers, &c.

Several cases had come to General Washington's attention of officers who were setting bad examples for their troops. When a captain found guilty of cowardice was sentenced to be discharged, the General used the occasion to exhort and warn all officers.

GENERAL ORDERS

Head Quarters, Cambridge, July 7th. 1775
Parole, Dorchester. CSign Exeter.

It is with inexpressible Concern that the General upon his first Arrival in the army, should find an Officer sentenced by a General Court-Martial to be cashier'd for Cowardice. A Crime of all others, the most infamous in a Soldier, the most injurious to an Army, and the last to be forgiven; inasmuch as it may, and often does happen, that the Cowardice of a single Officer may prove the Distruction of the whole Army: The General therefore (tho' with great Concern, and more especially, as the Transaction happened before he had the Command of the Troops) thinks himself obliged, for the good of the service, to approve the Judgment of the Court-Martial with respect to Capt. John Callender, who is hereby sentenced to be cashiered. Capt. John Callender is accordingly cashiered and dismissd from all farther service in the Continental Army as an Officer.

The General having made all due inquiries, and maturely consider'd this matter is led to the above determination not only from the particular Guilt of Capt. Callender, but the fatal Consequences of such conduct to the army and to the cause of america.

He now therefore most earnestly exhorts Officers of

Life of Benjamin Franklin BY O. L. HOLLEY, 1848

Benjamin Franklin, Thomas Lynch, and Benjamin Harrison were sent to Cambridge by Congress to arrange for the maintenance of the army.

all Ranks to shew an Example of Bravery and Courage to their men; assuring them that such as do their duty in the day of Battle, as brave and good Officers, shall be honor'd with every mark of distinction and regard; their names and merits made known to the General Congress and all America: while on the other hand, he positively declares that every Officer, be his rank what it may, who shall betray his Country, dishonour the Army and his General, by basely keeping back and shrinking from his duty in any engagment; shall be held up as an infamous Coward and punish'd as such, with the utmost martial severity; and no Connections, Interest or Intercessions in his behalf will avail to prevent the strict execution of justice.

Washington discovered, when he got an accurate count of his men, that his army was woefully weak to face the British, who could strike where and when they pleased with the support of the guns of their fleet. Moreover, his fortifications were flimsy and poorly planned. Near the end of July he sent his brother John Augustine a good summary of the situation.

Camp at Cambridge, about 5 miles from Boston,
July 27th. 1775.

On the 2d Instt. I arrived at this place after passing through a great deal of delightful Country, covered with grass.(although the Season has been dry) in a very different manner to what our Lands in Virginia are. I found a mixed multitude of People here, under very little discipline, order, or Government. I found the Enemy in Possession of a place called Bunkers Hill, on Charles Town Neck, strongly Intrenched & Fortifying themselves. I found part of our Army on two Hills (called Winter & Prospect Hills) about a Mile & quarter from the Enemy on Bunkers Hill, in a very insecure state; I found another part of the Army at this Village, and a third part at Roxbury, guarding the Entrance in and out of Boston. My whole time since I came here, has been Imployed in throwing up Lines of Defence at these three places; to secure in the first Instance, our own Troops from any attempts of the Enemy; and in the next, to cut of all Communications between their Troops and the Country; For to do this, & to prevent them from penetrating into the Country with Fire and Sword, & to harass them

Engraving of the Battle of Bunker Hill where Washington later found the enemy "strongly Intrenched"

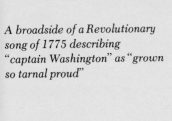

A broadside of a Revolutionary song of 1775 describing "captain Washington" as "grown so tarnal proud"

The YANKEY's return from CAMP.

FATHER and I went down to camp,
Along with Captain Gooding,
There we fee the men and boys,
As thick as hafty pudding.
Yankey doodle keep it up,
Chorus. Yankey doodle, dandy,
Mind the mufic and the ftep,
And wi' the girls be handy.
And there we fee a thoufand men,
As rich as 'Squire David ;
And what they wafted every day,
I wifh it could be faved.
Yankey doodle, &c.
The 'laffes they eat every day,
Would keep a houfe a winter :
They have as much that I'll be bound
They eat it when they're a mind to.
Yankey doodle, &c.

And ftuck a crooked ftabbing iron
Upon the little end on't.
Yankey doodle, &c.
And there I fee a pumpkin fhell
as big as mother's bafon,
And ev'ry time they touch'd it off,
They fcamper'd like the nation.
Yankey doodle, &c.
I fee a little barrel too,
The heads were made of leather,
They knock'd upon't with little clubs,
And call'd the folks together.
Yankey doodle, &c.
And there was captain Wafhington,
And gentlefolks about him,
They fay he's grown fo tarnal proud,
He will not ride without 'em.
Yankey doodle, &c.

if they do, is all that is expected of me; and if effected, must totally overthrow the designs of Administration, as the whole Force of Great Britain in the Town and Harbour of Boston, can answer no other end than to sink her under the disgrace and weight of the expence. Their Force, including Marines, Tories, &ca., are computed from the best Accts. I can get, at abt. 12,000 Men; ours, including Sick absent, &ca., at about 16,000; but then we have a cemi Circle of Eight or nine Miles to guard, to every part of wch. we are obliged to be equally attentive whilst they, situated as it were in the Centre of that Cemicircle, can bend their whole Force (having the entire command of the Water) against any one part of it with equal facility; this renders our Situation not very agreeable, though necessary; however, by incessant labour (Sundays not excepted) we are in a much better posture of defence now than when I first came. The Inclosed, though rough, will give you some small Idea of the Situation of Boston, & Bay on this side; as also of the Post they have Taken in Charles Town Neck, Bunker's Hill, and our Posts.

By very authentick Intelligence lately receivd out of Boston (from a Person who saw the returns) the number of Regulars (including I presume the Marines) the Morning of the Action on Bunkers Hill amounted to 7533 Men —their killed & wounded on that occasion amounted to

1043, whereof 92 were Officers. Our loss was 138 killed 36 Missing & 276 Wounded. The Enemy are sickly, and scarce of Fresh provisions — Beef, which is chiefly got by slaughtering their Milch Cows in Boston, sells from one shilling to 18d. Sterg. pr. lb.; & that it may not get cheaper, or more plenty, I have drove all the Stock within a considerable distance of this place back into the Country, out of the Way of the Men of War's Boats; In short, I have, & shall continue to do, every thing in my power to distress them. The Transports are all arrived & their whole Reinforcement Landed, so that I can see no reason why they should not if they ever attempt it, come boldly out and put the matter to Issue at once. If they think themselves not strong enough to do this, they surely will carry their Arms (having Ships of War & Transports ready) to some other part of the Continent, or relinquish the dispute; the last of which the Ministry, unless compelled will never agree to do. Our Works, & those of the Enemy, are so near & quite open between that we see every thing that each other is doing.

On August 1 Washington learned a shocking fact: his stock of powder, which he had been told was a barely adequate 308 barrels, was in fact a frighteningly meager ninety barrels — not enough for nine rounds per man, and with nothing for the artillery. The General enjoined the sternest kind of conservation, while carefully avoiding mention of a shortage.

GENERAL ORDERS

Head Quarters, Cambridge, August 4th. 1775
Parole, London. Countersign, Ireland.

It is with Indignation and Shame, the General observes, that notwithstanding the repeated Orders which have been given to prevent the firing of Guns, in and about Camp, that it is daily and hourly practised; that contrary to all Orders, straggling Soldiers do still pass the Guards, and fire at a Distance, where there is not the least probability of hurting the enemy, and where no other end is answer'd, but to waste Ammunition, expose themselves to the ridicule of the enemy, and keep their own Camps harrassed by frequent and continual alarms, to the hurt of every good Soldier, who is thereby disturbed of his natural rest, and will at length never be able to distinguish between a real, and a false alarm.

Brigadier General Horatio Gates

same offences; in short they are by no means such Troops, in any respect, as you are led to believe of them from the accts. which are published, but I need not make myself Enemies among them, by this declaration, although it is consistent with truth. I dare say the Men would fight very well (if properly Officered) although they are an exceeding dirty and nasty people; had they been properly conducted at Bunkers Hill (on the 17th of June) or those that were there properly supported, the Regulars would have met with a shameful defeat, and a much more considerable loss than they did, which is now known to be exactly 1057 killed and wounded; it was for their behaviour on that occasion that the above Officers were broke, for I never spared one that was accused of Cowardice but brot 'em to immediate Tryal.

There were endless harassing details to be taken care of. Although Brigadier General Horatio Gates, as Adjutant General, had taken charge of the administrative work of the staff and removed some of the burden from Washington, the primary responsibility was still the commander's.

GENERAL ORDERS

Head Quarters, Cambridge, July 14th. 1775
Parole, Hallifax. Countersign, Inverness.

As the Health of an Army principally depends upon Cleanliness; it is recommended in the strongest manner, to the Commanding Officer of Corps, Posts and Detachments, to be strictly diligent, in ordering the Necessarys [privies] to be filled up once a Week, and new ones dug; the Streets of the encampments and Lines to be swept daily, and all Offal and Carrion, near the camp, to be immediately buried. The Officers commanding in Barracks, or Quarters, to be answerable that they are swept every morning, and all Filth & Dirt removed from about the houses. Next to Cleanliness, nothing is more conducive to a Soldiers health, than dressing his provisions in a decent and proper manner. The Officers commanding Companies should therefore daily inspect the Camp Kitchens, and see the Men dress their Food in a wholesome way.

Head Quarters, Cambridge, August 22nd. 1775
The General does not mean to discourage the practice

of bathing, whilst the weather is warm enough to continue it; but he expressly forbids, any persons doing it, at or near the Bridge in Cambridge, where it has been observed and complained of, that many Men, lost to all sense of decency and common modesty, are running about naked upon the Bridge, whilst Passengers, and even Ladies of the first fashion in the neighbourhood, are passing over it, as if they meant to glory in their shame. The Guards and Centries at the Bridge, are to put a stop to this practice for the future.

Head Quarters, Cambridge, August 28th. 1775 As nothing is more pernicious to the health of Soldiers, nor more certainly productive of the bloody-flux; than drinking New Cyder: The General in the most possitive manner commands, the entire disuse of the same, and orders the Quarter Master General this day, to publish Advertisements, to acquaint the Inhabitants of the surrounding districts, that such of them, as are detected bringing new Cyder into the Camp, after Thursday, the last day of this month, may depend on having their casks stove.

With summer waning and the nip of early New England autumn in the air, Washington had to plan barracks for his men, provide warmer clothing, and even face the possibility that his army might melt away if the siege were not resolved before the end of the year. He expressed his forebodings to Congress in a letter to its president, John Hancock.

Camp at Cambridge, Septemr. 21st. 1775 The Connecticut & Rhode Island Troops stand engaged to the 1st. December only, & none longer than to the 1st. January. A Dissolution of the present Army therefore will take Place, unless some early Provision is made against such an Event. Most of the General Officers are of Opinion, the greater Part of them may be re-inlisted for the Winter or another Campaign, with the Indulgence of a Furlough to visit their Friends which may be regulated so as not to endanger the Service. How far it may be proper to form the new Army entirely out of the old for another Campaign, rather than from the Contingents of the several Provinces, is a Question which involves in it too many Considerations of Policy and Prudence for me to undertake to decide. It appears to be impos-

Israel Putnam (above) commanded the center division of Washington's reorganized army; Artemas Ward assumed command of the right wing.

sible to draw it from any other Source than the old Army this Winter; & as the Pay is ample, I hope a sufficient Number will engage in the Service for that Time at least: but there are various Opinions of the Temper of the Men on the Subject, & there may be great Hazard in deferring the Tryal too long.

[In the same letter, the Commander in Chief revealed that he had another campaign underway.]

I am now to inform the Honble. Congress, that encouraged by the repeated Declarations of the Canadians & Indians, & urged by their Requests; I have detached Col. Arnold with 1000 Men to penetrate into Canada by Way of Kennebeck River, & if possible, to make himself Master of Quebeck. By this manoeuvre, I propose, either to divert Carlton [Sir Guy Carleton, British commander] from St. Johns which would leave a free Passage to General Schuyler, or if this did not take Effect, Quebeck in its present defenseless State must fall into his Hands an easy Prey. I made all possible Inquiry as to the Distance, the Safety of the Rout, & the Danger of the Season, being too far advanced, but found nothing in either to deter me from proceeding, more especially, as it met with very General Approbation from all whom I consulted upon it. But that nothing might be omitted, to enable me to judge of its Propriety, & probable Consequences, I communicated it, by Express to General Schuyler, who approved of it in such Terms, that I resolved to put it into immediate Execution. They have now left this Place 7 Days, & if favoured with a good Wind, I hope soon to hear of their being safe in Kennebeck River.

Washington continued to extend and strengthen his lines, tightening his siege of Boston, which was then almost an island, connected to the mainland only by a narrow neck or peninsula. The army had been reorganized, formed into three "Grand Divisions," with the right wing, or division, under Artemas Ward, the left under Charles Lee, and the center commanded by Israel Putnam. After his powder supply had been somewhat replenished, Washington proposed to his general officers in September and again in October a concerted assault on the British lines to bring a decision. His officers disagreed, and he deferred to their opinion. To give his army more firepower, Washington assigned a special mission to Henry Knox, a twenty-five-year-old Boston bookseller, who had studied artillery and fortifications as a hobby and who would shortly become Washington's Chief of Artillery.

[Headquarters, Cambridge, November 16, 1775] You are immediately to examine into the state of the artillery of this army & take an account of the Cannon Motors, Shels, Lead & Ammunition, that are wanting. When you have done that, you are to proceed in the most expeditious manner to New York; There apply to the president of the provincial Congress, and learn of him whether Col. Reed did any thing, or left any orders &c. respecting these things & get him to procure such of them as can possibly be had there. The president if he can will have them immediately sent hither: If he cannot, you must put them in a proper Channel for being Transported to this Camp with dispatch before you leave New York. After you have procured as many of these Necessaries as you can there, you must go to Major General Schuyler & get the Remainder from Ticonderoga, Crown point, or St Johns—if it should be necessary, from Quebec; if in our Hands. The want of them is so great, that no trouble or expence must be spared to obtain them. I have wrote to General Schuyler, he will give you every necessary assistance, that they may be had & forwarded to this place, with the utmost dispatch. I have given you a Warrant to the paymaster General of the Continental army for a Thousand Dollars to defray the expence attending your Journey, & procuring these articles; An Account of which you are to keep & render upon your return.

Go: Washington

Endeavour to procure what Flints you can.

As the first of December neared—the date on which Connecticut troops insisted their enlistments expired—Washington expressed his despair to Joseph Reed, who had returned to his law practice in Philadelphia after having served as Washington's secretary during the first months at Cambridge.

Cambridge 28th. Novr., 1775. What an astonishing thing it is, that those who are employed to sign the Continental Bills should not be able, or Inclined to do it as fast as they are wanted. They will prove the destruction of the army if they are not more attentive and diligent. Such a dearth of Publick Spirit, & want of Virtue; such stock jobbing, and fertility in all the low Arts to obtain advantages, of one kind or another, in this great change of Military arrangemt. I never saw before, and pray God I may never be witness to again. What will be the ultimate end of these Maneuvres is beyond my Scan. I tremble at the prospect. We have been till this time Enlisting about 3500 Men. To engage these I have been obliged to allow Furloughs as far as 50 Men a Regiment, & the Officers, I am persuaded, endulge as many more. The Connecticut Troops will not be prevailed upon to stay longer than their term (saving those who have enlisted for the next Campaign, & mostly on Furlough) and such a dirty, Mercenary spirit pervades the whole, that I should not be at all surprizd at any disaster that may happen. In short, after the last of this Month, our lines will be so weakened that the Minute Men and Militia must be call'd in for their defence; these, being under no kind of Government themselves, will destroy the little subordination I have been labouring to establish, and run me into one evil, whilst I am endeavouring to avoid another; but the lesser must be chosen. Could I have foreseen what I have, & am like to experience, no consideration upon Earth should have induced me to accept this Command. A regiment or any subordinate department would have been accompanied with ten times the satisfaction, —perhaps the honour.

OLITAN MUSEUM OF ART, CHARLES ALLEN MUNN BEQUEST, 1924

Engraving of General Arnold's march through the Maine wilderness, from The Journal of Isaac Senter, *who accompanied the troops as surgeon*

Patriotic appeals and exhortations by Washington and other officers induced some men to re-enlist, but all but a handful of the Connecticut farmboy-soldiers insisted on going home. Washington held them until militia could arrive to fill some of the gaps, but on December 10 they left, amid general catcalls and pelting with clods. The next day, however, was one of the brightest Washington had experienced in many weeks. Martha arrived by carriage from Virginia, accompanied by her son Jack, his wife Nelly, and the wife of General Horatio Gates.

As the year drew to an end, there was good news from Canada: General Schuyler's force, led by his second in command, Brigadier General Richard Montgomery, had pushed north, captured British Forts St. John and Chambly, and then had taken Montreal. There was no news of Benedict Arnold, who had been moving with incredible hardships through the frozen wilderness of Maine toward Quebec; Washington, imminently expecting good news, would not learn for many weeks that on the last day of the year Montgomery and Arnold had joined in an unsuccessful attack on Quebec in which Montgomery had died and Arnold had been wounded.

On New Year's Day, 1776, Washington proclaimed the new army complete, with enlistments replacing all those that had expired. But far from having the twenty thousand men he considered a necessary minimum, Washington found his redoubts at some places entirely empty of defenders. Two days later King George's proclamation to Parliament, promising to crush the Colonial revolt, was first seen by the patriot army. Washington commented to Joseph Reed.

Original watercolor plan of Fort Ticonderoga made by Colonel John Trumbull at Washington's order in 1776, and then sent to Congress

Cambridge January 4th. 1776.

We are at length favoured with a sight of his Majesty's most gracious Speech, breathing sentiments of tenderness & compassion for his deluded American Subjects; the Echo is not yet come to hand; but we know what it must be; and as Lord North said, & we ought to have believed (& acted accordingly) we now know the ultimatum of British justice. The speech I send you. A volume of them was sent out by the Boston Gentry — and, farcical enough, we gave great joy to them (the red Coats I mean) without knowing or intending it, for on that day, the day which gave beginning to the new army (but before the proclamation came to hand) we had hoisted the Union Flag in compliment to the United Colonies but behold! it was received in Boston as a token of the deep Impression the Speech had made upon us, and as a signal of Submission — so we learn by a person out of Boston last night. By this time I presume they begin to think it strange that we have not made a formal surrender of our lines. Admiral Shuldham is arrivd at Boston. The 55th. and the greatest part, if not all, of the 17th. Regiment, are also got in there. The rest of the 5 Regiments from Ireland were intended for Halifax & Quebec; those for the first are arrived there, the others we know not where they are got to.

It is easier to conceive, than to describe the situation of My Mind for sometime past, & my feelings under our present Circumstances. Search the vast volumes of history through, & I much question whether a case similar to ours is to be found; to wit, to maintain a Post against the flower of the British Troops for Six Months together without [missing] and at the end of them to have one Army disbanded and another to raise within the same

A dramatic pencil sketch of the death of General Montgomery in the Battle of Quebec, also by Trumbull

distance of a Reinforced Enemy. It is too much to attempt. What may be the final issue of the last manoeuvre, time only can tell. I wish this month was well over our heads. The same desire of retiring into a Chimney-Corner seized the Troops of New Hampshire, Rhode Island, & Massachusetts, (so soon as their time expired) as had work'd upon those of Connecticut, notwithstanding many of them made a tender of their Services to continue till the lines could be sufficiently strengthned. We are now left with a good deal less than half rais'd Regiments, and about 5000 Militia who only stand Ingaged to the Middle of this Month; when, according to custom, they will depart, let the necessity of their stay be never so urgent. Thus it is that for more than two Months past, I have scarcely immerged from one difficulty before I have plunged into another. How it will end God in his great goodness will direct. I am thankful for his protection to this time. We are told that we shall soon get the army compleated, but I have been told so many things which have never come to pass that I distrust every thing.

On January 9, 1776, the first detailed rolls for the new army showed Washington that he had only about eighty-two hundred men, of whom some fifty-six hundred were present and fit for duty. Later it turned out that nearly two thousand men were without muskets. To add to his already heavy burdens, word came of the defeat of Montgomery and Arnold before Quebec. One bright spot: Henry Knox returned from Fort Ticonderoga with sixty-six pieces of artillery that he had brought across frozen rivers and over rugged countryside on ox-drawn sledges. When the army's manpower was temporarily increased by the arrival of several thousand short-term militia, Washington once more considered ways of getting at the British before his strength ebbed again. He reported one such plan to Congress in a letter to its president, John Hancock.

Cambridge, 18th. Feby. 1776.
The late freezing Weather having formed some pretty strong Ice from Dorchester point to Boston Neck, and from Roxbury to the Common, thereby affording a more expanded and consequently a less dangerous Approach to the Town, I could not help thinking, notwithstanding the Militia were not all come In, and we had little or no Powder to begin our Operation by a regular Cannonade & Bombardment, that a bold & resolute Assault upon the Troops in Boston with such Men as we had (for

it could not take many Men to guard our own Lines at a time when the Enemy were attacked in all Quarters) might be crown'd with success; and therefore, seeing no certain prospect of a supply of Powder on the one hand, and a certain dissolution of the Ice on the other, I called the General Officers together for their opinion (agreeably to the Resolve of Congress of the 22d. of December).

The Result will appear in the Inclosed Council of War [his officers decided such an attack would be unwise], and being almost unanimous, I must suppose to be right although, from a thorough conviction of the necessity of attempting something against the Ministerial Troops, before a Reinforcement should arrive and while we were favour'd with the Ice, I was not only ready, but willing and desirous of making the Assault; under a firm hope, if the Men would have stood by me, of a favourable Issue, notwithstanding the Enemy's advantage of Ground — Artillery, —&ca.

Perhaps the Irksomeness of my situation, may have given different Ideas to me, than those which Influenced the Gentlemen I consulted, and might have inclin'd me to put more to the hazard than was consistent with prudence. If it had, I am not sensible of it, as I endeavourd to give it all the consideration that a matter of such Importance required. True it is, & I cannot help acknowledging, that I have many disagreeable Sensations, on acct. of my Situation; for to have the Eyes of the whole Continent fixed, with anxious expectations of hearing of some great event, & to be restrain'd in every Military Operation for want of the necessary means of carrying it on, is not very pleasing; especially, as the means used to conceal my weakness from the Enemy conceals it also from our friends, and adds to their Wonder.

Major General Henry Knox by Stuart

By early spring Washington was in a position to carry out a less hazardous operation than sending his men across the ice to storm the British positions. He had accumulated enough powder to permit a modest bombardment, and on the night of March 4, 1776, began an operation that he described to his confidant Joseph Reed.

Cambridge, March 7, 1776.

The rumpus which every body expected to see between

Original drawing made by Archibald Robertson, entitled "View of Boston Showing the heights of Dorchester taken from Mount Whoredone, 1776"

the Ministerialists in Boston and our troops, has detained the bearer till this time. On Monday night I took possession of the Heights of Dorchester with two thousand men under the command of General Thomas. Previous to this, and in order to divert the enemy's attention from the real object, and to harass, we began on Saturday night a cannonade and bombardment, which with intervals was continued through the night—the same on Sunday, and on Monday, a continued roar from seven o'clock till daylight was kept up between the enemy and us. In this time we had an officer and one private killed, and four or five wounded; and through the ignorance, I suppose, of our artillery-men, burst five mortars (two thirteen inch and three ten inch), the "Congress," one of them. What damage the enemy has sustained is not known, as there has not been a creature out of Boston since. The cannonade, &c., except in the destruction of the mortars, answered our expectations fully; for although we had upwards of 300 teams in motion at the same instant, carrying on our fascines and other materials to the Neck, and the moon shining in its full lustre we were not discovered till daylight on Tuesday morning.

So soon as we were discovered, every thing seemed to be preparing for an attack, but the tide failing before they were ready, about one thousand only were able to embark in six transports in the afternoon, and these falling down towards the Castle, were drove on shore by a violent storm, which arose in the afternoon of that

123

Detail from a 1776 map showing the proximity of Dorchester Neck to Boston across a narrow strip of water

day, and continued through the night; since that they have been seen returning to Boston, and whether from an apprehension that our works are now too formidable to make any impression on, or from what other causes I know not, but their hostile appearances have subsided, and they are removing their ammunition out of their magazine, whether with a view to move bag and baggage or not I cannot undertake to say, but if we had powder (and our mortars replaced, which I am about to do by new cast ones as soon as possible) I would, so soon as we were sufficiently strengthened on the heights to take possession of the point just opposite to Boston Neck, give them a dose they would not well like.

We had prepared boats, a detachment of 4000 men, &c., &c., for pushing to the west part of Boston, if they had made any formidable attack upon Dorchester. I will not lament or repine at any act of Providence because I am in a great measure a convert to Mr. Pope's opinion, that whatever is, is right, but I think everything had the appearance of a successful issue, if we had come to an engagement on that day. It was the 5th of March, which I recalled to their remembrance as a day never to be forgotton [the anniversary of the Boston Massacre]; an engagement was fully expected, and I never saw spirits higher, or more prevailing.

Washington, in short, had seized the high ground known as Dorchester Heights under cover of darkness, and by daybreak his men had fortified their positions with fascines and other devices they had brought to minimize digging in the frozen ground. The British were apparently confused at finding the heights occupied at daybreak; indecision, a wrong tide, and finally a storm kept them from counterattacking until the American positions were too strong. Shortly thereafter there were signs that the British were making ready to quit Boston. Their position would soon be untenable; from Dorchester Heights the Americans could next move to a position called Nooks Hill, where their artillery could fire down into Boston and its harbor. Within ten days or so, Washington was able to send Congress, through John Hancock, the message he had been wanting for months to dispatch.

Head Quarters Cambridge March 19th. 1776
It is with the greatest pleasure I inform you that on Sunday last the 17th. Instant, about 9th O'Clock in the forenoon the Ministerial Army evacuated the Town of

Boston, and that the Forces of the United Colonies are now in actual Possession thereof. I beg leave to congratulate you Sir, and the Honorable Congress on this happy event, and particularly as it was effected without endangering the Lives and property of the remaining unhappy Inhabitants.

I have great reason to imagine their flight was precipitated by the appearance of the Work which I had ordered to be thrown up last Saturday night, on an eminence at Dorchester, which lay nearest to Boston Neck called Newks [Nooks] Hill. The Town although it has suffered greatly, is not in so bad a state as I expected to find it, and I have a particular pleasure in being able to inform you, Sir, that your House has received no damage worth mentioning, your furniture is in tolerable Order and the family pictures are all left entire and untouched. Captn. Cazneau takes charge of the whole until he receives further Orders from you.

As soon as the Ministerial Troops had quitted the Town, I ordered a Thousand men (who had had the small pox) under command of General Putnam, to take possession of the Heights, which I shall fortify in such a manner, as to prevent their return, should they attempt it; but as they are still in the Harbour, I thought it not prudent to march off with the main body of the Army, until I should be fully satisfied they had quitted the Coast. I have therefore only detached five Regiments besides the Rifle Battalion to New York, and shall keep the remainder here 'till all suspicion of their return ceases.

The situation in which I found their Works, evidently

A 1776 broadside celebrating British evacuation of the town of Boston

*Gold medal awarded to Washington
by Congress following Boston victory*

discovered that their retreat was made with the greatest precipitation. They have left their Barracks and other works of wood at Bunkers Hill &ca. all standing, and have destroyed but a small part of their Lines. They have also left a number of fine pieces of Cannon, which they first spiked up, also a very large Iron Mortar; and (as I am informed) they have thrown another over the end of your Wharf. I have employed proper Persons to drill the Cannon, and doubt not I shall save the most of them.

I am not yet able to procure an exact List of all the Stores they have left. As soon as it can be done I shall take care to transmit it to you. From an estimate already made, by the Quarter Master General, of what he has discovered, they will amount to 25 or 30,000 £.

Part of the Powder mentioned in yours of the 6th Instant has already arrived; The remainder I have ordered to be stop'd on the Road as we shall have no occasion for it here.

The British fleet lay in the outer harbor until March 27, causing some apprehension among the Americans that Howe might return and attack them. Then it sailed away, destination unknown. New York, however, was the strategic and logical place for the royal army to strike, and Washington had started a brigade on its way there even before Howe sailed. After the British fleet disappeared, Washington started the rest of his army moving toward New York. A letter went to Artemas Ward.

Cambridge, 29th. Mar. 76
As General Green is ordered to march with the next Brigade on Monday and as General Spencer will follow with the last (leaving four or five regiments in this department for Defense, Protection of the Stores, Erection of works &c.) I should be glad, if you are not afraid of the Small Pox & Incline to continue longer in the Service that you lately talk'd of, if you would remove into Boston tomorrow or next day, & take upon you the Command and direction of Matters there.

So Washington returned command of the Boston area to the man from whom he had taken it, General Artemas Ward. He then departed Boston on April 4, hastening toward New York. Both he and his army had new confidence. They had bested the British; they believed they could do it again.

First in War

EVE OF INDEPENDENCE

In 1746 Benjamin Franklin wrote to England to order "two setts of Popple's Mapps of N. America" (left) to hang in the Assembly room at Philadelphia; nearly thirty years passed before relations between the mother country and her American Colonies reached the state illustrated above. And in 1774 the map was still hanging in the Pennsylvania State House when the First Continental Congress met there. Stung by Britain's hardening attitude during the tense preceding decade—years that saw the hated Stamp Act imposed and repealed, the massacre at Boston, and the tea-dumping in Boston Harbor—Congress finally took a decisive stand. "The New England governments are in a state of Rebellion," declared King George III. "Blows must decide whether they are to be subject to this country or independent." But the "Female Combatants" were more blunt: "I'll force you to Obedience you Rebellious Slut," shouts an elegant Britannia. "Liberty Liberty for ever Mother while I exist," replies an aroused America.

BOSTON

CHARLES TOWN

THE FIRST ENCOUNTERS

On April 27, 1775, George Washington, at home in Mount Vernon, received the news of the Battle of Lexington (left, above), which had erupted a week before. It was not until the middle of June, however, that Washington, nominated by John Adams, was elected by the Second Continental Congress "to command all the Continental forces raised or to be raised for the defence of American liberty." On his way north, he learned of the burning of Charlestown and the bloody contest for Bunker Hill (left, below), which the British narrowly won with staggering casualties. His own first chance to confound the enemy came nine months later, when in one remarkable night he fortified Dorchester Heights with cannon dragged all the way from Fort Ticonderoga and forced the British to evacuate their then untenable position in Boston. The imposing portrait above by Gilbert Stuart commemorates Washington's first victory.

131

DISASTER IN NEW YORK

"I have brought the whole Army which I had in the New England Governments... to this place," Washington wrote in April, 1776. He knew that the British commander, General Howe (left), must have his eye on the Hudson River as the likeliest place to "stop the Intercourse between the northern and southern Colonies." Upon hearing of the Declaration of Independence in July, patriots toppled the statue of George III at Bowling Green (left, above). But for Washington things went from bad to worse. He suffered defeats on Long Island and at Kip's Bay before moving his army to Harlem Heights, after the British disembarked in New York—impressively Venetian as rendered at far left by a contemporary German artist. The final disaster came in November when the British took Fort Washington (above), while Washington watched in impotent fury from the New Jersey shore.

133

TEN DAYS OF VICTORY

The depths to which Washington had sunk between September, 1776, when he had written firmly from Harlem Heights, "I am resolved not to be forced from this ground while I have life," and December, when from a camp in Pennsylvania he cried, "I think the game is pretty near up," reveal the agonizing toll of his forced retreat south across New Jersey. He picked Christmas night to undertake a brilliant and dramatic stroke that was to have an electric effect on the morale of his "wretched remains of a broken army" and on the country as a whole. During the night, which he described to Congress as "very severe," he ferried his troops across the ice-clogged Delaware River, to which he points in the painting above, and totally surprised the drowsy, holiday-happy Hessian soldiers at Trenton. Their commander, Colonel Johann Rall, was killed, although the painting above, right, shows him surrendering to a Washington whose arm is extended to aid him. Washington hoped to strike again at once but encountered British reinforcements under Lord Cornwallis. While a few men kept his campfires burning in the night, Washington slipped out and struck the enemy's rear guard at Princeton. At right, Washington on horseback directs the artillery that routed the British redcoats and brought a second brilliant victory on January 3, 1777.

The Capture of the Hessians at Trenton BY JOHN TRUMBULL; YALE UNIVERSITY ART GALLERY

"A DREARY KIND OF PLACE"

The year following the Jersey victories was a dismal one. Battles at Brandywine Creek and Germantown were lost and Howe marched into Philadelphia. Washington chose Valley Forge, "a dreary kind of place" he called it, for his winter headquarters of 1777–78 (right). It was a rugged winter of suffering and despair, a point emphasized in the nineteenth-century painting below. The one good thing was the appearance of European professionals, including the Prussian drillmaster Baron von Steuben (left), who helped make Washington's army a far more viable force.

WASHINGTON AND HIS GENERALS

In this painting done after his death by an unknown hand, Washington is surrounded by his generals, among whom can tentatively be identified: Anthony Wayne (right foreground); Lafayette (in profile to his left); Greene and a round-faced Israel Putnam (to his right); Knox (far left).

CONFLICT AT MONMOUTH

Sir Henry Clinton (left, above) replaced Howe at Philadelphia in May, 1778, and decided to risk the long overland trek to New York. Determined to attack his enemy's strung-out lines, Washington put Charles Lee in charge of an advanced pursuit force that caught up with Clinton at Monmouth, New Jersey. Instead of pressing his attack, Lee for some still unknown reason ordered a retreat. A furious Washington, seen above at the moment of rallying the retreating soldiers, and "swearing like an angel from Heaven," removed Lee from command—hence *The Suspended General* (left) drawn by the famous Polish volunteer Thaddeus Kosciusko. Monmouth was the last major northern battle; after 1778, the emphasis shifted south, and French aid began to turn the tide of war.

141

VICTORY AT YORKTOWN

The young Marquis de Lafayette (right, above) was one of France's earliest volunteers in the American cause and a proud witness as the British troops passed in surrender between the French and American lines (above) following their defeat at Yorktown on October 19, 1781. Colonel David Humphreys, a Washington aide, had the honor of presenting the captured colors to Congress (right).

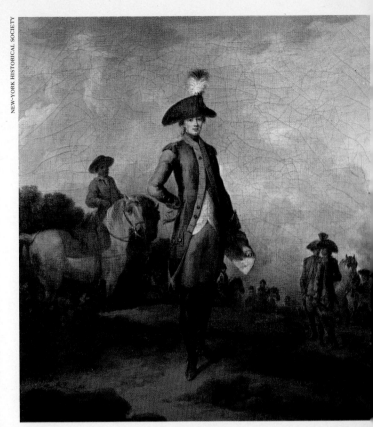

A SOLDIER'S ADIEU

More than a year passed between the British surrender at Yorktown and the signing of preliminary articles of peace at Paris in November, 1782; another year went by before the last British troops departed from New York. On December 4, 1783, Washington rode triumphantly back into the city he had been forced to retreat from in 1776 and there bade farewell to the officers who had served him so long and so faithfully. "Such a scene of sorrow and weeping I had never before witnessed," recalled one officer of the meeting in Fraunces Tavern (below). "That we should see his face no more in this world seemed to me utterly insupportable." After embracing each, Washington, too moved to speak, walked to the waterfront where a barge was waiting to take him across the Hudson River to the Jersey shore (left) and from which "out in the stream, our great and beloved General waved his hat and bid us a silent adieu."

Chapter **5**

Times That Tried
Men's Souls

Washington arrived in New York on April 13, 1776, afraid that he would find the sea-borne British already there. But Howe had taken his army to Halifax to reload and refit. The British had left Boston so hurriedly and had abandoned so much materiel that there was a great deal of sorting out to do, and shortages to be made up, before they would be ready for another campaign. General Charles Lee, now gone to South Carolina to ward off a British assault on Charleston, had started preparations for the defenses of New York, and Washington pushed on with the task. The entrance to the East River, which divides Manhattan and Long Island, was blocked with sunken vessels and other obstructions and was guarded by cannon on lower Manhattan and on the opposite high ground on Long Island known as Brooklyn Heights. On the west side of Manhattan the Hudson, or North, River was too wide and deep to be barred with sunken obstructions or effectively commanded by cannon fire; but that side of the island, unlike the East River shore, was mainly rocky and precipitous and unsuited for landings. In the city itself, which occupied only the lower tip of Manhattan, there were barricades on every street leading to the water, and trenches and earthworks laced the countryside above the town. While the American army waited and tried to make ready, Washington wrote to his brother John Augustine, once more giving him a good summary of the situation.

[New York, April 29, 1776]
Since my arrival at this place, I have been favour'd with two or three of your Letters, and thank you for your kind and frequent remembrance of me. If I shd. not write to you, as often as you do to me, you must attribute it to its true cause, and that is the hurry, and multiplicity of business in which I am constantly engaged from the time I rise out of my Bed till I go into it again.

I wrote to you a pretty full Acct. just before I left Cambridge of the movemts. of the two Armies, and now refer to it—since that, I have brought the whole Army which I had in the New England Governments (five Regiments excepted, & left behind for the defence of Boston and the Stores we have there) to this place; and Eight days ago, Detached four Regiments for Canada; and am now Imbarking Six more for the same place, as there are reasons to believe that a push will be made there this Campaign, and things in that Country not being in a very promising way, either with respect to the Canadians or Indian's. These Detachments have weaken'd us very considerably in this important post, where I am sorry to add, there are too many inimical persons; but as our Affairs in Canada can derive no support but what is sent to them, and the Militia may be called in here, it was thought best to strengthen that Quarter at the expence of this; but I am affraid we are rather too late in doing of it; from the Eastern Army (under my immediate Command) it was impossible to do it sooner.

We have already gone great lengths in fortifying this City & the Hudson River; a fortnight more will put us in a very respectable posture of Defence, the Works we have already constructed, and which they found we were about to erect, have put the King's Ships to flight; for instead of laying within Pistol shot of the Wharves, and their Centrys conversing with Ours (whilst they received every necessary that the Country afforded) they have now gone down to the Hook, near 30 Miles from this place, the last Harbour they can get to, and I have prevaild upon the Comee. of safety to forbid every kind of Intercourse between the Inhabitants of this Colony and the Enemy; this I was resolved upon effecting; but thought it best to bring it about, through that Channel, as I now can pursue my own measures in support of their resolves.

Mrs. Washington is still here, and talks of taking the Small Pox [infection with virus to produce a light—hopefully—case], but I doubt her resolution. Mr. and Mrs. Custis will set out in a few days for Maryland. I did not write to you by the 'Squire, because his departure in the first place, was sudden; in the next, I had but little to say. I am very sorry to hear that my Sister was

Washington's first headquarters in New York City were here on Pearl Street and later at 1 Broadway.

Indisposed with a sore Breast when you last wrote. I hope she is now recover'd of it, and that all your Family are well; that they may continue so, & that our once happy Country may escape the depredations & Calamities attending on War, is the fervent prayer of dr. Sir,

Go: WASHINGTON

Mrs. Washington, Mr. & Mrs. Custis join in love to my Sister the rest of the Family. With afn. G.W.

A month later New York was still waiting for the British, and Washington had occasion to send a short note to John Hancock about a subject of considerable interest.

New York, May 18. 1776

I do myself the honor to transmit to you the Inclosed letters and papers I received this morning in the state they now are, which contain sundry matters of Intelligence of the most Interesting nature.

As the Consideration of them may lead to important consequences and the adoption of several measures in the Military line, I have thought It advisable for Genl. Gates to attend Congress; he will follow to morrow and satisfie & explain to them some points they may wish to be informed of, in the course of their deliberations, not having an Opportunity at this time to submit my thoughts to them, upon these Interesting Accounts.

Among the "sundry matters of Intelligence of the most Interesting nature" that Washington enclosed were copies of treaties between England and the rulers of the petty German states of Hesse-Cassel, Brunswick, and Hanau, by which the German princes agreed to furnish soldiers to fight in America. These were the mercenaries who would be known and hated as Hessians, and their use by the Crown was to prove a last straw to many Americans who had still hoped that differences between motherland and Colonies could be conciliated. Washington expressed his own feelings about England and independence to his brother John Augustine after he learned that the Virginia Convention, the congress of that state, had voted unanimously to instruct its delegates in Philadelphia to propose that the Second Continental Congress declare the Colonies to be free and independent states.

Philadelphia, May 31, 1776.

Since my arrival at this place, where I came at the request of Congress, to settle some matters relative to the ensuing Campaign I have received your Letter of the 18th. from Williamsburg, & think I stand indebted to you for another, which came to hand sometime ago, in New York.

I am very glad to find that the Virginia Convention have passed so noble a vote, with so much unanimity — things have come to that pass now, as to convince us, that we have nothing more to expect from the justice of G. Britain — also, that she is capable of the most delusive Arts, for I am satisfied that no Commissioners ever were design'd, except Hessians & other Foreigners; and that the Idea was only to deceive, & throw us off our guard. The first it has too effectually accomplished, as many Members of Congress, in short, the representation of whole Provences, are still feeding themselves upon the dainty food of reconciliation; and tho' they will not allow that the expectation of it has any influence upon their judgments (with respect to their preparations for defence) it is but too obvious that it has an operation upon every part of their conduct and is a clog to their proceedings. It is not in the nature of things to be otherwise, for no Man, that entertains a hope of seeing this dispute speedily, and equitably adjusted by Commissioners, will go to the same expence, and run the same hazards to prepare for the worst event as he who believes that he must conquer, or submit to unconditional terms, & its concomitants, such as Confiscation, hanging, &c., &c.

German mercenaries (opposite, above, and below), who came to fight in America, were bitterly hated.

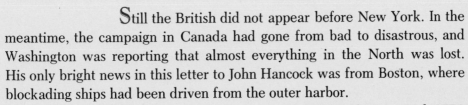

Still the British did not appear before New York. In the meantime, the campaign in Canada had gone from bad to disastrous, and Washington was reporting that almost everything in the North was lost. His only bright news in this letter to John Hancock was from Boston, where blockading ships had been driven from the outer harbor.

New York, June 23d. 1776

I herewith transmit you an extract of a Letter from Genl. Ward which came to hand by last nights post containing the agreeable Intelligence of their having Obliged the Kings Ships to leave Nantasket Road, and of Two Transports more being taken by our Armed Vessels with Two hundred and Ten Highland Troops on board.

I sincerely wish the like success had attended our Arms in another Quarter, but It has not. In Canada

In PROVINCIAL CONGRESS,
New-York, June 13, 1776.

Whereas this Congress have been informed
by the Continental Congress, and have great
Reason to believe that an Invasion of this Colony
will very shortly be made.

Resolved unanimously, That it be, and it is
hereby recommended to all the Officers in the Militia
in this Colony, forthwith to review the same, and
give Orders that they prepare themselves, and be
ready to march whenever they may be called upon.

Ordered, That the aforegoing Resolution be
published in the public News-Papers, and printed
in Hand-Bills to be distributed.

Extract from the Minutes,

ROBERT BENSON, Sec'ry.

*A June 13, 1776, broadside that
called on the militia to prepare was
followed in just over two weeks by
the British fleet's entry into New
York Harbor, as sketched at right.*

the situation of our Affairs is truly alarming. The Inclosed
Copies of Genls. Schuyler, Sullivan, & Arnold's Letters
will inform you, that Genl. Thompson has met with a
repulse at three Rivers, and is now a Prisoner in the
hands of Genl. Burgoyne, who these accounts say is
arrived with a considerable Army: nor do they seem to
promise an end of our misfortunes here; It is greatly
to be feared that the next advices from thence will
be, that our shattered, divided & broken Army, as you
will see by the return, have been obliged to abandon
the Country and retreat, to avoid a greater calamity,
that of being cut off or becoming prisoners. I will be
done upon the Subject & leave you to draw such con-
clusions, as you conceive from the state of facts are
most likely to result, only adding my apprehensions
that one of the. latter events, either that they are cutt
off or become Prisoners, has already happened If they
did not retreat while they had an opportunity.

150

Horatio Gates, formerly Adjutant General, had been made a major general and sent to Canada to try to save the situation, but he could do nothing. As the weeks passed, the defeat would become total: Benedict Arnold would be forced to give up Montreal as the rest of the American army, dispirited, sick, decimated by capture and smallpox, retreated into upper New York. Then on June 29 the first vessels of the British fleet came into New York Harbor; by the time all had dropped anchor there were 110 ships with some ten thousand men aboard. The Americans braced for action, but Howe only established camp on Staten Island. The word soon came in through the effective patriot spy system that the British general was waiting for another fleet under his older brother Admiral Richard Howe (Lord Howe) with troop transports carrying, among others, the first of the Hessians. To the dismay of Washington, the stream of reinforcements also included General Sir Henry Clinton and his forces, returned from their repulse at Charleston by Charles Lee. Rumors had spread that Congress had declared the Colonies independent of England, but not until July 9 was official word received in New York. Washington inserted a solemn announcement in the General Orders.

Head Quarters, New York, July 9th. 1776. The Hon. the Continental Congress, impelled by the dictates of duty, policy and necessity, having been pleased to dissolve the Connection which subsisted between this Country, and Great Britain, and to declare the United Colonies of North America, free and independent STATES: The several brigades are to be drawn up this evening on their respective Parades, at six OClock, when the declaration of Congress, shewing the grounds & reasons of this measure, is to be read with an audible voice.

The General hopes this important Event will serve as a fresh incentive to every officer, and soldier, to act with Fidelity and Courage, as knowing that now the peace and safety of his Country depends (under God) solely on the success of our arms: And that he is now in the service of a State, possessed of sufficient power to reward his

Johann Heinrich Ramberg, a German artist, drew his interpretation of the signing of the Declaration of Independence (above), while an American printmaker celebrated it by showing thirteen hands "Warm'd by one Heart, United in one Band."

merit, and advance him to the highest Honors of a free Country.

The Brigade Majors are to receive, at the Adjutant Generals Office, several of the Declarations to be delivered to the Brigadiers General, and the Colonels of Regiments.

The Declaration of Independence was read to all regiments, there was cheering, and in the evening a number of zealous patriots, among them some soldiers, toppled the equestrian statue of George III in Bowling Green. It was an act that the Commander in Chief deplored in his next General Orders.

Head Quarters, New York, July 10th. 1776.
'Tho the General doubts not the persons, who pulled down and mutilated the Statue, in the Broad way, last night, were actuated by Zeal in the public cause; yet it has so much the appearance of riot and want of order, in the Army, that he disapproves the manner, and directs that in future these things shall be avoided by the Soldiery, and left to be executed by proper authority.

On July 12 the British sent five ships up the Hudson River. Some American guns on the Manhattan bluffs opened fire, but in his General Orders the next day Washington remarked, more in sorrow than in anger, on the behavior of many of his cannoneers.

Head Quarters, New York, July 13th. 1776.
The General was sorry to observe Yesterday that many of the officers and a number of men instead of attending to their duty at the Beat of the Drum; continued along the banks of the North River, gazing at the Ships; such unsoldierly Conduct must grieve every good officer, and give the enemy a *mean* opinion of the Army, as nothing shews the brave and good Soldier more than in case of Alarms, cooly and calmly repairing to his post, and there waiting his orders; whereas a weak curiosity at such a time makes a man look mean and contemptible.

In other words, many American artillerymen had behaved like yokels, ignoring calls to man their guns and running instead to

153

gape at the ships sailing by. The enemy craft went up the Hudson as far as the wide reach called the Tappan Zee, where they cut off American communications between Albany and New York for six weeks—until frightened away by an American attack with fire rafts. British reinforcements kept arriving in New York Harbor through the second half of July and the first part of August. Washington was greatly outnumbered; moreover, a large part of his forces were militia, enlisted for two or three months, with little training, and most of them were ready to break for home if the going got hard. Approximately ten thousand American troops (a scourge of illness had laid low many others) opposed some thirty thousand trained enemy troops, although Washington's forces were later augmented by additional militia. With his small force, Washington had to defend a front of more than fifteen miles, from western Long Island to upper Manhattan. Howe could strike with his full force anywhere he chose, and he chose Long Island, with the American positions on rocky Brooklyn Heights as his objective. On August 22, in a smooth operation, he put ashore fifteen thousand men and equipment in a matter of hours. Later Washington described the Battle of Long Island to Hancock, without quite admitting that it had been a near disaster.

New York, Augt. 31st. 1776
Inclination as well as duty, would have Induced me to give Congress the earliest information of my removal and that of the Troops from Long Island & Its dependencies to this City the night before last, but the extreme fatigue, which myself and Family [his military staff] have undergone as much from the Weather since the Engagement of the 27th. rendered me & them entirely

unfit to take a pen in hand. Since Monday scarce any of us have been out of the Lines till our passage across the East River was effected yesterday morning & for Forty Eight Hours preceeding that I had hardly been of my Horse and never closed my Eyes so that I was quite unfit to write or dictate till this Morning.

Our Retreat was made without any Loss of Men or Ammunition and in better order than I expected from Troops in the situation ours were. We brought off all our Cannon & Stores, except a few heavy pieces, which in the condition the earth was by a long continued rain we found upon Trial impracticable. The Wheels of the Carriages Sinking up to the Hobs rendered It impossible for our whole force to drag them. We left but little Provisions on the Island except some Cattle which had been driven within our lines and which after many attempts to force across the water we found impossible to effect circumstanced as we were. I have Inclosed a copy of the council of War held previous to the Retreat, to which I beg leave to refer Congress for the reasons or many of them, that led to the adoption of that measure. Yesterday Evening and last Night a party of our Men were employed in bringing our Stores, Cannon, Tents &ca. from Governors Island, which they nearly compleated. Some of the Heavy Cannon remain there still, but I expect will be got away to day.

In the Engagement on the 27th. Generals Sullivan

Nineteenth-century engraving (above) of the American retreat from Long Island and a sketch (below) made by an English officer aboard one of Howe's ships in New York Harbor just after that disastrous defeat

Washington and His Generals, HEADLEY

General John Sullivan

& Stirling were made prisoners. The former has been permitted on his parole to return for a little time. From Lord Stirling I had a Letter by Genl. Sullivan, a Copy of which I have the Honor to transmit. That contains his Information of the Engagement with his Brigade. It is not so full and certain as I could wish, he was hurried most probably as his Letter was unfinished. Nor have I been yet able to obtain an exact amount of our Loss, we suppose it from 700 to a Thousand killed & taken. Genl. Sullivan says Lord Howe is extremely desirous of seeing some of the Members of Congress for which purpose he was allowed to come out & to communicate to them what has passed between him & his Lordship. I have consented to his going to Philadelphia, as I do not mean or conceive It right to withhold or prevent him from giving such Information as he possesses in this Instance.

I am much hurried & engaged in arranging and making new Dispositions of our Forces, The movements of the Enemy requiring them to be immediately had, and therefore have only time to add that I am with my best regards to Congress, and to you.

The British, using an unguarded road, had fallen on the rear of the regiments of General John Sullivan and the man the Americans knew as Lord Stirling for his claim to an extinct Scottish earldom. The enemy was suddenly on the slopes of Brooklyn Heights itself and might easily have carried the redoubts against the panicky, green defenders if Howe, probably with grim memories of Bunker Hill, had not held them back. Washington's water-borne rescue of his army—transported across the East River to Manhattan on a foggy night—was a marvel of secrecy, but no retreat is a cause for rejoicing. Through John Hancock, Washington gave Congress his views of a basic weakness of the Army.

New York, Septr. the 2d. 1776

As my Intelligence of late has been rather unfavorable and would be received with anxiety & concern, peculiarly happy should I esteem myself, were it in my power at this time to transmit such information to Congress, as would be more pleasing and agreeable to their wishes But unfortunately for me—unfortunately for them, It is not.

Our situation is truly distressing. The Check our Detachment sustained on the 27th. Ulto. has dispirited

John Glover's Marblehead regiment evacuated Washington's troops from Long Island, where General Israel Putnam had been in overall charge; Glover (above) in a facsimile of a Trumbull drawing and Putnam (below) from a Trumbull sketch.

too great a proportion of our Troops and filled their minds with apprehension and dispair. The Militia instead of calling forth their utmost efforts to a brave and manly opposition in order to repair our Losses, are dismayed, Intractable, and Impatient to return. Great numbers of them have gone off; in some instances almost by whole Regiments, by half ones & by Companies at a time. This circumstance of Itself, Independent of others, when fronted by a well appointed Enemy, superior in number to our whole collected force, would be sufficiently disagreeable, but when their example has Infected another part of the Army,—when their want of discipline & refusal of almost every kind of restraint & government, have produced a like conduct but too common to the whole, and an entire disregard of that order and subordination necessary to the well doing of an Army and which had been inculcated before, as well as the nature of our Military establishment would admit of, our condition is still more alarming, and with the deepest concern I am obliged to confess my want of confidence in the generality of the Troops. All these circumstances fully confirm the opinion I ever entertained and which I more than once in my letters took the liberty of mentioning to Congress, that no dependence could be put in a Militia or other Troops than those enlisted and embodied for a longer period than our regulations heretofore have prescribed. I am persuaded and as fully convinced, as I am of any one fact that has happened, that our liberties must of necessity be greatly hazarded, If not entirely lost If their defence is left to any but a permanent standing Army,—I mean one to exist during the War. Nor would the expence Incident to the support of such a body of Troops as would be competent almost to every exigency, far exceed that which is daily incurred by calling in succour and New Inlistments and which when effected are not attended with any good consequences. Men who have been free and subject to no controul, cannot be reduced to order in an Instant, and the priviledges & exemptions they claim and will have Influence the conduct of others, and the aid derived from them is nearly counterbalanced by the disorder, Irregularity and confusion they occasion. I can not find that the Bounty of Ten Dollars is likely to produce the desired effect. When men can get double that sum to engage for a month or two in the Militia & that Militia frequently called out, It is hardly to be expected. The addition of Land might have a considerable Influence on a permanent Inlistment. Our number of men at present fit for duty are under 20,000. They were so by the last returns and best accounts I could get after the Engagement on Long Island, — since which numbers have deserted.

Washington had a demonstration of the dismal weakness of poorly trained short-term militia when British and Hessians landed above New York on Kip's Bay (between 32nd and 38th Streets on the East River side of today's Manhattan) on September 15. Again he was reporting to John Hancock as president of Congress.

Head Qrs. at Col. Roger Morris's House,
September 16, 1776.

... about Eleven oClock [the enemy ships] in the East River began a most severe and heavy Cannonade to scour the Grounds and cover the landing of their Troops between Turtle Bay and the City, where Breast Works had been thrown up to oppose them. As soon as I heard the Firing, I road with all possible dispatch towards the place of landing when to my great surprize and mortification I found the Troops that had been posted in the Lines retreating with the utmost precipitation, and those ordered to support them, Parsons's & Fellows's Brigades, flying in every direction and in the greatest confusion, notwithstanding the exertions of their Generals to form them. I used every means in my power to rally and get them into some order but my attempts were fruitless and ineffectual and on the appearance of a

After the British had landed at Kip's Bay, as drawn on the spot (left), British officers used the Kip family mansion as headquarters (above), while Washington took refuge in the house of his friend Colonel Morris.

BOTH: *Pictorial Field-Book of the Revolution,* LOSSING

small party of the Enemy, not more than Sixty or Seventy, their disorder increased and they ran away in the greatest confusion without firing a single Shot. Finding that no confidence was to be placed in these Brigades and apprehending that another part of the Enemy might pass over to Harlem plains and cut of the retreat to this place, I sent orders to secure the Heights in the best manner with the Troops that were stationed on and near them, which being done; the retreat was effected with but little or no loss of Men, tho' of a considerable part of our Baggage occasioned by this disgraceful and dastardly conduct. Most of our Heavy Cannon and a part of our Stores and Provisions, which we were about removing was unavoidably left in the City, tho' every means after It had been determined in Council to evacuate the post had been used to prevent It. We are now encamped with the Main body of the Army on the Heights of Harlem, where I should hope the Enemy would meet with a defeat in case of an Attack, If the generality of our Troops would behave with tolerable bravery, but, experience to my extreme affliction has convinced me that this is rather to be wished for than expected. However I trust, that there are many who will act like men, and shew themselves worthy of the blessings of Freedom. I have sent out some reconoitring parties to gain Intelligence If possible of the disposition of the Enemy and shall inform Congress of every material event by the earliest Opportunity.

Although his forces were temporarily safe on rocky Harlem Heights in northern Manhattan, the Commander in Chief was thoroughly discouraged. Then, only the day after the disgraceful conduct of the militia at Kip's Bay, American units attacked and drove into retreat British forces that had ventured near Harlem Heights. The Battle of Harlem was a relatively minor clash, but it greatly raised patriot morale; the redcoats were not invincible. But one victory did not solve Washington's main problem; his forces were melting away as weary or homesick farm boys simply left and trudged the dirt roads leading home. Washington told his cousin Lund of his problems and his anguish.

Col. Morris's, on the Heights of Harlem.
September 30, 1776.

Your letter of the 18th., which is the only one received and unanswered, now lies before me. The amazement

159

which you seem to be in at the unaccountable measures which have been adopted by [Congress] would be a good deal increased if I had time to unfold the whole system of their management since this time twelve months. I do not know how to account for the unfortunate steps which have been taken but from that fatal idea of conciliation which prevailed so long—fatal, I call it, because from my soul I wish it may [not] prove so, though my fears lead me to think there is too much danger of it. This time last year I pointed out the evil consequences of short enlistments, the expenses of militia, and the little dependence that was to be placed in them. I assured [Congress] that the longer they delayed raising a standing army the more difficult and chargeable would they find it to get one, and that, at the same time that the militia would answer no valuable purpose, the frequent calling them in would be attended with an expense that they could have no conception of. Whether, as I have said before, the unfortunate hope of reconciliation was the cause, or the fear of a standing army prevailed, I will not undertake to say; but the policy was to engage men for twelve months only. The consequence of which, you have had great bodies of militia in pay that never were in camp: you have had immense quantities of provisions drawn by men that never rendered you one hour's service (at least usefully), and this in the most profuse

A contemporary, but highly fanciful, German engraving of the British troops marching into New York City

and wasteful way. Your stores have been expended, every kind of military [discipline?] destroyed by them; your numbers fluctuating, uncertain, and forever far short of report—at no one time, I believe, equal to twenty thousand men fit for duty. At present our numbers fit for duty (by this day's report) amount to 14,759, besides 3,427 on command, and the enemy within stone's throw of us. It is true a body of militia are again ordered out, but they come without any conveniences and soon return. I discharged a regiment the other day that had in it fourteen rank and file fit for duty only, and several that had less than fifty. In short, such is my situation that if I were to wish the bitterest curse to an enemy on this side of the grave, I should put him in my stead with my feelings; and yet I do not know what plan of conduct to pursue. I see the impossibility of serving with reputation, or doing any essential service to the cause by continuing in command, and yet I am told that if I quit the command inevitable ruin will follow, from the distraction that will ensue. In confidence I tell you that I never was in such an unhappy, divided state since I was born. To lose all comfort and happiness on the one hand, whilst I am fully persuaded that under such a system of management as has been adopted, I cannot have the least chance for reputation, nor those allowances made which the nature of the case requires; and to be

Another fanciful view by the same artist of the disastrous fire that swept New York after Howe's entry

In this engraving of the Battle of Harlem Heights, one of Washington's only successes in New York, the 42nd Highlanders are seen scurrying over a fence in disorganized retreat.

told, on the other, that if I leave the service all will be lost, is, at the same time that I am bereft of every peaceful moment, distressing to a degree. But I will be done with the subject, with the precaution to you that it is not a fit one to be publicly known or discussed. If I fall, it may not be amiss that these circumstances be known, and declaration made in credit to the justice of my character. And if the men will stand by me (which by the by I despair of), I am resolved not to be forced from this ground while I have life; and a few days will determine the point, if the enemy should not change their plan of operations; for they certainly will not—I am sure they ought not—to waste the season that is now fast advancing, and must be precious to them. I thought to have given you a more explicit account of my situation, expectation, and feelings, but I have not time. I am wearied to death all day with a variety of perplexing circumstances—disturbed at the conduct of the militia, whose behavior and want of discipline has done great injury to the other troops, who never had officers, except in a few instances, worth the bread they eat. My time, in short, is so much engrossed that I have not leisure for corresponding, unless it is on mere matters of public business.

On October 12, 1776, Howe landed troops at Throgs Neck in what is now the Bronx, with the obvious intent of cutting the American line of communication with the country to the north. Washington skillfully evaded the trap by withdrawing. He later gave John Augustine Washington an account of subsequent events.

White Plains [New York], November 6, 1776. Whilst we lay at the upper end of York [Manhattan] Island (or the heights of Harlem) How suddenly Landed from the best accts. we cd. get, about 16,000 Men above us, on a place called Frogs point on the East River, or Sound, this obliged Us, as his design was evidently to surround us, & cut of our Communication with the Country, thereby stopping all Supplies of Provisions (of which we were very scant) to remove our Camp and out Flank him, which we have done, & by degrees got strongly posted on advantageous Grounds at this place....

Novr. 19, at Hackensac [New Jersey]. I began this Letter at the White plains as you will see by the first part of it; but by the time I had got thus far the Enemy advanced a Second time (for they had done it once before, & after engaging some Troops which I had posted on a Hill, and driving them from it with the loss of abt. 300 killed & wounded to them, & little more than half the number to us) as if they meant a genel. Attack but finding us ready to receive them, & upon such ground as they could not approach without loss, they filed of & retreated towards New York.

As it was conceived that this Manoeuvre was done with a design to attack Fort Washington (near Harlem heights) or to throw a body of Troops into the Jersey's, or what might be still worse, aim a stroke at Philadelphia, I hastend over on this side [New Jersey] with abt. 5000 Men by a round about March (wch. we were obliged to take on Acct. of the shipping opposing the passage at all the lower Ferries) of near 65 Miles, but did not get hear time enough to take Measures to save Fort Washington tho I got here myself a day or two before it surrendered, which happened on the 16th. Instt. after making a defence of about 4 or 5 hours only....

This is a most unfortunate affair, and has given me great Mortification as we have lost not only two thousand Men that were there, but a good deal of Artillery, & some of the best Arms we had. And what adds to my Mortification is that this Post, after the last Ships went past it, was held contrary to my Wishes & opinion; as I conceived it to be a dangerous one: but being determind on by a full Council of General Officers, and recieving a resolution of Congress strongly expressive of their desires, that the Channel of the River (which we had been labouring to stop for a long while at this place) might be obstructed, if possible, & knowing that this could not be done unless there were Batteries to protect the Obstruction I did not care to give an absolute Order for withdrawing the Garrison till I could get round & see the Situation of things & then it became too late as the Fort was Invested.

General Nathanael Greene

The grievous loss of men and supplies at Fort Washington must be laid at the Commander in Chief's door. Washington had believed this last American stronghold on Manhattan should be abandoned; General Nathanael Greene, who was in command of the fort, wanted to defend it. Washington, as he so often did, yielded. His reluctance to impose his decisions was a flaw in leadership; it would disappear only as he came to recognize that since his was the ultimate responsibility, his must also be the final decision. Troubles multiplied. Reporting to the president of Congress on the situation in New Jersey, Washington had not finished his letter before he was forced to tell of a fresh disaster.

This map of New York Island, drawn by a man who served under General Howe, shows Fort Washington almost dead center with Fort Lee across the Hudson River in New Jersey.

[Hackensack] November 21. The unhappy affair of the 16th. has been succeeded by further Misfortunes.

Yesterday Morning a large body of the Enemy landed between Dobb's Ferry and Fort Lee. Their object was evidently to inclose the whole of our Troops and stores that lay between the North and Hackensack Rivers, which form a narrow neck of Land. For this purpose they formed and Marched, as soon as they had ascended the Heights towards the Fort. Upon the first information of their movements, our men were ordered to meet them, but finding their numbers greatly superior and that they were extending themselves It was thought proper to withdraw our Men, which was effected and their retreat secured over Hackensack Bridge. We lost the whole of the Cannon that was at the Fort except two twelve pounders, and a great deal of Baggage, between two & three hundred Tents, about a thousand Barrels of Flour and other stores in the Quarter Master's Department. This loss was inevitable. As many of the stores had been removed, as circumstances & time would admit of. The Ammunition had been happily got away. Our present situation between Hackensack & Passaick Rivers, being exactly similar to our late one, and our force here by no means adequate to an Opposition, that will promise the smallest probability of Success, we are taking measures to retire over the Waters of the latter, when the best dispositions will be formed, that Circumstances will admit of.

The Commander in Chief's spare words did not tell the entire dramatic story. He himself had galloped to warn the garrison of Fort Lee (across the Hudson from Fort Washington) that the British were coming and had hurried the men out so fast that those preparing a meal could not wait for kettles to cool enough to pack. Even so, they barely won a race with the enemy to a bridge over the Hackensack River and escape. Washington now wrote to General Charles Lee, who had been left in command of a force north of Manhattan, directing him to rejoin the main army in New Jersey. Unknown to the commander, another letter had been inserted with his by Joseph Reed, his former secretary and confidant and now Adjutant General. "I do not mean to flatter or praise you at the expense of any other," Reed wrote in part to Lee, "but I confess I do think it is entirely owing to you that this army, and the liberties of America, so far as they are dependent on it, are not totally cut off." Reed heaped more praise on Lee, whose self-esteem as a professional soldier was already monumental, blamed Washington for the loss of Fort Washington, and declared, "Oh! General, an indecisive mind is one of the greatest misfortunes that can befall an army; how often have I lamented it in this campaign." Washington sent several urgent messages to Lee, all in the same vein.

Engraving after an original water color of the landing of the British forces in New Jersey on November 20

New Ark [New Jersey], Novemr. 27th. 1776.
I last night received the favour of your Letter of the 25th. My former Letters were so full and explicit, as to the Necessity of your Marching, as early as possible, that it is unnecessary to add more on that Head. I confess I expected you would have been sooner in motion. The force here, when joined by yours, will not be adequate to any great opposition; at present it is weak, and it has been more owing to the badness of the weather, that the Enemy's progress has been checked, than any resistance we could make. They are now pushing this way, part of 'em have passed the Passaic. Their plan is not entirely unfolded, but I shall not be surprized, if Philadelphia should turn out the object of their Movement. The distress of the Troops, for want of Cloaths, I feel much, but what can I do? Having formed an enterprize against Roger's &c. I wish you may have succeeded.

But Lee was not obeying the order to bring his forces to New Jersey. Lee's motives are still obscure. He may have hoped for a victory of his own over British forces in his area, which would enhance his military reputation at Washington's expense. Undoubtedly he also feared the effect of the march on his own disintegrating army. And he strongly disagreed with his commander's current military plans. In the meantime he wrote to Joseph Reed, thanking the Adjutant General for his kind letter and saying, among other things, "Lament with you that fatal indecision of mind which in war is a much greater disqualification than stupidity, or even want of personal courage." Reed was away when the letter arrived, and Washington, thinking it some Army matter, opened it. He recognized it, as he later put it, as "an echo" of one Reed must have written to Lee, but sent it on to Reed with an apology.

Brunswick [New Jersey], Novr. 30th. 1776.
The inclosed was put into my hands by an Express from the White Plains. Having no Idea of its being a Private Letter, much less suspecting the tendency of the correspondence, I opened it, as I had done all other Letters to you, from the same place and Peekskill, upon the business of your Office, as I conceived and found them to be.

This, as it is the truth, must be my excuse for seeing the contents of a Letter, which neither inclination or intention would have prompted me to.

I thank you for the trouble and fatigue you have undergone in your Journey to Burlington, and sincerely wish that your labours may be crowned with the desired success.

Reed sent his resignation to Congress; Washington urged him to stay on for the good of the country. Reed did remain, but it was a long time before the tension between the two was eased. As the ragged American Army retreated across New Jersey, its Jersey militiamen melted away, and citizens hastened to buy immunity from British reprisals by swearing allegiance to King George. In early December the Army reached temporary safety when it crossed the Delaware into Pennsylvania, taking every boat it could find to hamper pursuit. And all the while Washington was calling on Charles Lee to hurry to his assistance, while that self-seeking man now argued that he could do more good hanging on the flanks of Howe's army. In one of his periodic letters to his cousin Lund, Washington described his dangerous situation and imparted the news of Lee's capture.

Falls of the Delaware, Southside,
December 10, 1776.

Dear Lund:

I wish to Heaven it was in my power to give you a more favorable account of our situation than it is. Our numbers, quite inadequate to the task of opposing that part of the army under the command of General Howe, being reduced by sickness, desertion, and political deaths (on or before the 1st. instant, and having no assistance from the militia,) were obliged to retire before the enemy, who were perfectly well informed of our situation till we came to this place, where I have no idea of being able to make a stand, as my numbers, till joined by the Philadelphia militia, did not exceed three thousand men fit for duty. Now we may be about five thousand to oppose Howe's whole army, that part of it excepted which sailed under the command of Gen. Clinton. I tremble for Philadelphia. Nothing, in my opinion, but Gen. Lee's speedy arrival, who has been long expected, though still at a distance (with about three thousand men,) can save it. We have brought over and destroyed all the boats we could lay our hands on upon the Jersey shore for many miles above and below this place; but it is next to impossible to guard a shore for sixty miles, with less than half the enemy's numbers; when by force or strategem they may suddenly attempt a passage in many different places. At present they are encamped or quartered along the other shore above and below us (rather this place, for we are obliged to keep a face towards them) for fifteen miles.

December 17, ten miles above the Falls. I have since moved up to this place, to be more convenient to our great and extensive defences of this river. Hitherto, by our destruction of the boats, and vigilance in watching the fords of the river above the falls (which are now rather high,) we have prevented them from crossing; but how long we shall be able to do it God only knows, as they are still hovering about the river. And if every thing else fails, will wait till the 1st. of January, when there will be no other men to oppose them but militia, none of which but those from Philadelphia, mentioned in the first part of the letter, are yet come (though I am told some are expected from the back counties). When I say none but militia, I am to except the Virginia regiments and the shattered remains of Smallwood's, which, by fatigue, want of clothes, &c., are reduced to nothing — Weedon, which was the strongest, not having more than between one hundred and thirty to one hundred and forty men fit for duty, the rest being in the hospitals. The unhappy policy of short enlistments and a dependence upon militia will, I fear, prove the downfall of our cause, though early pointed out with an almost prophetic spirit! Our cause has also received a severe blow in the captivity of Gen. Lee. Unhappy man! Taken by his own imprudence, going three or four miles from his own camp, and within twenty of the enemy, notice of which by a rascally Tory was given, a party of light horse seized him in the morning after travelling all night, and carried him off in high triumph and with

General Joseph Reed

167

every mark of indignity, not even suffering him to get his hat or surtout coat. The troops that were under his command are not yet come up with us, though they, I think, may be expected to-morrow. A large part of the Jerseys have given every proof of disaffection that they can do, and this part of Pennsylvania are equally inimical. In short, your imagination can scarce extend to a situation more distressing than mine. Our only dependence now is upon the speedy enlistment of a new army. If this fails, I think the game will be pretty well up, as, from disaffection and want of spirit and fortitude, the inhabitants, instead of resistance, are offering submission and taking protection from Gen. Howe in Jersey.

The capture of General Charles Lee by a British scouting party was mourned by many prominent patriots and celebrated by the British as a loss to the American cause of its best trained and most competent general. In fact, Washington was well rid of a man whom even he had described as "fickle," though he was as bemused as everyone else by Lee's self-proclaimed military talents. As 1776 drew to a close, Washington gave way to despair; to his brother John Augustine he suggested that the American cause might well be lost.

Camp, near the Falls of Trenton,
December 18, 1776.

Since I came on this side, I have been join'd by about 2000 of the City Militia, and understand that some of the Country Militia (from the back Counties,) are on their way; *but we are in a very disaffected part of the Provence, and between you and me, I think our Affairs are in a very bad situation; not so much from the apprehension of Genl. Howe's Army, as from the defection of New York, Jerseys, and Pensylvania. In short, the Conduct of the Jerseys has been most Infamous. Instead of turning out to defend their Country and affording aid to our Army, they are making their submissions as fast as they can. If they the Jerseys had given us any* support, we might have made a stand at Hackensack and after that at Brunswick, but the few Militia that were in Arms, disbanded themselves and left the poor remains of our Army to make the best we could of it.

I have no doubt but that General Howe will still make an attempt upon Philadelphia this Winter. I see nothing to oppose him a fortnight hence, as the time

Capture of Charles Lee

General Sir William Howe

of all the Troops, except those of Virginia (reduced almost to nothing,) and Smallwood's Regiment of Maryland, (equally as bad) will expire in less than that time. In a word my dear Sir, *if every nerve is not strain'd* to recruit the New Army with all possible expedition, *I think the game is pretty near up, owing, in a great measure, to the insidious Arts of the Enemy, and disaffection of the Colonies before mentioned, but* principally to the accursed policy of short Inlistments, and placing too great a dependence on the Militia the Evil consequences of which were foretold 15 Months ago with a spirit almost Prophetick.

The soldiers of the weary little Army were ragged, hungry, cold, often sick, and much of Washington's effort was devoted to obtaining for them the common necessities of life. To Robert Morris, who had remained in Philadelphia to procure supplies for the Army after the other members of Congress had fled to Baltimore, he made a plea for clothing for his troops.

> Camp above the Falls at Trenton,
> Decr. 22d. 1776.
>
> Your favour of yesterday [a letter saying 856 blankets were being sent to the Army] came duely to hand, and I thank you for the several agreeable articles of Intelligence therein contain'd. For godsake hurry Mr. Mease [James Mease, Clothier-General of the Army] with the Cloathing as nothing will contribute more to facilitate the recruiting Service than warm & comfortable Cloathing to those who engage.

On the day he wrote to Morris, Washington sent the Pennsylvania Council of Safety a message even more eloquent in what it said of the state of the patriot Army.

> Head Quarters, Buck County,
> December 22, 1776.
>
> Your Collection of old cloathes for the use of the army, deserves my warmest thanks; they are of the greatest use and shall be distributed where they are most wanted. I think if the Committee or some proper persons were appointed to go thro' the County of Bucks and make a Collection of Blankets &c., in the manner you have done in Philadelphia, it would be better than doing it in a

Military Way by me; for many people, who would be willing to contribute or sell, if asked so to do by their Neighbours or Acquaintances, feel themselves hurt when the demand is made, backed by an Armed force. But I would at the same time remark, that if any, who can spare without inconvenience, refuse to do it, I would immediately give proper assistance to take from them.

I have not a Musket to furnish the Militia who are without arms, this demand upon me makes it necessary to remind you, that it will be needless for those to come down who have no Arms, except they will consent to work upon the Fortifications instead of taking their Tour of Military Duty; if they will do that, they may be most usefully employed.

By the end of 1776 the American cause was indeed at low ebb. On December 23 there appeared a pamphlet, the first of Thomas Paine's *Crisis* papers, which began, "These are the times that try men's souls." But three days later, the morning after Christmas, Washington struck at the celebration-befuddled Hessian camp at Trenton. He made a happy report to Congress.

Head Quarters, Newton, December 27, 1776.
I have the pleasure of Congratulating you upon the success of an enterprize which I had formed against a Detachment of the Enemy lying in Trenton, and which was executed yesterday Morning. The Evening of the 25th. I ordered the troops intended for this service to parade back of McKonkey's Ferry, that they might begin to pass as soon as it grew dark, imagining we should be able to throw them all over, with the necessary Artillery, by 12 O'Clock, and that we might easily arrive at Trenton by five in the Morning, the distance being about nine miles. But the Quantity of Ice, made that Night, impeded the passage of the Boats so much, that it was three o'clock before the Artillery could all be got over, & near four, before the troops took up their line of march.

This made me despair of surprizing the Town, as I well knew we could not reach it before the day was fairly broke, but as I was certain there was no making a retreat without being discovered, and harassed on repassing the river, I determined to push on at all Events. I formed my detachments into two divisions

The War of Independence BY BENSON J. LOSSING, 1850

Engraving of Washington crossing the Delaware from Lossing's The War of Independence, *1850 (above); a German engraving (below) shows the prisoners taken at Trenton being marched through Philadelphia.*

one to March by the lower or river road, the other by the upper or Pennington Road. As the divisions had nearly the same distance to march, I ordered each of them, immediately upon forcing the out guards, to push directly into the Town, that they might charge the enemy before they had time to form. The upper division arrived at the enemy's advanced post, exactly at eight oclock, and in three minutes after I found from the fire on the lower road that, that division had also got up. The Out guards made but small opposition tho' for their numbers, they behaved very well, keeping up a constant retreating fire from behind houses. We presently saw their main body formed, but from their motions, they seemed undetermined how to act.

Being hard pressed by our troops, who had already got possession of part of their Artillery, they attempted to file off by a road on their right leading to Princeton, but perceiving their intention, I threw a body of troops in their way which immediately checked them. Finding from our disposition that they were surrounded, and that they must inevitably be cut to pieces if they made any further resistance, they agreed to lay down their arms. The number, that submitted in this manner, was 23 Officers and 886 Men. Col. Rall the commanding officer with seven others were found wounded in the town. I dont exactly know how many they had killed, but I fancy not above twenty or thirty, as they never made any regular stand. Our loss is very trifling indeed, only two officers and one or two privates wounded.

I find, that the detachment of the enemy consisted of the three Hessian Regiments of Lanspatch, Kniphausen and Rohl amounting to about 1500 Men, and a troop of British light horse, but immediately upon the begining of the attack, all those who were not killed or taken, pushed directly down the Road towards Burdentown. These would likewise have fallen into our hands, could my plan have been compleatly carried into execution. Genl. Ewing was to have crossed before day at Trenton ferry, and taken possession of the bridge leading out of town but the quantity of Ice was so great, that tho he did every thing in his Power to effect it, he could not get over.

This difficulty also hindered General Cadwallader from crossing with the Pennsylvania militia, from Bristol, he got part of his foot over, but finding it impossible to embark his artillery, he was obliged to desist. I am fully confident, that could the troops under Generals Ewing and Cadwallader have passed the river, I should have been able, with their assistance, to have driven the enemy from all their posts below Trenton. But the number I had with me, being inferior to theirs below me, and a strong battalion of light infantry at Princeton above me I thought it most prudent to return the same evening with my prisoners and the artillery we had taken. We found no stores of any consequence in the Town. In justice to the officers and men, I must add, that their behaviour upon this occasion, reflects the highest honor upon them. The difficulty of passing the river in a very severe night, and their march thro' a violent storm of snow and hail, did not in the least abate their ardour. But when they came to the charge, each seemed to vie with the other in pressing forward, and were I to give a preference to any particular corps, I should do great injustice to the others.

Colonel Baylor, my first Aid de Camp, will have the honor of delivering this to you, and from him you may be made acquainted with many other particulars; his spirited behaviour upon every occasion, requires me to recommend him to your particular notice. I have the honor to be with great respect Sir your most Obedt. Servt.

G. WASHINGTON

P.S. Inclosed you have a particular list of the prisoners, artillery and other stores.

General Hugh Mercer, who was killed in the Battle of Princeton, 1777

The effect on both civilian and Army morale was electric. Men whose terms of enlistment were to have expired at the end of the year agreed to stay on for another six weeks to see the campaign through. The next battle of that campaign came on January 2, when Lord Cornwallis, one of Howe's generals, confronted Washington on Assunpink Creek near Trenton as night fell. The American position was precarious, but Washington had a few men keep the American campfires blazing during the night, while the patriot Army circled the enemy camp, attacked and defeated a British force at Princeton, and then retired before Cornwallis could bring his main army to the rescue. The American Army then went into winter quarters at Morristown, in a region protected by natural defenses of rocky hills. It was a location that threatened the enemy supply line if the British attempted any move toward Philadelphia, and so forced

Howe to retire into eastern New Jersey. Washington busied himself with the details of command, from recruiting his depleted ranks to prodding Congress for pay and clothing for his men. No problem was more onerous than that of dealing with an influx of French officers, many claiming commissions conferred by Congress or by Silas Deane, the American representative in Paris, most speaking no English, all expecting high rank. He complained to Congress.

Preliminary drawing by Trumbull for his painting Battle of Princeton

Head Quarters, Morristown,
February 11, 1777.

I was yesterday waited upon by two French Gentlemen, Monsr. Romand de Lisle, and Robillard. The first produced a Commission signed by you in Novemr. last appointing him a Major of Artillery, but, by the inclosed Letter from him to me, he claims much higher Rank under the promise of Congress, that of Commandant of the Continental Artillery. Whether any such promise was made, I leave you to determine.

Robillard claims a Captaincy of Artillery, but, upon what he grounds his pretentions, I do not know. I never saw him but once before, and that was upon his way from Boston to Philada.

The War of Independence. LOSSING

Washington's headquarters at Morristown, New Jersey

You cannot conceive what a weight these kind of people are upon the Service, and upon me in particular, few of them have any knowledge of the Branches which they profess to understand, and those that have, are entirely useless as officers, from their ignorance of the English Language. I wish it were possible to make them understand, when Commissions are granted to them, that they are to make themselves Masters of the english Language in some degree, before they can be attached to any particular Corps.

Not all the French volunteers were useless baggage. Some, experts in military engineering, Washington could not have done without. The Marquis de Lafayette, an arrival during the summer of 1777, whom Congress saw fit to make a major general although he was not yet twenty and had had no military experience, soon became a confidant of Washington's. Martha came to Morristown in mid-March, 1777, for a two-month stay that relieved the tedium of winter quarters. There were occasional clashes between American and enemy units but nothing decisive. Then on June 30, 1777, Howe left Amboy, his last base in New Jersey. A week or so later came dispiriting news: General John Burgoyne, moving down from Canada, had captured Fort Ticonderoga without firing a shot, opening the way south to the Hudson. Washington was sure Howe would move up the Hudson to meet Burgoyne and thus split New England from the rest of the nation, but the British commander only engaged in a game of hide-and-seek that kept the puzzled American leader shuttling his army here and there. He told John Augustine Washington about it.

Mount Vernon. LOSSING

Washington's camp-chest

Germantown, near Philada., Augt. 5th., 1777. Your favors of the 21st. of June from Westmoreland, and 10th. ulto. from Fredericksburg, are both to hand. Since Genl. Howes remove from the Jerseys, the Troops under my Command have been more harrassed by Marching, & Counter Marching, than by any thing that has happend to them in the course of the Campaign.

After Genl. Howe had Imbarkd his Troops, the presumption that he woud operate upon the North [Hudson] River, to form a junction with General Burgoyne, was so strong, that I removed from Middle Brook to Morristown, & from Morristown to the Clove (a narrow pass leading through the Highlands) about 18 Miles from the River. Indeed, upon some pretty strong presumptive evidence, I threw two divisions over the North River. In this Situation we lay till about the 24th. ulto., when,

Receiving certain Information that the Fleet had actually Saild from Sandy hook (the outer point of New York harbour) and the concurring Sentiment of every one, (tho I acknowledge my doubts of it were strong) that Philadelphia was the object We counter Marchd, and got to Coryells Ferry on the Delaware (abt. 33 Miles above the City) on the 27th. where I lay till I receiv'd Information from Congress that the Enemy were actually at the Capes of Delaware. This brought us in great haste to this place for defence of the City, but in less than 24 hours after our arrival we got Accts. of the disappearance of the Fleet on the 31st.; since which nothing having been heard of them, we remain here in a very irksome state of suspense. Some imagine that they are gone to the Southward, whilst a Majority (in whose opinion upon this occasion I concur) are satisfied they are gone to the Eastward. The fatigue however, & Injury, which Men must Sustain by long Marches in such extreme heat as we have felt for the last five days, must keep us quiet till we hear something of the destination of the Enemy.

The Marquis de Lafayette by Peale

Howe's transports at last showed up on Chesapeake Bay south of Philadelphia, where the British disembarked and began moving toward the capital. Washington chose to make his stand on a creek called the Brandywine, twenty miles or so from the city. His first brief report of the clash to John Hancock was made the night of the battle.

At Midnight, Chester, September 11, 1777.
I am sorry to inform you, that in this day's engagement we have been obliged to leave the enemy masters of the field. Unfortunately the intelligence received of the enemy's advancing up the Brandywine, and crossing at a ford about six miles above us, was uncertain and contradictory, notwithstanding all my pains to get the best. This prevented my making a disposition adequate to the force with which the enemy attacked us on the right; in consequence of which the troops first engaged, were obliged to retire before they could be reinforced. In the midst of the attack on our right, that body of the enemy which remained on the other side of Chad's Ford, crossed it, and attacked the division there under the command of General Wayne, and the light Troops under Genl. Maxwell who, after a severe conflict, re-

175

The Battle of Germantown, 1777

tired. The Militia under the command of Major Genl. Armstrong, being posted at a ford, about two Miles below Chad's, had no opportunity of engaging. But altho' we fought under many disadvantages and were from the causes above mentioned obliged to retire, yet our loss of Men is not, I am persuaded, very considerable, I beleive much less than the enemys. We have also lost about seven or eight pieces of cannon, according to the best information I can at present obtain. The baggage having been previously moved off is all secure, saving the men's Blankets; which being at their backs, many of them doubtless are lost.

I have directed all the Troops to Assemble behind Chester, where they are now arranging for the night. Notwithstanding the misfortune of the day, I am happy to find the troops in good spirits; and I hope another time we shall compensate for the losses now sustained.

The Marquis La Fayette was wounded in the leg, and Genl. Woodford in the hand. Divers other Officers were wounded, and some slain; but the number of either cannot now be ascertained. I have the honor To be Sir Your obedient hub. Servant

Go: WASHINGTON

P.S. It has not been in my power to send you earlier intelligence; the present being the first leisure moment I have had since the action.

While it was true that the Americans were outnumbered and that many of Washington's troops were local militia of questionable dependability, nevertheless the battle was poorly fought by Washington. He had done little reconnaissance and so was unable to evaluate reports of the enemy movements. One of his biographers says he fought like a man in a daze. Later, as the two armies maneuvered, Howe feinted the Americans out of position and sent Cornwallis's division to take unopposed possession of Philadelphia. As for Washington, he awaited his opportunity and struck on October 4 against Howe's main forces at Germantown. It was an audacious move; the American troops attacked at dawn and were rolling back the enemy in confused fighting in heavy fog when, for some unknown reason, panic spread through the patriot forces and sent them tumbling to the rear. The headlong flight was checked, but the advantage of surprise was lost and Washington was forced to retreat. In the midst of war, Washington and General Howe maintained a formal correspondence on such matters as prisoner exchange—and one nonmilitary subject.

October 6, 1777.
General Washington's compliments to General Howe. He does himself the pleasure to return him a Dog, which accidentally fell into his hands, and by the inscription on the Collar, appears to belong to General Howe.

On October 15, 1777, Washington announced to his troops the defeat of General Burgoyne by Horatio Gates at the Battle of Saratoga in upper New York. Washington had heard of the victory only indirectly; no word had come from Gates, who should have reported to his superior officer. Writing to congratulate Gates, Washington mildly reproved his subordinate officer.

Head Qrs. near White Marsh 15 Miles from Philada.
Octobr. 30 1777
By this Opportunity, I do myself the pleasure to congratulate you on the signal success of the Army under your command, in compelling Genl. Burgoyne and his whole force, to surrender themselves prisoners of War. An event that does the highest honor to the American Arms, and which, I hope, will be attended with the most extensive and happy consequences. At the same time, I cannot but regret, that a matter of such magnitude and so interesting to our general operations, should have reached me by report only, or thro' the Channel of Letters, not bearing that authenticity, which the importance of it required, and which it would have received by a line under your signature, stating the simple fact.

View of General Burgoyne's army encamped on the west bank of the Hudson River before his defeat

Gates's failure to inform Washington had been no oversight. His victory and his soaring popularity had opened new vistas. He saw himself as the commander of a northern department coequal with Washington's southern command—and very likely he would soon be called upon to take supreme command to save the nation. When Gates finally did write to Washington, he loftily notified the Commander in Chief that henceforth he would report directly to Congress, which—Gates suggested—would keep Washington sufficiently informed. When Horatio Gates had sent his first report of the victory at Saratoga to Congress, his courier had been his aide, Colonel James Wilkinson, a young man of sociable habits. Wilkinson tarried on his errand for an evening of conviviality at an inn where several of Washington's officers were staying. His tongue was loosened, and he boasted that General Gates had received a letter from one of Washington's brigadier generals, Thomas Conway, an Irish-born Frenchman, in which Conway had made remarks derogatory to the Commander in Chief. One of Washington's loyal officers reported the incident to the commander. Although Washington was well aware that he had detractors, the letter from Conway to Gates, men who he did not know were even acquainted with each other, was his first indication of a widespread intrigue to discredit him and have him ousted. It would become known as the Conway Cabal, more for reasons of euphony than because its leading figure was Brigadier General Thomas Conway.

For the moment, Washington had more pressing problems. Hard winter was coming on, and the Army had to find cold-weather quarters. Washington chose a region protected by streams and bluffs not only because it was easily defensible, but because, less than twenty miles from Philadelphia, the nearness of his Army would keep the British on the qui vive. On December 20, for the first time, he used the date line "Valley Forge" from the new winter headquarters.

Medal struck in honor of General Gates for his victory at Saratoga

Pictorial Field-Book of the Revolution, LOSSING

Chapter **6**

The Long Road
to Yorktown

General Howe took the British army into snug winter quarters in Philadelphia on December 9, 1777. Washington's men found no comforts when they trudged through the snow to their own winter quarters at Valley Forge shortly after the middle of December. Valley Forge lay about twenty miles northwest of Philadelphia, an area of rolling land in the angle where Valley Creek joins the Schuylkill River, protected by bluffs on all sides. Its natural defenses were strong, but it offered no amenities except for a few farms and plenty of timber for firewood and cabins. Getting his men into "huts" was one of the Commander in Chief's first considerations. Two days before he arrived at Valley Forge, he had laid down specifications for housing.

Head Quarters, at the Gulph, Decr. 18, 1777. The Colonels, or commanding officers of regiments, with their Captains, are immediately to cause their men to be divided into squads of twelve, and see that each squad have their proportion of tools, and set about a hut for themselves: And as an encouragement to industry and art, the General promises to reward the party in each regiment, which finishes their hut in the quickest, and most workmanlike manner, with *twelve* dollars. And as there is reason to believe, that boards, for covering, may be found scarce and difficult to be got—He offers *One hundred* dollars to any officer or soldier, who in the opinion of three Gentlemen, he shall appoint as judges, shall substitute some other covering, that may be cheaper and quicker made, and will in every respect answer the end.

The Soldier's huts are to be of the following dimensions —viz—fourteen by sixteen each—sides, ends and roofs made with logs, and the roof made tight with split slabs, or in some other way—the sides made tight with clay—fireplace made of wood and secured with clay on the inside eighteen inches thick, this fire place to be in the rear of the hut—the door to be in the end next the street—the doors to be made of split oak-slabs, unless boards can be procured—Side-walls to be six and a half feet high—the officers huts to form a line in the rear of the troops, one hut to be allowed to each General Officer, one to the staff of each brigade—one to the field officers of each regiment—one to the staff of each regiment—one to the commissioned officers of two companies, and one to every twelve non-commissioned officers and soldiers.

It is doubtful if the British army could have housed itself without lumber and nails, but the Americans were largely farm boys, skilled with an axe. Even so, building log cabins for eleven thousand men takes time, and meanwhile the icy chill of canvas tents could have been borne with a better will if the men had not lacked everything else. In a letter to Congress, Washington gave way to frustration and anger over the sad state of affairs.

Valley Forge December 23d. 1777.
Full as I was in my representation of matters in the Commissary's department yesterday, fresh and more powerful reasons oblige me to add, that I am now convinced, beyond a doubt, that unless some great and Capital change suddenly takes place in that line, this Army must inevitably be reduced to one or other of these three things; starve, dissolve or disperse in order to obtain subsistence in the best manner they can; rest assured Sir, this is not an exaggerated picture, and that I have abundant reason to support what I say.

Yesterday afternoon, receiving information that the Enemy, in force, had left the City and were advancing towards Derby, with apparent design to forage, and draw subsistance from that part of the Country, I ordered the Troops to be in readiness, that I might give every opposition in my power; when behold, to my great mortification, I was not only informed, but convinced, that the Men were unable to stir on Acct. of Provision, and that a dangerous mutiny, begun the night before, and which with difficulty was suppressed by the spirited exertion of some Officers, was still much to be apprehended for want of this article.

"Washington forma il Campo a Valle-fucina"—an Italian version of log-cabin building at Valley Forge

This brought forth the only Commissary in the purchasing line, in this Camp; and with him, this melancholy and alarming truth, that he had not a single hoof of any kind to slaughter, and not more than 25. Barrels of Flour! From hence form an opinion of our situation, when I add, that he could not tell when to expect any.

The huts were not completed until about mid-January, and only when all the men were housed did Washington move from his own hut into the farmhouse that he made his headquarters. Many of the huts were still without straw to cover the cold earthen floors, the men were ill-supplied with blankets, most were in rags. In the midst of his other troubles, Washington had to contend with the Conway Cabal, that collection of oddly assorted characters whose common denominator was a wish to see a new Commander in Chief: Horatio Gates, or possibly the still-captive Charles Lee, or even the loudmouthed braggart Conway. The faction had enough influence in Congress to have Conway promoted to Major General in December, 1777, although Washington was emphatically opposed to such an advance in rank. Conway was made Inspector General of the Army, charged with putting into effect a new system of drill and maneuver. The intriguers hoped that an outraged Washington would resign, but when Conway presented himself at headquarters, Washington merely sent him a blunt letter concerning his appointment.

Head Qurs., Decemr. 30th. 1777.

I am favoured with your Letter of Yesterday, in which you propose (in order to loose no time) to begin with the instructions of the Troops.

You will observe by the Resolution of Congress relative to your appointment, that the Board of War is to furnish a set of Instructions, according to which the Troops are to be Manoeuvred. As you have made no mention of having received them, I suppose they are not come to you. When they do, I shall issue any Orders which may be judged necessary to have them carried into immediate Execution.

Your appointment of Inspector General to the Army, I believe has not given the least uneasiness to any Officer in it. By consulting your own feelings upon the appointment of the Baron De Kalb [whom Conway claimed he had outranked in France] you may judge what must be the Sensations of those Brigadiers, who by your promotion are superceded. I am told they are determined to remonstrate against it; for my own part

Horatio Gates, drawn from life by Du Simitière, engraved by Prevost

I have nothing to do in the appointment of Genl. Officers, and shall always afford every Countenance and due respect to those appointed by Congress, taking it for granted, that prior to any Resolve of that nature, they take a dispassionate view, of the merits of the Officer to be promoted, and consider every consequence that can result from such a procedure; nor have I any other wish on that Head, but that good attentive Officers may be chosen, and no Extraordinary promotion take place, but where the merit of the Officer is so generally acknowledged as to obviate every reasonable cause of dissatisfaction thereat.

Conway vented his frustration with a couple of insulting letters to Washington, who did not deign to answer. Close on the heels of this episode, General Gates wrote to Washington. He had just learned that the commander knew about the letter from Conway that his aide Colonel Wilkinson had talked about so freely one evening in a tavern. The letter had been "stealingly copied," he said. Not so, replied Washington.

Valley Forge January 4th. 1778.
Your Letter of the 8th. Ulto. came to my hands a few days ago, and to my great surprise informed me, that a copy of it had been sent to Congress, for what reason, I find myself unable to account; but, as some end doubtless was intended to be answered by it, I am laid under the disagreeable necessity of returning my answer through the same channel, lest any member of that Honble. Body, should harbour an unfavourable suspicion of my having practiced some indirect means to come at the contents of the confidential Letters between you and General Conway.

I am to inform you then, that Colo. Wilkinson in his way to Congress in the month of October last, fell in with Lord Stirling at Reading; and, not in confidence that I ever understood, informed his Aid de Camp Major McWilliams that General Conway had written thus to you,

"Heaven has been determined to save your Country; or a weak General and bad Counsellors would have ruined it."

Lord Stirling from motives of friendship, transmitted the account with this remark. "The inclosed was communicated by Colo. Wilkinson to Major McWilliams; such wicked duplicity of conduct I shall always think

Pictorial Field-Book of the Revolution, LOSSING

House of Isaac Potts, Washington's headquarters at Valley Forge

*Colonel James Wilkinson
by Charles Willson Peale*

it my duty to detect."

In consequence of this information, and without having any thing more in view than merely to shew that Gentleman, that I was not unapprized of his intriguing disposition, I wrote him a Letter in these words. "Sir. A Letter which I received last night contained the following paragraph.

"In a Letter from Genl. Conway to Genl. Gates he says, Heaven has been determined to save your Country; or a weak General and bad Counsellors (one of whom, by the bye, he was) would have ruined it. "I am Sir &ca."

Neither this Letter, nor the information which occasioned it was ever, directly, or indirectly communicated by me to a single officer in this Army (out of my own family) excepting the Marquis De la Fayette, who, having been spoken to on the Subject by General Conway, applied for, and saw, under injunctions of secresy, the Letter which contained Wilkenson's information; so desirous was I of concealing every matter that could, in its consequences, give the smallest Interruption to the tranquility of this Army, or afford a gleam of hope to the Enemy by dissentions therein.

Thus Sir, with an openess and candour which I hope will ever characterize and mark my conduct, have I complied with your request. The only concern I feel upon the occasion, finding how matters stand, is, that in doing this, I have necessarily been obliged to name a Gentleman whom I am persuaded (although I never exchanged a Word with him upon the Subject) thought he was rather doing an act of Justice, than committing an act of infidility; and sure I am, that, till Lord Stirling's Letter came to my hands, I never knew that General Conway (whom I viewed in the light of a stranger to you) was a correspondent of yours, much less did I suspect that I was the subject of your confidential Letters. Pardon me then for adding, that so far from conceiving that the safety of the States can be affected, or in the smallest degree injured, by a discovery of this kind, or, that I should be called upon in such solemn terms to point out the author, that I considered the information as coming from yourself, and given with a friendly view to forewarn, and consequently forearm me, against a secret enemy, or in other words, a dangerous incendiary; in which character, sooner or later, this

Country will know General Conway. But, in this, as in other matters of late, I have found myself mistaken.

The matter led to a quibbling debate by letter that was unlike Washington, but in the end Gates disengaged himself by disclaiming any personal connection with Conway and denying ties with any faction. Washington, probably with tongue in cheek, accepted the proffered olive branch.

Valley Forge Feby. 24th., 1778.
I yesterday received your favor of the 19th. Instt. I am as averse to controversy, as any man, and had I not been forced into it, you never would have had occasion to impute to me, even the Shadow of a disposition towards it. Your repeatedly and Solemnly disclaiming any offensive views, in those matters, which have been the subject of our past correspondence, makes me willing to close with the desire, you express, of burying them hereafter in silence, and as far as future events will permit, oblivion. My temper leads me to peace and harmony with all men; and it is peculiarly my wish, to avoid any personal feuds or dissentions with those, who are embarked in the same great national interest with myself; as every difference of this kind must in its consequences be very injurious.

There were influential men in the Conway Cabal, but most of the Army and probably most of the nation remained staunchly loyal to Washington. A number of brigadier generals protested to Congress the promotion of Conway over the heads of abler men. "We have commanded [with?] him in the field and are totally unacquainted with any superior Act of Merit which could entitle him to rise above us," they wrote. Collectively, the brigadiers had enough political influence in their states to make many members of Congress back away from Conway. In January the intriguers, through the Board of War, which they dominated, conceived a winter attack on Canada to be led by the Marquis de Lafayette with General Thomas Conway second in command. But Lafayette absolutely refused to have Conway and threatened Congress with his resignation and those of a number of other French officers if the Board insisted. Later, when he reached Albany, he found supplies for a winter campaign so miserably inadequate that he castigated the Board of War for even thinking about an invasion, to the extreme discomfiture of that body. By early spring the Conway Cabal was in confusion and retreat. Wilkinson and Gates had almost fought a duel. Thomas Mifflin, Washington's former aide, onetime Quartermaster General, and a leading intriguer, publicly proclaimed that the Commander in Chief was the best friend he ever had. And Conway, who often threatened resignation to frighten Congress into giving him what he wanted, did it once too often and found his bluff called by delegates disenchanted with him. While he fenced with the Conway Cabal, Washington had to cope with the privation that marked Valley Forge. Two months after having moved to the encampment he was still crying crisis in a joint letter to three supply officers.

> Head Qurs. Valley Feby. 15th. 1778.
> I am constrained to inform you, that the situation of the Army is most critical and alarming for want of provision of the Meat kind. Many of the Troops for four days and some longer, have not drawn the smallest supplies of this Article. This being the case, it is needless to add [more] to convince you of their distress. They have been on the point of dispersing and without the earliest releif, no address or authority will be sufficient to keep them long together. Their patience and endurance are great, but the demands of nature must be satisfied. I must therefore, Gentlemen, in the most urgent terms, request and entreat your immediate and more active exertions to procure and forward to Camp, as expeditiously as possible, all the provision of the Meat kind which it may be in your power to obtain. I would not have you wait till you collect a large quantity, but wish you to send on supplies, as fast as you can get them. The troops must have instant relief or we shall have reason to apprehend the worst consequences. I need not mention to you the necessity of secrecy in an affair of such delicacy. Your own prudence and discretion will point it out....
> P.S. The State of Forage is the same with that of provision, and a supply is materially wanted. Without it and very speedily, we shall have not a Horse left.

Major General Thomas Conway

The darkness lightened. On March 12, 1778, Washington wrote Governor George Clinton of New York that "by the exertions of our Friends in different quarters, the Army has been pretty well supplied" since mid-February. Martha had been at Valley Forge since early February, creating, as always, some bit of social gaiety among the small circle of officers' wives. Washington, though beset by problems, was not too busy to spare a moment for a young woman.

Camp-Valley-Forge 18th. Mar. 1778
General Washington having been informed, lately, of the honor done him by Miss Kitty Livingston in wishing for a lock of his Hair, takes the liberty of inclosing one, accompanied by his most respectful compliments.

The day before he sent Miss Livingston the lock of hair, the Commander in Chief issued a brief General Order that was going to have far-reaching effects on the Continental Army.

Pictorial Field-Book of the Revolution, LOSSING

Banner of Washington's Life Guard

Head-Quarters V. Forge
March 17th. 1778. Tuesday.
Parole Robinson. Countersigns Radnor, Ringwood.

One hundred chosen men are to be annexed to the Guard of the Commander in Chief for the purpose of forming a Corps to be instructed in the Manoeuvres necessary to be introduced in the Army and serve as a Model for the execution of them. As the General's guard is composed intirely of Virginians the one hundred draughts are to be taken from the troops of the other States.

What it meant was that the Baron von Steuben, former officer under Frederick the Great of Prussia, was now drillmaster of the American Army. His system of training and reorganizing the Army, starting with the squad of one hundred as a model, created for the first time a disciplined American armed force. Also, France had for some time been sending arms and supplies to the new nation, and official recognition was expected. When Washington received formal notification of the alliance from Congress, he issued orders to the Army for celebration.

GENERAL ORDERS

Head-Quarters V. Forge Tuesday May 5th. 1778.
It having pleased the Almighty ruler of the Universe propitiously to defend the Cause of the United American States and finally by raising us up a powerful Friend among the Princes of the Earth to establish our liberty and Independence upon lasting foundations, it becomes us to set apart a day for gratefully acknowledging the divine Goodness & celebrating the important Event which we owe to his benign Interposition.

The several Brigades are to be assembled for this Purpose at nine o'Clock tomorrow morning when their Chaplains will communicate the Intelligence contain'd

In CONGRESS, 29th March, 1779.

CONGRESS judging it of the greatest importance to prescribe some invariable rules for the order and discipline of the troops, especially for the purpose of introducing an uniformity in their formation and manœuvres, and in the service of the camp:

ORDERED, *That the following regulations be observed by all the troops of the United States, and that all general and other officers cause the same to be executed with all possible exactness.*

By Order,

JOHN JAY, PRESIDENT.

Attest.

CHARLES THOMPSON,
Secretary.

Two pages, above and below, of the special presentation copy given to Washington by Baron von Steuben of his manual, Regulations for the Order and Discipline of the Troops of the United States

in the Postscript to the Pennsylvania Gazette of the 2nd. instant and offer up a thanksgiving and deliver a discourse suitable to the Occasion. At half after ten o'Clock a Cannon will be fired, which is to be a signal for the men to be under Arms. The Brigade Inspectors will then inspect their Dress and Arms, form the Battalions according to instructions given them and announce to the Commanding Officers of Brigades that the Battalions are formed. The Brigadiers or Commandants will then appoint the Field Officers to command the Battalions, after which each Battalion will be ordered to load & ground their Arms.

At half after eleven a second Cannon be fired as a signal for the march upon which the several Brigades will begin their march by wheeling to the right by Platoons & proceed by the nearest way to the left of their ground in the new Position; this will be pointed out by the Brigade Inspectors. A third signal will be given upon which there will be discharge of thirteen Cannon; When the thirteen has fired a runing fire of the Infantry will begin on the right of Woodford's and continue throughout the whole front line, it will then be taken on the left of the second line and continue to the right. Upon a signal given, the whole Army will *Huzza!* "Long Live the King of France." The Artillery then begins again and fires thirteen rounds, this will be succeeded by a second general discharge of the Musquetry in a runing fire — *Huzza!* — "And long live the friendly European Powers." Then the last discharge of thirteen Pieces of Artillery will be given, followed by a General runing fire and *Huzza!* "To the American States".

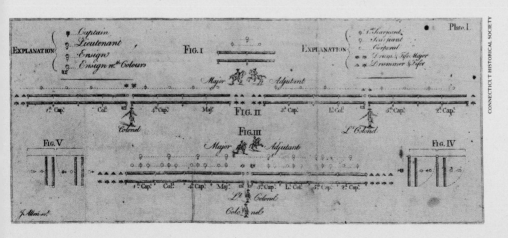

The English print above condemns the Americans for their alliance with France, while the French print at right shows Washington holding the Declaration of Independence and the formal treaty signed in 1778.

The review was the first showing of the Steuben-trained Army and went off smoothly. A disciplined soldiery was one of the good things to come out of Valley Forge; it would soon have a chance to prove its mettle. With the coming of spring, Major General Charles Lee returned after a year and a half as a prisoner, freed in exchange for a British officer. Washington had feared that Lee, a onetime British officer, might be hanged as a traitor; in fact, Lee and Lord Howe had been on such friendly terms that Lee had worked out for the British a plan for defeating the American Army. On June 18 the British army—now commanded by Sir Henry Clinton, who had succeeded Howe in May—left Philadelphia and started overland toward New York. The next day Washington led his forces out of Valley Forge in cautious pursuit. When he proposed to his generals that an attack be made on the rear of the strung-out enemy column, General Lee was so vehemently opposed that he at first declined to lead the attack force, although he was the ranking officer. Americans, he said, could not possibly stand up to European soldiers in open battle. He changed his mind and accepted the command only when it was offered to Lafayette. The clash took place near Monmouth Court House (now Freehold), New Jersey. Washington's first report to Congress was simply a statement that an encounter was shaping up in almost intolerably hot weather.

Before the Army left Valley Forge, Congress directed Washington to administer an oath of allegiance to each of his officers. This one is signed by Major General Stirling.

English Town, 6 Miles from Monmouth Court House
June 28th. 1778. 1/2 after 11.A.M.

I am now here with the main body of the Army and presing hard to come up with the Enemy. They encamped yesterday at Monmouth Court House, having almost the whole of his front, particularly his left wing, secured by a marsh and thick wood and his rear by a difficult defile, from whence he moved very early this morning. Our advance, from the rainy weather and the intense heat when it was fair (tho' these may have been equally disadvantageous to the Enemy) has been greatly delayed. Several of our men have fallen Sick from these causes, and a few unfortunately have fainted and died in a little time after. We have a select and strong detachment more forward under the general Command of Major Genl. Lee, with orders to attack their rear, if possible. Whether it will be able to come up with them, is a matter of some doubt; especially before they get into strong grounds. Besides this, Morgan with his Corps and some bodies of Militia are on their flanks. I cannot determine yet at what place they intend to embark. Some think they will push for Sandy Hook, whilst other suppose they mean to go to shoal harbour. The latter opinion seems to be founded in the greatest probability, as from intelligence several Vessels and Craft are lying there. We have made a few prisoners, and they have lost a good many men by desertion. I cannot ascertain their number, as they came in to our advanced parties & pushed immediately into the [Country]. I think five or Six hundred at least, have come in the whole. The deserters are chiefly foreigners.

The following day, the Commander in Chief sent Congress a brief and strangely uninformative account of the battle.

Fields near Monmouth Court House
29th. June 1778.

I have the honor to inform you that about seven OClock yesterday Morning both Armies advanced on each other. About 12 they met on the Grounds near Monmouth Court House, when an action commenced. We forced the Enemy from the Field and encamped on the Ground. They took a strong post in our front, secured on both flanks by Morasses and thick Woods, where they remained till about 12 at Night, and then retreated. I cannot at this time go into a detail of Matters. When opportunity will permit I shall take the liberty of transmitting Congress a more particular account of the proceedings of the day.

Plan of the Battle of Monmouth

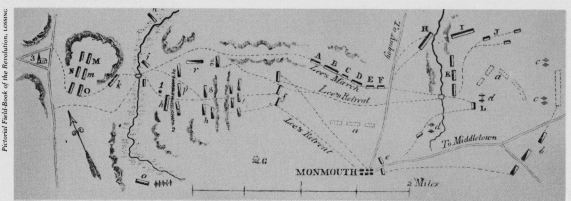

Pictorial Field-Book of the Revolution, LOSSING

Washington made a complete report two days later, but in his detailed recounting of the movements of regiments and brigades, the curious actions of General Lee were obscured. To his brother Jack he was more outspoken.

Sir Henry Clinton

RADIO TIMES HULTON PICTURE LIBRARY, LONDON

Brunswick in New Jersey July 4th. 1778. Your Letter of the 20th Ulto. came to my hands last Night. Before this will have reached you, the Acct. of the Battle of Monmouth probably will get to Virginia; which, from an unfortunate, and bad beginning, turned out a glorious and happy day.

The Enemy evacuated Philadelphia on the 18th. Instt.—at ten oclock that day I got intelligence of it, and by two oclock, or soon after, had Six Brigades on their March for the Jerseys, & followed with the whole Army next Morning. On the 21st. we compleated our passage over the Delaware at Coryells ferry (abt. 33 Miles above Philadelphia) distance from Valley forge near 40 Miles. From this Ferry we moved down towards the Enemy, and on the 27th. got within Six Miles of them.

General Lee having the command of the Van of the Army, consisting of full 5000 chosen Men, was ordered to begin the Attack next Morning so soon as the enemy began their March, to be supported by me. But, strange to tell! when he came up with the enemy, a retreat commenced; whether by his order, or from other causes, is now the subject of enquiry, & consequently improper to be discanted on, as he is in arrest, and a Court Martial sitting for tryal of him. A Retreat however was the fact, be the causes as they may; and the disorder arising from it would have proved fatal to the Army had not that bountiful Providence which has never failed us in the hour of distress, enabled me to form a Regiment or two (of those that were retreating) in the face of the Enemy, and under their fire, by which means a stand was made long enough (the place through which the enemy were pursuing being narrow) to form the Troops that were advancing, upon an advantageous piece of Ground in the rear. Hence our affairs took a favourable turn, & from being pursued, we drove the Enemy back, over the ground they had followed us, recovered the field of Battle, and possessed ourselves of their dead—but, as they retreated behind a Morass very difficult to pass, & had both Flanks secured with thick Woods, it was found impracticable with Men fainting with fatigue, heat, and want of water, to do any thing more that Night. In the Morning we expected to renew the Action, when behold the enemy had stole off as Silent as the Grave in the Night after having sent away their wounded. Getting a Nights March of us, and having but ten Miles to a strong post, it was judged inexpedient to follow them any further, but move towards the North River least they should have any design upon our posts there.

Major General Charles Lee

Lee had almost turned the Battle of Monmouth into a disaster. After one brief clash in which an American regiment turned back an enemy cavalry charge, Lee had ordered a retreat but told only the regiment next to him, leaving other units to discover that they had been left unsupported. Washington had come up just in time to stem the withdrawal. Lee had babbled about saving the Army from disaster by his retreat, but Washington, unconvinced, had Lee court-martialed. Lee was found guilty of disobeying orders, of misbehavior before the enemy, and of disrespect for the Commander in Chief, but was given the strangely light sentence of suspension from command for one year. However, he wrote a letter so insulting to Congress that those gentlemen took his commission away entirely.

France and Britain went to war in June; a joint Franco-American action in July against a British garrison in Rhode Island ended abortively when a storm scattered the French fleet. Otherwise the summer and fall of 1778 passed rather uneventfully, and in December Washington went into winter quarters at Middlebrook (Bound Brook), New Jersey. The Army passed the cold months "better clad and more healthy than they had ever been since the formation of the army," according to Washington, although food was hardly in bountiful supply yet. In the spring of 1779 Washington sent one of his periodic summaries to his brother Jack.

> Middlebrook May 12th. 1779.
> [It is] my opinion, that the enemy will strain every nerve to push the War with vigor this Campaign. By Accts. from England as late as March it appears evident that Seven Regiments besides two of the new raised scotch Corps, recruits for the Guards, & for other Regiments now in America were on the Point of embarking. The whole it is said would amt. to 12 or 1300 Men; but whether they will go to the West Indies, Georgia, or New York or in part to all, remains to be determined. My own opinion of the matter is, that they will Garrison New York & Rhode Isld. strongly, & push their successes to the Southward vigorously.... By a Bill which has passed both Houses of Parliament every parish in the Kingdom is called upon to furnish two Men. These it is said will be immediately had, & will amount in the whole to 27000 recruits for their Army. In aid of these, all the Indians from the extremest North to the South, are bribed to cut our throats, & have already begun the work of devastation in most places on our frontiers. We, on the other hand, have been dreaming of Peace and Independence, and striving to enrich ourselves on the spoils & ruin of our Country, by preying upon the very vitals of it. In a word, our

This engraving of the siege of Rhode Island in 1778 appeared in Gentleman's Magazine *the next year.*

conduct has been the very reverse of the enemy's, for while they were doing every thing to prepare vigorously for the Campaign now opening, we were doing nothing—nay, worse than nothing—but considering how cautious I intended to be, I have said more than enough; & shall add no more on this head, but lament, which I do most pathetically that decay of public virtue with which people were inspired at the beginning of this contest. Speculation—peculation—with all their concomitants, have taken such deep root in almost every Soil, that little else but money making is attended to—the great business may get forward as it can. . . .

I am very apprehensive for the fate of Charlestown. A detachment of between 3 & 4000 Men left New York the 5th. Instt. intended, as is conjectured, to reinforce the enemy in Georgia. This will leave them abt. 8 or 9000 strong at New York and abt. 5000 at Rhode Isld. which they can unite in a few hours at any time. I have ordered all the Virginia levies to Georgia under the command of Genl. Scott. They are to be formed into Regiments, & Officers go from the Troops of that State, in this Camp, to command them. It is much to be feared that this aid will prove very inadequate without vigorous measures are adopted by Virginia & No. Carolina to assist their Sister State. Let them bear in mind how much better it is to oppose the enemy at a distance than at their own homes.

We have, and still do flatter ourselves, with an acknowledgment of our Independance by Spain; and that she will take an active part against G. Britain. Should an event of this kind take place, it would, I should hope, give a decisive turn to our affairs—but as my imagination is not sufficiently fertile to suggest a good reason for the delay, I am inclined to think that the Ministry hath hit upon some device to keep Spain amused while she tries the issue of another Campaign; if not with a view of conquest—to obtain better terms. This campaign is certainly big of events; & requires all our exertions—wisdom—fortitude—& virtue.

Except for a minor but morale-building action in July against a fort at Stony Point on the Hudson, there was little military action in which Washington had any direct part during 1779, and little had been

193

accomplished by the time cold weather came once more. Washington again made his headquarters at Morristown, New Jersey, where he had spent the winter of 1776–77. It was to be Valley Forge all over again, only worse. The soldiers huddled in tents while huts were being built. An officer wrote that "many a good lad [had] nothing to cover him from his hips to his toes, save his blanket." To cap everything, the winter was one of the most bitterly cold in memory. Washington early warned Congress that the situation was desperate, and he sent letters in like vein to the governors of New York, New Jersey, Pennsylvania, Delaware, and Maryland.

Head Qurs. Morris Town 16th. Decr. 1779. The situation of the Army with respect to supplies is beyond description alarming. It has been five or Six weeks past on half allowance: and we have not more than three days bread at a third allowance on hand, nor any where within reach. When this is exhausted, we must depend on the precarious gleanings of the neighbouring country. Our Magazines are absolutely empty every where and our commisaries entirely destitute of Money or Credit to replenish them. We have never experienced a like extremity at any period of the War. We have often felt temporary want, from accidental delay in forwarding supplies; but we always had something in our Magazines and means of procuring more. Neither one nor the other is at present the case. This representation is the result of a minute examination of our resources. Unless some extraordinary and immediate exertions be made by the States, from which we draw our supplies, there is every appearance that the Army will infallibly disband in a fortnight. I think it my duty to lay this candid view of our situation before your Excellency and to entreat the vigorous interposition of the State to rescue us from the danger of an event, which if it did not prove the total ruin of our affairs, would at least give them a shock, from which they would not easily recover and plunge us into a train of new and still more perplexing embarrassments, than any we have hitherto felt.

Pictorial Field-Book of the Revolution. LOSSING

View of Stony Point

On the day before Christmas, Washington had to order that corn meant for horses be ground into meal for the men. On the second day of 1780, a violent and deadly two-day blizzard began, piling drifts as high as six feet. Hungry soldiers took to raiding at night, pillaging farmers of food until Washington organized a system of requisitioning grain and

Washington was elected a member of the American Philosophical Society of Philadelphia in March of 1780.

cattle and paying for them in the Continental currency the farmers would not accept voluntarily. The measure helped for a while, but destitution lasted far into the spring—with serious consequences. Washington wrote to Governor Jonathan Trumbull of Connecticut about an incident involving troops from his state.

Head Qurs. Morris Town May 26th. 1780. It is with infinite pain I inform you, that we are reduced to a situation of extremity for want of meat. On several days of late the troops have been entirely destitute of any, and for a considerable time past they have been at best, at a half, a quarter, an Eighth allowance of this Essential Article of Provision. The Men have borne their distress with a firmness and patience never exceeded, and every possible praise is due the Officers for encouraging them to it, by precept, by exhortation, by example. But there are certain bounds beyond which it is impossible for human Nature to go. We are arrived at these. The want of provision last night produced a Mutiny in the Army of a very alarming kind. Two Regiments of the Connecticut line got under Arms and but for the timely notice and exertions of their Officers, it is most likely it would have been the case with the whole, with a determination to return home. After a long expostulation by their Officers and some of the Pennsylvania line who had come to their assistance they were prevailed on to go into their Huts. But this without relief can only be momentary. I will not dwell longer upon this melancholy subject, being fully convinced that Your Excellency will hasten to us every possible relief in your power.

The Connecticut soldiers who mutinied had had no meat in ten days; neither they nor any other troops had been paid for five months. The Army was melting away, with state governments doing little about replacement recruiting. One bright spot for Washington was the return in May, 1780, of Lafayette from a year-and-a-half furlough in France. The young marquis, whose relationship with Washington had become almost that of father and son, brought the inspiriting news that six French men-of-war and six thousand troops were on their way to America. Then, to counter these good tidings came the grim word from South Carolina that on May 12 Charleston had fallen to General Clinton, with fifty-five hundred prisoners taken, the worst American defeat of the war. The day after having learned of the loss of Charleston, Washington wrote to Joseph Jones, delegate to Congress from Virginia, to express himself—as he would many times in coming years—on the need for the states to surrender some of their prerogatives to create a stronger Congress.

Morristown May 31st. 1780.

I have been honoured with your favour in answer to my Letter respecting the appointment of a Committee; and with two other of later date—the last containing General Woodford's account of the situation of things at Charlestown, at the time of his writing. I thank you for them all. Unhappily that place (Charles town) the Garrison in it, &c. (as appears by the New York account, which I have transmitted to Congress) have been in the hands of the Enemy since the 12th. Instant.

Certain I am, that unless Congress speaks in a more decisive tone; unless they are vested with powers by the several States, competent to the great purposes of War, or assume them as matter of right; and they, and the States respectively, act with more energy than they hitherto have done, that our cause is lost. We can no longer drudge on in the old way. By ill-timing the adoption of measures; by delays in the execution of them or by unwarrantable jealousies, we incur enormous expences, and derive no benefit from them. One State will comply with a requisition of Congress, another neglects to do it. A third executes it by halves, and all differ, either in the manner; the matter; or so much in point of time, that we are always working up Hill and ever shall (while such a System as the present one, or rather want of one prevails) be unable to apply our strength or resources to any advantage.

This, My Dear Sir, is plain language to a Member of Congress; but it is the language of Truth and friendship.

Detail of a map of the siege of Charleston from Stedman's history of the American Revolution, 1794

It is the result of long thinking, close application, and strict observation. I see one head gradually changing into thirteen. I see one Army branching into thirteen; and instead of its looking up to Congress, as the supreme controuling power of the United States, are considering themselves as dependent on their respective States. In a word, I see the powers of Congress declining too fast for the consequence and respect which is due to them as the Great representative Body of America, and am fearful of the consequences.

British General Clinton returned to New York from Charleston, leaving General Cornwallis to carry on the campaign in the South. Washington braced for action, but Clinton, after a bit of skirmishing in New Jersey, again settled down in New York City. Transports with a French army under the Comte de Rochambeau arrived at Newport, Rhode Island, but almost immediately were bottled up by a blockading British fleet. As for the American Army, by mid-August it had received only six thousand of the 16,500 recruits the states had been asked to supply. The states were equally remiss in providing supplies, so much so that the Army was forced to requisition its own food from the countryside; in a land heavy with a bountiful harvest the men were still hungry and half naked. Washington sent letters of implied warning to the governors of the New England and Middle Atlantic States.

Head Quarters near the liberty Pole Bergen County
27th. August 1780

A contemporary engraving caricatured Rochambeau reviewing French troops.

The Honorable the Committee of cooperation having returned to Congress, I am under the disagreeable necessity of informing Your Excellency, that the army is again reduced to an extremity of distress for want of Provision. The greater part of it had been without meat from the 21st. to the 26th. To endeavour to obtain some relief, I moved down to this place, with a view of stripping the lower parts of the Country of its Cattle, which, after a most rigorous exaction, is found to afford between two and three days supply only, and those consisting of milch cows and calves of one or two years old. When this scanty pittance is consumed, I know not what will be our next resource, as the Commissary can give me no certain information of more than 120 head of Cattle expected from Pennsylvania, and about 150 from Massachusetts. I mean in time to supply our immediate wants.

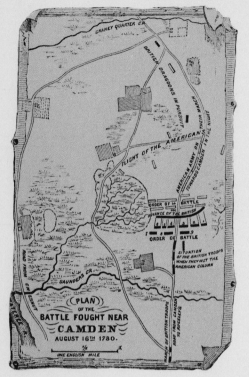

Plan of the battle fought near the town of Camden, S.C., August, 1780

Military coercion is no longer of any avail, as nothing further can possibly be collected from the Country in which we are obliged to take a position, without depriving the Inhabitants of the last morsel. This mode of subsisting, supposing the desired end could be answered by it, besides being in the highest degree distressing to individuals, is attended with ruin to the morals and discipline of the Army. During the few days which we have been obliged to send out small parties to procure Provisions for themselves, the most enormous excesses have been committed.

It has been no inconsiderable support of our cause, to have had it in our power to contrast the conduct of our army with that of the Enemy, and to convince the Inhabitants that while their rights were wantonly violated by the British Troops, by ours they were respected. This distinction must unhappily now cease, and we must assume the odious character of the plunderers, instead of the protectors of the People, the direct consequence of which must be to alienate their minds from the army, and insensibly from the cause.

We have not yet been absolutely without flour, but we have *this* day but *one* days supply in Camp, and I am not certain that there is a single barrel between this and Trenton. I shall be obliged therefore to draw down one or two hundred barrels, from a small Magazine which I had endeavoured to establish at West Point, for the security of the Garrison in case of a sudden investiture.

From the above state of facts, it may be foreseen that this army cannot possibly remain much longer together, unless very vigorous and immediate measures are taken by the States to comply with the requisitions made upon them. The Commissary General has neither the means nor the power of procuring supplies. He is only to receive them from the several Agents. Without a speedy change of circumstances, this dilemma must be involved; either the Army must disband, or what is, if possible, worse, subsist upon the plunder of the People.

I would fain flatter myself that a knowledge of our situation will produce the desired relief—not a relief of a few days, as has generally heretofore been the case, but a supply equal to the establishment of magazines for the Winter. If these are not formed, before the Roads are broken up by the Weather, we shall certainly experience the same difficulties and distresses the ensuing Winter, which we did the last. Altho' the Troops have upon every occasion hitherto, borne their wants with unparalled patience, it will be dangerous to trust too often to a repetition of the causes of discontent.

There was more bad news from the South, where General Horatio Gates, sent to recoup American fortunes, had been so badly defeated at Camden, South Carolina, that he did not stop retreating for 180 miles. In September, Washington went to Hartford, Connecticut, to meet General Rochambeau and discuss future joint strategy. On his return he stopped at West Point to inspect the vital Hudson River fortress and to pay a call on his friend General Benedict Arnold. He arrived at the Beverly Robinson house across the river from West Point, where Arnold made his headquarters, to find a puzzling situation that grew ominous as the day progressed. He summarized it for Congress the next day.

Robinsons House in the Highlands
Septr. 26th. 1780.

I have the honour to inform Congress, that I arrived here yesterday about 12 O'Clock on my return from Hartford. Some hours previous to my arrival, Major General Arnold went from his quarters which were at this place and as it was supposed, over the River to the Garrison at West point, whither I proceeded myself in order to visit the Post. I found General Arnold had not been there during the day, and on my return to His Quarters he was still absent. In the mean time a packet had arrived from Lieut. Colo. Jamison announcing the capture of a John Anderson who was endeavouring to go to New York, with the several interesting and important papers, mentioned below, all in the hand writing of General Arnold. This was also accompanied with a letter from the Prisoner, avowing himself to be Major John Andre Adjutant General of the British Army relating the manner of his capture and endeavouring to shew that he did not come under the description of a Spy. From these several circumstances and information that the General seemed to be thrown into some degree of agitation, on receiving a letter a little time before he went from his Quarters, I was led to conclude immediately that he had heard of Major Andre's captivity and that he would, if possible, escape to the Enemy and

The War of Independence, LOSSING

The Beverly Robinson house, in which General Arnold had his headquarters

An engraving of West Point, as it appeared at the close of war, from the old New York Magazine

accordingly took such measures as appeared the most probable to apprehend him. But he had embarked in a barge and proceeded down the River under a flag to the Vulture Ship of War which lay some miles below Stony and Verplank's Points. He wrote me after he got on board, a letter of which the inclosed is a Copy. Major Andre is not arrived yet, but I hope he is secure and that he will be here to day. I have been and am taking proper precautions, which I trust will prove effectual, to prevent the important consequences which this conduct on the part of Genl. Arnold was intended to produce. I do not know the party that took Major Andre, but it is said it consisted only of a few Militia, who acted in such a manner upon the Occasion, as does them the highest honour and proves them to be Men of great Virtue. They were offered, I am informed, a large sum of Money for his release and as many Goods as they would demand, but without any effect.

Washington's inspection had revealed the West Point defenses to be woefully neglected and the garrison so disposed that it could have put up little effective resistance to an enemy attack. The reasons why one of Washington's most brilliant and dependable combat generals should have turned traitor are complex and even today are not entirely understood, but one contributory cause was that on three or four occasions in the past, promotions Arnold had abundantly earned had gone to lesser men because of the workings of state politics, leaving him deeply embittered. Arnold had escaped. Major André was not so fortunate. The decision of the court-martial in his case was inevitable.

GENERAL ORDERS

Head Quarters Orangetown
Sunday October 1st. 1780.

The Board of General officers appointed to examine into the Case of Major Andre have reported.

1st. "That he came on shore from the Vulture sloop of War in the night of the 21st. of September last on an interview with General Arnold in a private and secret manner."

2dly. "That he changed his dress within our Lines and under a feigned name and in a disguised habit passed our works at Stoney and Vere-Planks Points the Evening of the 22d. of September last at Tarrytown in a disguised habit being then on his way to New York;

The capture of Major André

and when taken he had in his possession several Papers which contain'd intelligence for the Enemy."

The Board having maturely considered these Facts do also report to his Excellency General Washington

"That Major Andre Adjutant General to the British Army ought to be considered as a spy from the Enemy and that agreeable to the Law and usage of nations it is their opinion he ought to suffer Death."

The Commander in Chief directs the execution of the above Sentence in the usual way this afternoon at five o'clock precisely.

André, young, handsome, chivalrous, was greatly disturbed that he was to be hanged like a criminal rather than shot like an officer and a gentleman. He pleaded with Washington to die before a firing squad, but he had been captured in civilian clothes, and the military code is rigid. His execution was delayed one day when General Clinton made a

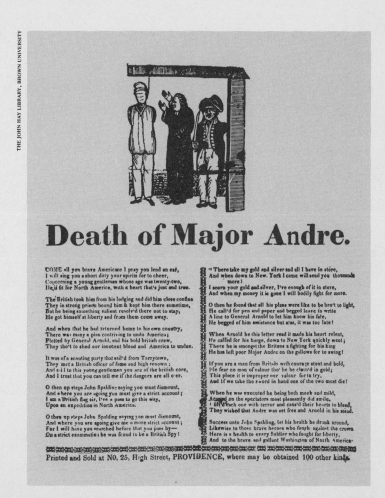

THE JOHN HAY LIBRARY, BROWN UNIVERSITY

A broadside printed in Providence, Rhode Island, after death of André

201

special appeal for his young adjutant; Washington offered to trade André for Arnold, but the deal was unacceptable, and André died on the gallows.

The Army went into winter quarters in December as usual, with Washington's headquarters at New Windsor near West Point, although units were spread from West Point to Morristown to ease the supply problem. Food and clothing scarcities were so severe that for the first time Washington made no attempt to hold troops through the winter but directed his officers to let men drift away as their enlistments expired in order to diminish the number of hungry mouths. Then early in January, 1781, occurred an event the Commander in Chief had been dreading. Among those to whom he later sent a report were the New England governors, in a circular letter.

> Head Qurs. New Windsor 5th. Janry. 1781.
> It is with extreme anxiety and pain of mind, I find myself constrained to inform *your Excellency,* that the event I have long apprehended would be the consequence of the complicated distresses of the Army, has at length taken place. On the night of the 1st. instant, a mutiny was excited by the non Commissioned Officers and Privates of the Pennsylvania Line, which soon became so universal as to defy all opposition; in attempting to quell this tumult, in the first instance, some Officers were killed, others wounded, and the lives of several common Soldiers lost. Deaf to the arguments, entreaties & utmost efforts of *all their Officers* to stop them, they moved off from Morris Town the place of their cantonment, with their Arms, and Six pieces of Artillery. And from accounts just received by General Wayne's Aid de Camp, they were still in a body, on their March to Philadelphia to demand a redress of their grievances. At what point this defection will stop, or how extensive it may prove, God only knows; at present the troops at the important Posts in this vicinity remain quiet, not being acquainted with this unhappy and alarming affair, but how long they will remain so cannot be ascertained, as they labor under some of the pressing hardships with the troops who have revolted.
>
> The aggravated Calamities and distresses that have resulted from the Total want of Pay for nearly twelve months, the want of Clothing at a severe Season, and not unfrequently the want of Provisions, are beyond description. The circumstances will now point out much more forcibly what ought to be done, than any thing that can possibly be said by me on the subject.

Letter from Washington to Congress,
describing the mutiny of his troops

The mutiny had been caused by resentment over food, pay, terms of enlistment, and bounties. These grievances led to action. Pennsylvania authorities negotiated with the mutineers, ending the rebellion, but at a cost of discharging more than half the twenty-four hundred men of the Pennsylvania division, men who swore that they had served more than three years (written records were sketchy). Inspired by the success of the Pennsylvanians as well as by their own misery, New Jersey troops mutinied on January 20, 1781. But Washington's attitude differed from that of the Pennsylvania authorities; his orders to Major General Robert Howe at West Point were unequivocal.

[West Point, January 22, 1781]

You are to take the command of the detachment, which

Cornwallis Retreating!

PHILADELPHIA, April 7, 1781.

Extract of a Letter from Major-General *Greene*, dated
CAMP, at *Buffelo Creek, March* 25, 1781.

"ON the 16th Inftant I wrote your Excellency, giving an Account of an Action which happened at Guilford Court-Houfe the Day before. I was then perfuaded that notwithstand-ing we were obliged to give up the Ground, we had reaped the Advantage of the Action. Circumftances fince confirm me in Opinion that the Enemy were too much gauled to improve their Succefs. We lay at the Iron-Works three Days, prepar-ing ourfelves for another Action, and expecting the Enemy to advance : But of a fudden they took their Departure, leaving behind them evident Marks of Diftrefs. All our wounded at Guilford, which had fallen into their Hands, and 70 of their own, too bad to move, were left at New-Garden. Moft of their Offi-cers fuffered—Lord Cornwallis had his Horfe fhot under him—Col. Steward, of the Guards was killed, General O Hara and Cols. Tarlton and Webfter, wounded. Only three Field-Officers efcaped, if Reports, which feem to be authentic, can be relied on.

Our Army are in good Spirits, notwithstanding our Sufferings, and are advancing towards the Enemy; they are retreating to Crofs-Creek.

In South-Carolina, Generals Sumpter and Marian have gained feveral little Advantages. In one the Enemy loft 60 Men, who had under their Care a large Quantity of Stores, which were taken, but by an unfortunate Miftake were afterwards re taken.

Publifhed by Order,
CHARLES THOMSON, Secretary.

§§ : Printed at N. Willis's Office.

*Broadside containing an extract of
a letter from General Nathanael
Greene, telling of enemy's retreat*

has been ordered to march from this Post against the Mutineers of the Jersey line. You will rendezvous the whole of your command at Ringwood or Pomptons as you find best from circumstances. The object of your detachment is to compel the Mutineers to unconditional submission, and I am to desire you will grant no terms while they are with Arms in their hands in a state of resistance. The manner of executing this I leave to your discretion according to circumstances. If you succeed in compelling the revolted Troops to a surrender you will instantly execute a few of the most active and incendiary leaders.

You will endeavour to collect such of the Jersey Troops to your standards as have not followed the pernicious example of their associates, and you will also try to avail yourself of the services of the Militia, representing to them how dangerous to Civil Liberty the precedent is of Armed Soldiers dictating terms to their Country.

The mutinous troops were taken by surprise, two ring-leaders summarily executed, their officers restored to command. Then Washington appointed a commission to look into their grievances.

More and more the South became the main arena of war. General Nathanael Greene, who had replaced the defeated Horatio Gates the previous December, reorganized his army and fought so skillfully, though outnumbered and unable to win a decisive battle, that he forced the British out of all Georgia and the Carolinas, except the seaport towns of Savannah and Charleston. Meanwhile, Washington wanted to strike at New York; the French General Rochambeau, at Cornwallis's army in Virginia. The decision was taken out of Washington's hands when word came that the French Admiral the Comte de Grasse would bring his West Indies fleet into Chesapeake Bay in August and be available to help in a Virginia campaign but would not venture north to New York. The overland movement of the allied armies was carefully designed to leave Clinton in the dark as to its objective until the last moment; not till they were on their way did Washington even inform Congress.

Head Quarters Chatham 27th. Augst. 1781
I have the Honor to inform Congress, that my Expectation of the Arrival of the Fleet of Monsr. De Grasse, in the Chesapeak Bay—with some other Circumstances, of which Congress were informed in my Letter of the 2d. of Augt. & in which very little Alterations have since taken place—have induced me to make an Alteration

in the concerted Operations of this Campaign. I am now on my March with a very considerable Detachment of the American Army and the whole of the French Troops, for Virginia.

As I expect a few Days will bring me to Philadelphia, I shall then have the Honor to open my Motives & Intentions to Congress, more fully than it may be prudent to do by Letter at this Distance.

Washington wrote ahead to Lafayette, who commanded a small force harassing Cornwallis at Yorktown, Virginia, telling him to hold fast. More notable than what he said was the location from which he wrote.

Mount Vernon Septr. 10th. 1781.
We are thus far, My Dear Marquis, on our way to you. The Count De Rochambeau has just arrived: General Chattelus will be here and we propose (after resting tomorrow) to be at Fredericksburg on the Night of the 12th.: The 13th. we shall reach New Castle, and the next Day we expect the pleasure of seeing you at your Encampment.

Should there be any danger as we approach you, I shall be obliged if you will send a party of Horse towards New Kent Court House to meet us. With great personal regd etc.

P.S. I hope you will keep Lord Cornwallis safe, without Provisions or Forage untill we arrive. Adieu.

French view of de Grasse's fleet

Washington spent three days at Mount Vernon, the first since he had become Commander in Chief six years earlier. He met his three stepgranddaughters and an infant stepgrandson for the first time. And his stepson, Jack Custis, announced that he had decided to serve his country by joining Washington's staff. Cornwallis had taken his army to Yorktown on Chesapeake Bay, expecting support by a British fleet. Instead, de Grasse's fleet arrived at the end of August, established a blockade, and landed troops to join Lafayette's small force. On September 28 Washington and Rochambeau marched in with the allied armies and began the siege of Yorktown. Two days later, as Washington wrote to George Weedon, a Brigadier General, Cornwallis's lines were already being forced in.

Camp before York 30th. Septr. 1781.
I have just received your favor of Yesterday. Last Night the Enemy evacuated their exterior Works, and have left

A French engraving of "Le General Washington" has an inset view of the "Journée mémorable" of surrender. Opposite: a battle plan drawn in 1781 by a New York artilleryman

us in full possession of Pigeon Quarter, and some other work which they had occupied, contracting their defence near the Town. The circumstance has created a jealousy in some Minds similar to yours, that Lord Cornwallis may throw himself with his Troops upon the Gloucester side [the town of Gloucester was across the James River from Yorktown], and endeavour, by a rapid movement, to attempt an Escape: I can hardly persuade myself that he will make such a push: He ought to be watched however on every point. You will therefore pay the utmost attention to all their movements approaching as near as you can with safety and prudence so as not to hazard too much. In case any intention of an escape should be discovered, you will give me the most instantaneous information, and at the same time give immediate Notice to the Inhabitants to remove from their probable Route all the Cattle and Horses that can be of use to them; and at the same time give every impediment to their march that you possibly can, that I may have time to throw my Army in their Front.

I am this Day informed that some Troops are crossing to Glosesster; whether these are to replace a Corps of Germans which are said to have come from that side Yesterday, or for some other purpose I cannot say. Three Boats with Men I saw cross myself.

From then on, Washington's reports to Congress were always of constricting lines drawing closer to Yorktown, of siege guns battering Cornwallis's defenses. At last he received from the British commander a message he had awaited for years; it asked for a twenty-four-hour cessation of hostilities. His reply was terse.

Camp before York 17. Octr. 1781.
I have had the honour of receiving your Lordships letter of this date.

An ardent desire to spare the further effusion of Blood, will readily incline me to listen to such terms for the surrender of your Posts of York & Gloucester, as are admissible.

I wish previously to the meeting of Commissioners that your Lordships proposals in writing, may be sent to the American Lines, for which purpose a suspension of hostilities during two hours, from the Delivery of this letter will be granted.

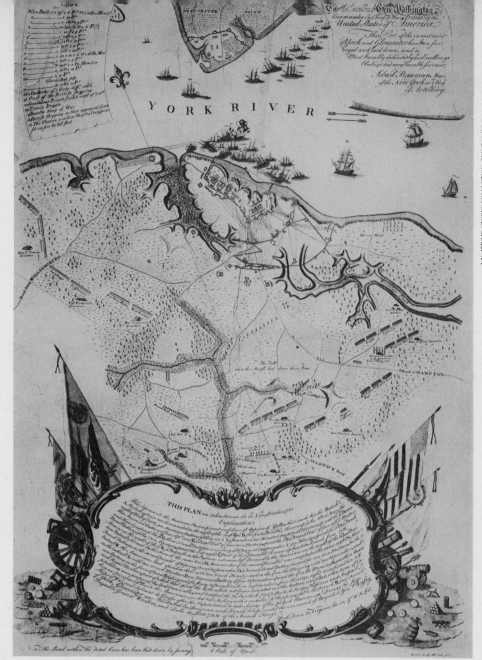

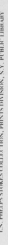

The surrender terms were worked out, the capitulation was signed on October 19, 1781, and the next day the British army, almost eight thousand strong, marched out between the ranked allied armies to give up their arms, with the immaculately uniformed French on one side and the ragged Continentals on the other. Cornwallis, bitter with humiliation, did not appear at the ceremony but sent his second in command. As for Washington, now that a magnificent victory was his, he found himself with surprisingly little to say in his report to Congress.

Head Quarters near York 19th. Octr. 1781.

I have the Honor to inform Congress, that a Reduction

207

of the British Army under the Command of Lord Cornwallis, is most happily effected. The unremitting Ardor which actuated every Officer & Soldier in the combined Army on this Occasion, has principally led to this Important Event, at an earlier period than my most sanguine Hopes had induced me to expect.

The singular Spirit of Emulation, which animated the whole Army from the first Commencement of our Operations, has filled my Mind with the highest pleasure & Satisfaction—and had given me the happiest presages of Success.

On the 17th. instant, a Letter was received from Lord Cornwallis, proposing a Meeting of Commissioners, to consult on Terms for the Surrender of the Posts of York & Gloucester. This Letter (the first which had passed between us) opened a Correspondence, a Copy of which I do myself the Honor to inclose; that Correspondence was followed by the Definitive Capitulation, which was agreed to, & Signed on the 19th. Copy of which is also herewith transmitted—and which I hope, will meet the Approbation of Congress.

On October 24 General Clinton arrived off Chesapeake Bay with a relieving army of seven thousand but put back to New York when he found he was too late to help Cornwallis. De Grasse and the French fleet prepared to return to the West Indies, while the French army planned to go into winter quarters in Virginia. But Washington made ready to return north; the war was not over as long as Clinton and the main British army remained in New York.

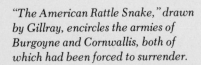

"The American Rattle Snake," drawn by Gillray, encircles the armies of Burgoyne and Cornwallis, both of which had been forced to surrender.

When
leizure (if [...]
with give yo[...]
of this quar[...]
my view & re[...]
I shall conte[...]
exp you, that [...]
join very sinc[...]
your health,
—and that I [...]
ticrate estee[...]
G. W[...]

Colo Humphrey,